TROUBLING CHILDREN

SOCIAL PROBLEMS AND SOCIAL ISSUES

An Aldine de Gruyter Series of Texts and Monographs

SERIES EDITOR

Joel Best

Southern Illinois University at Carbondale

Joel Best (*editor*), **Images of Issues: Typifying Contemporary Social Problems**

Joel Best (*editor*), **Troubling Children: Studies of Children and Social Problems**

James A. Holstein, **Court-Ordered Insanity: Interpretive Practice and Involuntary Commitment**

James A. Holstein and Gale Miller (*editors*), **Reconsidering Social Constructionism: Debates in Social Problems Theory**

Gale Miller and James A. Holstein (*editors*), **Constructionist Controversies: Issues in Social Problems Theory**

Philip Jenkins, **Intimate Enemies: Moral Panics in Contemporary Great Britain**

Philip Jenkins, **Using Murder: The Social Construction of Serial Homicide**

Valerie Jenness, **Making It Work: The Prostitutes' Rights Movement in Perspective**

Stuart A. Kirk and Herb Kutchins, **The Selling of *DSM*: The Rhetoric of Science in Psychiatry**

Bruce Luske, **Mirrors of Madness: Patrolling the Psychic Border**

Leslie Margolin, **Goodness Personified: The Emergence of Gifted Children**

William B. Sanders, **Gangbangs and Drivebys: Grounded Culture and Juvenile Gang Violence**

Wilbur J. Scott, **The Politics of Readjustment: Vietnam Veterans since the War**

Wilbur J. Scott and Sandra Carson Stanley (*editors*) **Gays and Lesbians in the Military: Issues, Concerns, and Contrasts**

Malcolm Spector and John I. Kitsuse, **Constructing Social Problems**

TROUBLING CHILDREN
Studies of
Children and Social Problems

JOEL BEST
Editor

ALDINE DE GRUYTER
New York

About the Editor

Joel Best is Professor and Chair of Sociology at Southern Illinois University at Carbondale. Dr. Best is the editor of *Images of Issues: Typifying Contemporary Social Problems*, and coeditor of the *Satanism Scare* (both Aldine de Gruyter). He is the author of numerous journal articles specializing in social problems and deviance.

ALDINE DE GRUYTER
A division of Walter de Gruyter, Inc.
200 Saw Mill River Road
Hawthorne, New York 10532

This publication is printed on acid-free paper

Library of Congress Cataloging-in-Publication Data

Troubling children : studies of children and social problems / Joel
   Best, editor.
      p.   cm. — (Social problems and social issues)
   Includes bibliographical references and index.
      ISBN 0-202-30491-4 (alk. paper). — ISBN 0-202-30492-2 (pbk. :
   alk. paper)
      1. Children—Social conditions. 2. Social problems. I. Best,
   Joel. II. Series.
   HQ767.9.T76   1994
   305.23—dc20   93-50052
                                                                              CIP

Manufactured in the United States of America

10 9 8 7 6 5 4 3 2 1

Contents

PART IV.   FAMILIES AND CHILDREN

PART V.   SCHOOLS AND CHILDREN

PART VI.   CHILDREN'S PERSPECTIVES ON SOCIAL PROBLEMS

Part I

INTRODUCTION

Chapter 1

Troubling Children: Children and Social Problems

Joel Best

Children make up about one-quarter of the U.S. population. This apparently simple statement contains an implicit definition: A child is anyone under 18 years of age. Different definitions would produce different statistics: In 1990, about 29 percent of the U.S. population was under age 20, 22 percent under 15, and 15 percent under 10 years of age (U.N. Department of Economic and Social Development 1992).

Because most Third World countries have higher birth rates and higher death rates than Western, industrialized countries like the United States, children account for a much larger proportion of Third World populations. For instance, recent statistics from three African countries—the Congo, Mali, and Cameroon—put the proportion of their populations under 20 at 55 to 56 percent, while 45 to 46 percent are under age 15, and 32 to 35 percent are under 10 years of age (U.N. Department of Economic and Social Development 1992). Obviously, regardless of how we define childhood, children represent a large share of the world's population.

The simple fact that there are so many children might lead us to expect that there would be many sociological studies of children. We would be correct—so long as we defined childhood broadly. There are thousands of sociological studies of young people, including such classics as *The Unadjusted Girl* (Thomas 1923), *The Gang* (Thrasher 1927), *Elmstown's Youth* (Hollingshead 1949), *Delinquent Boys* (A. Cohen 1955), and *The Adolescent Society* (Coleman 1961). But the great majority of these studies (including all of the classic titles just listed) deal with older children—adolescents or teenagers. This emphasis on adolescents in sociologists' discussions of children is not new; much of Francis J.

3

Brown's 1939 book, *The Sociology of Childhood*, concerns teenagers. Nor should the intense interest in adolescents surprise us. Far more than younger children, teenagers engage in deviant behaviors that trouble adults, behaviors such as delinquency, drinking, and drug use. Adolescence is when most young people enter the labor market, become sexually active, begin driving, and decide to drop out or stay in school. Teenagers' choices are consequential; they set the direction for the youths' adult lives. Naturally, adolescence has been the subject of intense sociological study.

In contrast, younger children have received remarkably little attention from sociologists, and most of that attention has focused on only two aspects of childhood, family life and education. Of course, families and schools are central institutions in most preadolescent children's lives, but there is a tendency for sociologists studying these institutions to concentrate on their adult members (e.g., parents and teachers) rather than the children. There are probably more studies of how adults deal with children than of children themselves. By largely ignoring younger children, sociologists have virtually surrendered the study of those children to child psychologists, who concentrate on the individual, psychological processes that characterize childhood development, rather than focusing on children as social beings.

There are signs that sociology's neglect of younger children is ending. It is during childhood that we learn how to behave as members of society (Denzin 1977), and sociologists have begun to pay more attention to this process of socialization. Thus, studying children's arguments offers a way of understanding how children learn to use language in their interactions with others (Maynard 1985); research on Little League baseball teams can help show how children develop group cultures (Fine 1987); and observations of boys and girls in school playgrounds reveal how children come to understand what it means to be male or female (Thorne 1993). Sociological interest in childhood is growing. In 1992, the American Sociological Association (ASA) formally acknowledged this interest, establishing a section for members interested in the sociology of children. The new section, which publishes a newsletter and organizes sessions for the ASA's annual meeting, will encourage more sociologists to conduct research on childhood.

Much of this new interest in children is motivated by sociologists' concerns about children and social problems. Sociologists write about child abuse, juvenile delinquency, missing children, childhood poverty, children carrying guns to school, and other social problems of childhood. But even studies that, at first glance, may not seem to be about social problems often reflect such concerns. For instance, Thorne (1993) studied boys' and girls' behavior on playgrounds because she sought to understand how children learn and reproduce society's patterns of gender inequality through play. She examined play, a seemingly innocent activity, to understand the roots of a social problem—sexism. Although there is growing interest in the sociology of children in general and in children and social problems in particular, this interest usually takes the form of case studies of particular problems. There have been few attempts to discuss the general relationships between children and social problems. To do so, we must begin by giving separate consideration to the nature of childhood and the nature of social problems.

THE MEANING OF CHILDREN

We know remarkably little about the history of childhood prior to the nineteenth century. The most influential book on pre–nineteenth-century children, *Centuries of Childhood* by Philippe Ariès (1962), a French social historian, argues that traditional European societies' view of children evolved over time:

> In medieval society the idea of childhood did not exist; this is not to suggest that children were neglected, forsaken or despised. The idea of childhood is not to be confused with affection for children: it corresponds to an awareness of the particular nature of childhood, that particular nature which distinguishes the child from the adult, even the young adult. In medieval society this awareness was lacking. That is why, as soon as the child could live without the constant solicitude of his mother, his nanny or his cradle-rocker, he belonged to adult society. (Ariès 1962:128)

Ariès argues that the meaning of childhood underwent a gradual transformation in Europe from the twelfth to the eighteenth centuries. At the beginning of this period, children past infancy mingled freely with adults. Life was hard: Disease, hunger, and exploitation killed many children. The psychohistorian Lloyd deMause emphasizes these hardships (1974:1): "The history of childhood is a nightmare from which we have only recently begun to awaken. The further back in history one goes, the lower the level of child care, and the more likely children are to be killed, abandoned, beaten, terrorized, and sexually abused." The brutality of life—and the precariousness of children's lives in particular—led adults to view children with what historian Edward Shorter (1975) calls "traditional indifference."

Over time, however, the basic conditions of social life gradually improved. In particular, improvements in agricultural methods increased production. This meant that, on average, people were better fed and healthier; more efficient agriculture also made laborers, no longer needed on the land, available for manufacturing, and the growth in manufacturing further improved the standard of living. These changes did not occur all at once or without significantly disrupting many people's lives; in general, people of higher social status experienced the benefits of change first and most fully. However, over centuries, these changes transformed most social arrangements, including family life and especially the lives of children.

The Sentimental Perspective

By the eighteenth—certainly by the nineteenth—century, the meaning of childhood had been redefined: Childhood became sentimentalized. This redefinition did not occur all at once. It involved a gradual change in attitudes toward children. In general, the new meanings originated among the more privileged, then slowly spread throughout the social structure. This redefinition caused people to speak less of children's utility, their ability to contribute to the family economy; instead, they emphasized children's need for nurturing. The family had become a more private sphere, a center of sentiment; within the family, children received and returned love (Shorter 1975; Wishy 1968; Zelizer 1985). Although we will never have a full understanding of historical childhood, we know a good deal more about developments over the past two centuries, when this sentimental definition of childhood emerged and flourished. During the nineteenth century, more people became literate and printing technology improved, causing a dramatic rise in publishing books, periodicals, and other printed material. As a result, there is a far richer historical record concerning daily life, and this record suggests that Europe and the United States underwent an important transformation in attitudes toward children, redefining childhood in sentimental terms.

The new, idealized, sentimentalized vision of childhood spread beyond its initial focus in family life. Reformers began to draw attention to problems facing children in the larger society, problems that previously had been ignored. For instance, Charles Dickens's novels portrayed children's hardships in sympathetic terms. By the middle of the nineteenth century, the campaign to establish public schools in the United States was well established; by the end of the century, the law made schooling compulsory, and the age at which children could legally leave school was rising. The great crusade on behalf of children during the late nineteenth and early twentieth centuries was the campaign against child labor, but there were many other Progressive Era causes:

movements to establish child protection laws, juvenile courts, training schools, child welfare programs, playgrounds, and settlement houses emerged during this period, and all of these movements reflected a sentimental vision of children. That is, the reformers viewed children as vulnerable, needing and deserving society's protection.

The late nineteenth and early twentieth centuries also saw a variety of other developments that shaped attitudes toward children. One deserves special mention: the emergence of psychoanalysis in the work of Sigmund Freud and his followers. Psychoanalysis argued that events in early childhood shaped adults' personalities, that parents, in particular, affect their children's psychological development. This basic insight became commonplace as awareness of psychoanalysis spread during the twentieth century. Although relatively few people understood the perspective well, many realized that this new science held parents responsible for the development of their children's personalities and in particular for their problems and failings. Children's vulnerability made them susceptible to harm, even within the haven of family life. Thus, the sentimental perspective made it easy to link children with social problems.

THE NATURE OF SOCIAL PROBLEMS

Any discussion of children and social problems must consider the nature of social problems, as well as the nature of childhood. The preceding discussion reveals that, although every culture tends to assume that it understands the nature of childhood, those understandings vary across cultures and over time. Childhood is not an objective, natural category. Rather, the meaning of childhood is subjective, a product of particular cultures and social structures. Thus, our essentially sentimental vision of childhood reflects relatively recent historical developments in Western society.

Sociologists inevitably confront a tension between two approaches to understanding social life. On the one hand, the *objectivist* viewpoint assumes that people simply recognize and understand objective reality, that the nature of the world shapes meaning. For example, many discussions of children make a commonsensical assumption that childhood can be defined according to some objective criterion or set of criteria. For instance, we might define a child as anyone under age 21, 18, 13, or whatever. We have already suggested some of the problems with such definitions. Some societies make a clear distinction between childhood and adulthood, often marking the transition into adulthood with a formal ceremony anthropologists call a rite of passage. Contemporary U.S.

society has no such ceremony: Does childhood end when an individual can legally drink (at 21 in most states), vote (18), or drive an automobile (usually 16)? Does childhood end only when an individual completes his or her schooling, achieves sexual maturity, or what? Obviously, for our society, there is no agreement on the correct answer. Not only does the definition of childhood vary among societies, but also it varies within our society. We may be able to agree about how old a person is, but the definition of childhood is *subjective,* and, as noted, discussions of the nature of childhood are even more subjective.

The distinction between objectivist and subjectivist stances also characterizes sociologists' discussions of social problems. On the one hand, some sociologists assume that social problems such as crime and poverty are objective phenomena, that people naturally recognize these conditions as social problems. The difficulty with this objectivist argument is that definitions of social problems, like definitions of childhood, vary over time and among cultures. Prior to 1962, sociologists writing about social problems paid little attention to parents' physical assaults on children. However, following the publication of reports by medical researchers about what they initially called the "battered child syndrome," sociologists (like other members of society) began to perceive and treat child abuse as a serious social problem (Nelson 1984; Pfohl 1977). This example suggests that definitions of social problems are subjective. When some people draw attention to a particular phemonenon by claiming that it is somehow troubling, we come to define that phenomenon as a social problem. Parental violence against children had a long history, but child abuse only became considered a significant social problem in the contemporary United States when activists in the child protection movement began making claims—and others began responding to those claims. Sociologists refer to this process of claimsmaking as the construction of social problems, and sociologists who study this process are often called *constructionists.*

Constructionists study the emergence and evolution of social problems (Best 1989; Holstein and Miller 1993; Spector and Kitsuse 1977). A typical constructionist analysis traces the history of claims—who said what, and how others responded. There are constructionist studies of several social problems involving children, including research on child abuse (Howitt 1992; Pfohl 1977); child sexual abuse (Weisberg 1984), missing children (Best 1990), hyperkinesis (Conrad 1975), learning disabilities (Erchak and Rosenfeld 1989), and sudden infant death syndrome (SIDS) (Johnson and Hufbauer 1982). These studies seek to explain how and why particular issues regarding children came to public attention.

Constructionist analyses tend to focus on claimsmakers' *rhetoric*. Rhetoric is persuasive communication. All claimsmakers seek to persuade, to convince others that some condition is a social problem, that it has undesirable effects and needs to be addressed through new social policies. Of course, this rhetoric emerges within a social structural and cultural context. Claimsmakers' rhetoric must match this context; people must find it convincing, or else they will ignore the claims. Claimsmaking is a political activity, in which claimsmakers try to muster enough resources—convincing rhetoric, but also money, members, allies in other causes, public opinion, and the like—to compel policymakers to accept their definition of a social problem and institute appropriate policies to address the problem.

The objectivist and constructionist approaches to studying social problems ask different sorts of questions and produce different sorts of answers. The objectivist approach is more familiar; its focus on social conditions and their consequences may seem more commonsensical. In contrast, the constructionist stance concentrates on claimsmaking, on the ways in which issues emerge and evolve through discourse. Both approaches are useful for addressing particular issues.

SOCIAL PROBLEMS AND CHILDREN

Conceptions of social problems involving children, then, reflect a society's definitions of both childhood and social problems. The sentimental vision of childhood remains dominant in contemporary U.S. society, and it encourages certain patterns in claimsmaking about children. Claims about social problems and children tend to depict children in particular ways, and different sorts of claims tend to come from particular categories of claimsmakers.

Varieties of Troubled Children

Our culture tends to focus on four sorts of social problems involving children (Best 1990). Each of these sets of claims characterizes children through distinctive imagery. The first image is the *rebellious child*. Rebellious children reject adults' expectations; they run away from home, have sex, break the law, and adopt disturbing tastes in music or dress. In short, rebellious children make troublesome choices, and reformers usually respond to rebellion by trying to control the children's choices. Often, the solutions proposed for problems of rebellion invoke legal authority (e.g., the juvenile justice system) to compel children to make the right choices. Rebellion is probably the central image when adults express concern about adolescents, but it is less important in discussions of younger children. Sentimentality suggests that children—particularly the uncorrupted young—are basically good. And goodness means, in part, conforming to adult expectations. When younger children do act in ways that might be characterized as rebellious, their behavior is often is explained in terms of some external cause that "makes" the naturally good child behave badly.

The second image is the *deprived child*. Deprived children face poverty, disability, family problems, and other constraints on their lives. These are matters of circumstance, not choice. Even with circumstances for which adults are held responsible (e.g., poverty), blame rarely extends to children, and this is especially true for younger children. Reformers seek to help children overcome their deprivations, to make their childhood more complete, more like the happy, innocent childhoods the sentimental perspective idealizes. Here the reformers' goal is to compensate for what is missing, to minimize the damage to the child. If rebellion often leads to calls for legal solutions, the proposed solutions to deprivation usually involve social welfare institutions.

A third image has become increasingly important as medical science advanced during the twentieth century. The *sick child* has a medical problem. In the late twentieth century, we believe in the efficacy of medical science, and we presume that medical problems can be solved. Reformers turn to medical professionals in hopes of caring for—and curing—sick children. The near eradication of polio, whooping cough, smallpox, and other once-devastating childhood diseases has encouraged reformers to mount campaigns against other medical problems, such as SIDS and muscular dystrophy. Note that a wide range of conditions can be—and are—defined as medical problems. Sociologists term this process *medicalization* (Conrad and Schneider 1992). For instance, children's problems in school (Conrad 1975; Erchak and Rosenfeld 1989) and family violence (Pfohl 1977) have been medicalized by some claimsmakers. Because our culture usually does not blame people for their illnesses, medicalization is consistent with the sentimental vision of the innocent, blameless child.

The child-victim is a fourth image. Menaced by deviants, child-victims are vulnerable to harms intentionally inflicted by kidnappers, child molesters, child abusers, and other malicious adults. Like deprived and sick children, child-victims are not held responsible for their plight; their vulnerability is consistent with the sentimental view of childhood. Reformers seek to protect child-victims, both by helping children protect themselves and by cracking down on those who would harm them.

Because the child-victim menaced by the adult deviant is a particularly dramatic, emotionally powerful image, claimsmakers sometimes adopt the language and imagery of child-victims when describing children threatened by poverty or other impersonal social conditions.

Claims in Child-Saving's History

These four images reappear throughout the history of claimsmaking about child welfare. Concern for children is not a recent development. American history has featured numerous social movements on behalf of children. A partial list would include: the spread of orphan asylums and houses of refuge in the 1830s (Rothman 1971); the antebellum campaign to establish public schools (Katz 1968); the Progressive Era's many child-saving movements, most notably the campaign to abolish child labor, but also efforts that led to the establishment of juvenile courts, training schools, settlement houses, supervised playgrounds, and the Boy Scouts and other, similar youth organizations (R. Cohen 1985); on through contemporary child-saving focused on child abuse and neglect, missing children, child sexual abuse, and many other causes.

Virtually all nineteenth- and twentieth-century child-saving movements derived their rhetoric from the modern sentimental conception of childhood. Such claims draw attention to children's vulnerability. During the Progressive Era, reformers such as Jacob Riis (1894) drew attention to the plight of "street Arabs" and "the bitter cry of the children" (Spargo 1913, see also Payne 1916). Similarly, because many people are more willing to help innocent, vulnerable children than they are to aid adults (who may be considered partly to blame for their own problems), contemporary claimsmakers often find it useful to focus attention on how some social condition affects children, even when affected adults outnumber affected children. Thus, recent books focus on examples of children to typify such social problems as urban poverty (Kotlowitz 1991), homelessness (Kozol 1988), and even the threat of nuclear war (La Farge 1987). Because the sentimental perspective emphasizes both children's value and their vulnerability, claims that can construct a social problem as endangering children are rhetorically powerful.

What motivates claimsmakers? Histories that celebrate social reformers often imply that altruism is the key motivation, that reformers simply want to do good by helping children. But sociological interpretations often note that reformers have something to gain from their campaigns' outcomes. Analysts of a radical bent suggest that reformers and their reforms serve elite interests: In this view, public schooling created a better-educated work force to meet an industrializing economy's demands for better-trained workers (Katz 1968), and the juvenile justice system emerged to control the disorderly poor (Platt 1969). For these critics, social reforms, even apparently altruistic reforms aimed at helping children, are best understood as mechanisms to reduce the threat of political and economic revolution and to maintain the status quo. The difficulty with such interpretations, of course, is that they turn reformers into little more than the pawns of a manipulative elite.

An alternative sociological interpretation notes that claimsmakers have more personal interests in the outcomes of their campaigns. In particular, successful claimsmakers can achieve what Joseph Gusfield calls *ownership*—"the ability to create and influence the public definition of a problem" (1981:10). Thus, after claimsmaking by physicians medicalized the problem of child abuse in the early 1960s, at least for several years, discussions of child-abuse policy tended to turn to physicians for leadership (Pfohl 1977). Claimsmaking does not merely draw attention to a problematic social condition, but also gives the problem shape, characterizing it as a particular sort of problem (e.g., rebellion, deprivation, disease, or victimization) that in turn requires particular sorts of policy responses. In many cases, claimsmakers depict social problems in terms that, if accepted, will give the claimsmakers ownership of the problem. Several of the papers in this book reveal how claimsmakers struggled to control the definitions of social problems involving children.

PLAN OF THE BOOK

The chapters in this book are case studies of preadolescent children and social problems. Aside from that shared focus, they reflect considerable diversity. Although most concern children in the United States, some of the papers deal with children in three other, very different countries (Albania, Japan, and Kenya). Although several adopt versions of the constructionist stance, others make objectivist assumptions. The papers' topics range from the effects of prenatal experiences on children to the concerns of children on the verge of adolescence, from the clearly political (e.g., the effects of societal economic crises) to the apparently personal (e.g., parents choosing appropriate toys). Certainly, this collection makes no claim to being encyclopedic, to examining all aspects of the broad topic "children and social problems." Rather, it is meant to offer a sense of the diversity of current research in the field.

The essays are grouped within five sections: children in societal crises; pregnancy and infancy; families and children; schools and children; and children's perspectives on social problems.

Children in Societal Crises

Compared to adults, children are small, weak, frail, and inexperienced; they are relatively vulnerable to disease, malnutrition, and abuse, and they depend on adults for protection and support. In Western industrial societies, there is a presumption that most children should and will receive adequate care. Those who suffer are somehow exceptional: They may come from unusually poor or dysfunctional families, or through some genetic predisposition or simple ill luck they fall victim to disease or some other misfortune. In these societies, discussions of children's problems tend to focus on finding ways to give all children the protection they deserve.

But what of children who belong to societies undergoing major crises? Wars, epidemics, and severe political or economic crises can affect many—sometimes nearly all—of a society's members. In such circumstances, a large proportion of a society's children may face conditions far more severe than those experienced by all but a few children in Western societies. Many children lack access to adequate food, shelter, basic medical care, and education; they find themselves vulnerable to disease, violence, lives of perpetual poverty, and other devastating problems.

The first two chapters deal with children in societies undergoing severe crises. In Chapter 2, York Bradshaw, Claudia Buchmann, and Paul N. Mbatia explore the problems of children in Kenya, an East African country beset by poverty, unstable political and social institutions, and serious health problems, including an AIDS epidemic. Perhaps more than any other paper in this collection, this chapter demonstrates the vulnerability of children in societies that cannot offer adequate protections. Such studies reveal a limitation in the constructionist perspective. Surely, claimsmakers (including the chapter's authors) construct Kenyan children's problems, but even if no one paid attention to the conditions affecting children, even if no one considered those conditions troubling, the children's lives would be affected. In such cases, the objectivist's focus on the conditions affecting children seems more significant that the constructionist's concern with social problems' emergence and evolution.

Similarly, Marion Kloep's paper (Chapter 3) examines preadolescents in Albania. This small Eastern European country has suffered severe economic dislocations following the collapse of the Soviet bloc. Never prosperous by Western standards, Albanians' standard of living has become precarious, and Kloep argues that economic insecurity reverberates throughout children's lives, affecting their schooling, leisure, and family lives. In Albania, Kenya, and other countries in the Second and Third Worlds, today's crises endanger children in ways likely to shape the lives of those who survive into adulthood.

Pregnancy and Infancy

Children's vulnerability declines with age. Older children are relatively hardy, but infants are incapable of fending for themselves; they depend completely on older people for protection and nurturance. The first year of life is the most dangerous; infants' vulnerability puts them at great risk of death from disease, accident, abuse, or neglect. Historians argue that the high infant mortality rates of past centuries hardened adults to children's suffering (Shorter 1977). However, improved medical care has made it possible to protect infants from many formerly lethal dangers and, with the spread of the sentimental definition of children, concern for the well-being of the very young has grown.

This concern for the vulnerable young sometimes extends into the period before birth, focusing on the well-being of the fetus during pregnancy. This is most evident in the pro-life movement's campaign against abortion. Pro-life rhetoric depicts the fetus as an especially vulnerable child, terming abortion "murder" and "the ultimate form of child abuse." Not everyone agrees with these claims, and the debate over abortion is bitter and acrimonious, but social concern regarding other issues of prenatal care is less controversial. In her essay (Chapter 4) Carol Brooks Gardner explores one set of widely accepted claims about the problems of pregnancy. Specifically, she examines contemporary warnings about precautions a pregnant woman should take to avoid endangering the fetus.

During the 1980s, such concerns about the problems of pregnancy became focused on the dangers the pregnant woman's drinking and drug use might pose for the fetus. Discussions of Fetal Alcohol Syndrome and "crack babies" argued that a woman's substance abuse during pregnancy could cause irreparable damage to her child; the effects would leave the child disadvantaged throughout life. In Chapter 5, Jacquelyn Litt and Maureen McNeil examine claims about crack babies. These dramatic claims, widely accepted when the crack problem emerged in the mid-1980s, now seem less convincing. Litt and McNeil argue that these claims served not only to label drug-using mothers as deviant but also to blame them for a broad range of social problems. Claims about crack babies and other forms of fetal endangerment are especially interesting because claimsmakers' rhetoric emphasizes protecting the child, but, as Gardner and Litt and McNeil point out, the rhetoric's consequences are further constraints on pregnant women.

Families and Children

Most children live and grow within families. The sentimental vision of childhood celebrates the family as a haven for children. At the same time, following the lead of psychoanalysis, we also define the family as the probable cause of many difficulties in the child's later life. Adults who have personality problems, who drink or use drugs, or who encounter other difficulties may be told that their problems should be blamed on their upbringing. In fact, some claimsmakers argue that virtually all families are dysfunctional, and therefore virtually all children are in danger of being damaged by their family experiences (Kaminer 1992).

Such claims set the stage for considerable parental anxiety. Having been told that parental behavior shapes—and may well damage—their children, parents continually find themselves making decisions that they sense may have unintended, but harmful, consequences. Parents must make choices, even while surrounded by warnings that their choices may damage their children. In Chapter 6, Shan Nelson-Rowe examines one arena in which parents make such choices, educational toys. Claimsmakers often charge toys—children's playthings—with corrupting children in various ways: Barbie dolls supposedly reinforce traditional gender roles; war toys are said to encourage violence; and so on. In trying to select appropriate, educational toys, Nelson-Rowe argues, parents seek to protect their children from several sorts of dangers. Furthermore, he suggests, making these decisions offers parents a sense of control over their children's destiny.

Choosing toys, however difficult it may be for some parents, seems trivial compared to the need to discipline children. As Phillip W. Davis points out in Chapter 7, there is—and for some time has been—considerable debate over the propriety of spanking and other forms of physical discipline. Spanking's advocates claim that it is effective and causes no lasting harm, but there have always been critics who disagree, warning of spanking's damaging effects. In recent years, these critics have adopted new rhetoric; they increasingly depict spanking as abusive, yet another threat to child-victims. By tracing the changing claims and counterclaims about spanking, Davis illustrates how the construction of social problems can evolve as broader definitions of childhood shift.

The third paper in Section IV addresses another common focus of parental concern, popular culture. In the contemporary United States, children's exposure to commercial entertainment seems ubiquitous—and troubling. Although critics worry about the consequences of exposure to virtually all forms of popular culture, even including toys and children's books (Engelhardt 1991), most claimsmaking focuses on the impact of television viewing and listening to popular music. Attacks on the music favored by the young have a particularly long history (Gray 1989); there is a longstanding suspicion that popular music encourages delinquency, sexual misbehavior, and other forms of rebellion. In Chapter 8, Joseph A. Kotarba offers a counterargument. In contrast to rock music's many critics, he suggests that the claimsmakers have ignored the positive functions rock has for family life. At least in this case, Kotarba suggests, parents' concern over child-rearing choices seems exaggerated.

Schools and Children

Although many young children spend virtually all of their infancy and much of their early years within the family, virtually all older children spend a substantial proportion of their time in schools. Schools affect children in various ways. Most obviously schools teach children a variety of formal lessons about reading, arithmetic, and so on, but they also bring children into contact with other children, sometimes from very different backgrounds, forcing them to learn how to deal with non-family members. Moreover, schools place children under the supervision of adults outside the family, adults who see themselves as professionals. Teachers and the other adults who work in schools typically have special training, and they often view themselves as being experts in dealing with children and their problems. Obviously, these professionals are likely to define children and their problems differently from family members.

One of the most striking recent transformations in education has been the growing number of very young children—pre-kindergarteners—placed in preschools and daycare centers. Daycare's growth has been caused by both push and pull factors. The principal force pushing children into daycare has been the growing number of women—particularly mothers—in the work force. As more mothers work, more families find it difficult to arrange care for their young children at home, and childcare facilities have expanded to meet this need. But daycare is more than a place to put children; parents are pulled or attracted to daycare by the presumed benefits—exposure to other children, opportunities to learn age-appropriate lessons, and so on. In Chapter 9, Donileen R. Loseke and Spencer E. Cahill trace the history of claimsmaking about daycare, demonstrating that the rationale for daycare shifted as definitions of childhood changed.

Schools have proven unable to serve all children equally well. Much of the literature within education concerns the problems posed by particular sorts of students, such as the disabled, those with learning disorders (Erchak and Rosenfeld 1989), hyperkinetic children (Conrad 1975), the gifted (Margolin 1994), and so on. In (Chaper 10) Atsushi Yamazaki examines another catgeory of students that schools find troublesome, but this time the example comes from Japan. Japanese education attracted considerable attention during the 1980s, when many U.S. claimsmakers argued that Japanese students outscored their U.S. counterparts on objective tests, and that superior Japanese schools were the force behind Japan's surging economy. Yamazaki looks at a side of Japanese education that receives far less attention in the U.S. press. He chronicles the "school refusal" problem—young Japanese students who refuse to attend schools. Initially viewed as truancy, school refusal was redefined as a medical problem, then redefined yet again as school refusal students came to be seen as evidence of the limitations of Japanese education. Yamazaki reminds us that definitions of children's social problems reflect the social structural and cultural context within which claims are made.

Children's Perspectives on Social Problems

In the final paper (Chapter 11) our focus shifts dramatically. The preceding chapters all implicitly adopt the perspective of some adults—parents, schools, experts, or even the sociological analyst—framing the social problem in the adults' terms. In contrast, Donna Lee King attempts to study young children's constructions of one social problem—environmental crisis. Children learn about environmental problems from various sources: In formal lessons in school; through didactic popular culture (e.g, the eco-warriors on the television cartoon series "Captain Planet and the Planeteers" [King 1994]); by family members' example; and in informal discussions with peers. Children must take what they learn from these various sources and construct their own meanings for this and other social problems. We know surprisingly little about this process. King, who analyses children's drawings, offers one method of trying to understand what children think about social problems.

Overview

The chapters in this book certainly do not exhaust the topic of children and social problems. Beyond their narrowly focused substantive findings, these studies illustrate some approaches—particularly constructionist approaches—sociologists may find useful in trying to study other issues. If young children continue to attract sociological attention, these papers may help suggest directions for other researchers.

REFERENCES

Ariès, P. 1962. *Centuries of Childhood*. New York: Knopf.
Best, J. (ed.). 1989. *Images of Issues*. Hawthorne, NY: Aldine de Gruyter.
_____. 1990. *Threatened Children*. Chicago: University of Chicago Press.
Brown, F. J. 1939. *The Sociology of Childhood*. Englewood Cliffs, NJ: Prentice-Hall.
Cohen, A. K. 1955. *Delinquent Boys*. Glencoe, IL: Free Press.
Cohen, R. D. 1985. "Child-Saving and Progressivism, 1885–1915." Pp. 273–309 in *American Childhood*, edited by J. M. Hawes and N. R. Hiner. Westport, CT: Greenwood.
Coleman, J. S. 1961. *The Adolescent Society*. New York: Free Press.
Conrad, P. 1975. "The Discovery of Hyperkinesis." *Social Problems* 23:12–21.
Conrad, P., and J. Schneider. 1992. *Deviance and Medicalization*, 2nd ed. Philadelphia: Temple University Press.
deMause, L. 1974. *The History of Childhood*. New York: Psychohistory Press.
Denzin, N. K. 1977. *Childhood Socialization*. San Francisco: Jossey-Bass.
Engelhardt, T. 1991. "Reading May Be Harmful to Your Kids." *Harper's* 282 (June):55–62.
Erchak, G. M., and R. Rosenfeld. 1989. "Learning Disabilities, Dyslexia, and the Medicalization of the Classroom." Pp. 79–97 in *Images of Issues*, edited by J. Best. Hawthorne, NY: Adline de Gruyter.
Fine, G. A. 1987. *With the Boys: Little League Baseball and Preadolescent Culture*. Chicago: University of Chicago Press.
Gray, H. 1989. "Popular Music as a Social Problem." Pp. 143–58 in *Images of Issues*, edited by J. Best. Hawthorne, NY: Adline de Gruyter.
Gusfield, J. R. 1981. *The Culture of Public Problems*. Chicago: University of Chicago Press.
Hollingshead, A. B. 1949. *Elmtown's Youth*. New York: Wiley.
Holstein, J. A., and G. Miller (eds.). 1993. *Reconsidering Social Constructionism*. Hawthorne, NY: Aldine de Gruyter.
Howitt, D. 1992. *Child Abuse Errors*. New Brunswick, NJ: Rutgers University Press.
Johnson, M., and K. Hufbauer. 1982. "Sudden Infant Death Syndrome as a Medical Research Problem since 1945." *Social Problems* 30:65–81.
Kaminer, W. 1992. *I'm Dysfunctional, You're Dysfunctional*. Reading, MA: Addison-Wesley.
Katz, M. B. 1968. *The Irony of Early School Reform*. Boston: Beacon Press.
King, D. L. 1994. "Captain Planet and the Planeteers: Kids, Environmental Crisis, and Competing Narratives of the New World Order." *Sociological Quarterly* 35:103–20.
Kotlowitz, A. 1991. *There Are No Children Here*. New York: Doubleday.

Kozol, J. 1988. *Rachel and Her Children*. New York: Crown.

La Farge, P. 1987. *The Strangelove Legacy*. New York: Harper & Row.

Margolin, L. 1994. *Goodness Personified*. Hawthorne, NY: Aldine de Gruyter.

Maynard, D. W. 1985. "On the Functions of Conflict among Children." *American Sociological Review* 50:207–23.

Nelson, B. J. 1984. *Making an Issue of Child Abuse*. Chicago: University of Chicago Press.

Payne, G. H. 1916. *The Child in Human Progress*. New York: Putnam's.

Phofl, S. J. 1977. "The 'Discovery' of Child Abuse." *Social Problems* 24:310–23.

Platt, A. M. 1969. *The Child Savers*. Chicago: University of Chicago Press.

Riis, J. A. 1894. *How the Other Half Lives*. New York: Scribner's.

Rothman, D. 1971. *The Discovery of the Asylum*. Boston: Little, Brown.

Shorter, E. 1977. *The Making of the Modern Family*. New York: Basic Book.

Spargo, J. 1913. *The Bitter Cry of the Children*. New York: Macmillan.

Spector, M., and J. I. Kitsuse. 1977. *Constructing Social Problems*. Menlo Park, CA: Benjamin Cummings.

Thomas, W. I. 1923. *The Unadjusted Girl*. Boston: Little, Brown.

Thorne, B. 1993. *Gender Play*. New Brunswick, NJ: Rutgers University Press.

Thrasher, F. M. 1927. *The Gang*. Chicago: University of Chicago Press.

U.N. Department of Economic and Social Development, Statistical Division. 1992. *1991 Demographic Yearbook*. New York: United Nations.

Weisberg, D. K. 1984. "The 'Discovery' of Sexual Abuse." *U.C. Davis Law Review* 18:1–57.

Wishy, B. 1968. *The Child and the Republic*. Philadelphia: University of Pennsylvania Press.

Zelizer, V. A. 1985. *Pricing the Priceless Child*. New York: Basic Books.

Part II

CHILDREN IN SOCIETAL CRISES

Chapter 2

A Threatened Generation: Impediments to Children's Quality of Life in Kenya

York W. Bradshaw, Claudia Buchmann, and Paul N. Mbatia

Africa observed the Day of the African Child on June 16, 1993, stressing the "Need for a Fresh Start." Unfortunately, the day passed with little official or unofficial fanfare, not because the continent undervalues children, but because the circumstances facing its children are so formidable. Kenya's most influential newspaper, the *Daily Nation*, ran an urgent editorial describing childrens' situation as "horrendous" and "extremely bleak." The editorial further noted: "Today, the continent commemorates Day of the African Child, and honest observers can only say that unless local governments and the international community take deliberate, practical steps to curb poverty and the deterioration of health and educational infrastructure, the children are truly and firmly candidates for 'endangered species'" (*Daily Nation* 1993:6).

Since the 1980s, a lethal combination of circumstances have emerged that severely threatens the next generation of African children. Growing poverty, structural adjustment policies, ethnic violence, AIDS, external indebtedness, corruption, mismanagement, educational decline, and overpopulation are only a few of the conditions that harm children. Although African children have long faced significant obstacles, they have perhaps never faced such a threatening combination of circumstances. After 20 or 30 years of experiencing improved health, African children are now less healthy and dying in larger numbers than just a few years ago. Years of development have been reversed, and children are among the primary victims of this deterioration.

This chapter focuses on the plight of children in the East African country of Kenya. Like other countries on the continent, Kenya has a large percentage of children (16% of Kenyans are under 5 years of age) and a declining standard of living. We first survey three topics that illustrate the deteriorating state of children in the country: health, education, and homelessness. Next, we examine several factors that contribute to the poor quality of life of children, including economic decline, ethnic violence, and AIDS. Finally, we discuss what (if anything) can be done to improve the deteriorating situation for children in Kenya. A variety of organizations—based inside and outside the country—have attempted to implement programs to help children, but only a few programs have made a positive impact.

THE CONTEMPORARY SITUATION FACING KENYAN CHILDREN

Sickness and Death

It is a well-known fact that child mortality rates in the Third World declined substantially over the last several decades. Kenya's decline has been especially impressive; the number of children dying before age 5 dropped from over 200 (out of 1,000 births) in 1960 to the current estimate of 105 (Government of Kenya [GOK] and UNICEF 1992:57). Unfortunately, however, Kenya is experiencing a reversal of several decades of progress. Preliminary estimates from the 1989 census clearly show that the country's child mortality rate is increasing. It is estimated that, by the end of the 1990s, the under-5 mortality rate will jump to 189 (GOK and UNICEF 1992:43).

A major cause of this increase is AIDS, which is very prevalent in Kenya. A newly published report states unequivocally that "AIDS alone threatens to eliminate 30 years of steady progress in reducing child death rates in Kenya" (GOK and UNICEF 1992:43). Kenya is not an aberration, of course. The *World Development Report* shows that other African countries with high levels of HIV infections are also experiencing growing child mortality rates (World Bank 1993). Moreover, the HIV epidemic will likely become much worse before it has any chance of slowing. By the year 2000, an estimated 95 percent of all HIV cases will be in the Third World, up from the current rate of 80 percent (World Bank 1993:99). The World Bank notes: "Historians will look back on the latter half of this century as having had one great medical triumph, the eradication of smallpox, and one great medical tragedy, AIDS" (World Bank 1993:99).

Although AIDS is killing a growing number of children, it is only one cause of death among Kenya's young. The vast majority of child deaths are caused by one of the following diseases: *malaria* (responsible for 30% of child deaths in some areas of Kenya), *acute respiratory infections* (responsible for over 40% of child deaths in some areas of Kenya), and *diarrheal diseases* (responsible for about 20% of child deaths nationwide). Furthermore, vaccine-preventable diseases such as measles, polio, tuberculosis, and neonatal tetanus kill and maim thousands of Kenyan children annually (GOK and UNICEF 1992:57–61). As in many regions of the Third World, most of these diseases can be cured or prevented with the proper resources and knowledge. Immunization is already fairly high in Kenya, where an estimated 71 percent of children are immunized against the major childhood killers. This is still below the target figure of 75 percent, however, and these rates vary widely by region of the country (GOK and UNICEF 1992:61–62).

In fact, physical quality of life for Kenyan children varies widely throughout the country. Important factors affecting the health of children include a region's level of wealth, climate, elevation, vegetation, and geographic location. The incidence of malaria is one example of variability by region. Table 1 shows (1) the under-5 mortality rate for the country's eight provinces; (2) the percentage of hospital outpatients diagnosed as suffering from malaria; and (3) an index measuring the severity of malaria experienced in each province. Malaria is transmitted when a mosquito carrying malaria parasites bites a person. Thus, malar-

Table 1. Province-Level Data on Various Development Indicators, 1979 (Provinces Arranged According to Lowest Level of Child Mortality)

	Under-5 child mortality	Malaria patients (%)	Malaria index
Central	85	7	1
Nairobi	104	0	0
Rift Valley	132	15	2
Eastern	128	19	3
North Eastern	160	20	3
Western	187	30	4
Coast	206	23	3
Nyanza	220	30	5
National average	*153*	*18*	*3*

Note: Under-5 mortality rate represents the number of children that die before age 5 per 1,000 births; malaria patients represents the percentage of hospital outpatients diagnosed with malaria; malaria index measures the severity of malaria in a region—0 shows that malaria is not endemic, and 5 shows that malaria is highly endemic.

Source: Bradshaw 1993.

ia is most problematic in regions that are heavily infested with mosquitoes (labeled "5" in the table) and least problematic in regions that do not have many mosquitoes (labeled "0" in the table). Not surprisingly, there is a high correlation between the prevalence of malaria and child mortality. Central Province and Nairobi Province are in high-altitude regions that have relatively few mosquitoes and relatively low child mortality rates, whereas Western, Coast, and Nyanza Provinces are in hot, humid regions that breed malaria-transmitting mosquitoes. A recent quantitative study found that the relationship between malaria and child mortality is strong even after a variety of other factors are controlled in multiple regression analysis (Bradshaw 1993).

Many diseases that afflict children are a direct result of lack of access to clean water. The majority of Kenyans live in rural areas, and, as shown in Table 2, only 42 percent of these people have access to safe drinking water. A substantial number of urban Kenyans live in slum areas, including 60 percent of Nairobi residents, and they also have limited access to safe water. Very few slum dwellers (under 2%) have piped water in their homes; instead, they must rely on communal water pipes and informal vendors who sell water. Despite these sources of water, a substantial number of urban slum dwellers have no access to safe water, including 63 percent of the population in Mombasa, Kenya's second largest city (GOK and UNICEF 1992:87).

Closely related to unsafe water is lack of basic sanitation facilities. Water contaminated by human waste is one of the most significant health problems confronting Kenya and other poor countries. Only 35 percent of Kenya's population has access to adequate sewerage facilities,

Table 2. Province-Level Data on Percentage of Population with Access to Safe Drinking Water in Planned Urban Areas, Urban Slums, and Rural Areas, 1989

Province	Planned urban areas	Urban slums	Rural areas
Central	92	54	68
Nairobi	100	56	0
Rift Valley	88	56	30
Eastern	100	55	30
North Eastern	75	62	37
Western	76	60	55
Coast	100	42	25
Nyanza	100	59	45
National average	92	53	42

Source: GOK and UNICEF 1992.

such as a septic tank, pour or flush latrine, or some type of pit latrine (GOK and UNICEF 1992:88). Poor sanitation contributes directly to a variety of diseases and intestinal parasites such as worms. Thousands of children could be saved each year if more people had access to basic sewerage facilities.

Poor sanitation also contributes to malnutrition among children, because parasites compete with the body for food. It is estimated that about 20 percent of Kenya's under-5 population suffers from physical stunting due to malnutrition, although this number varies widely according to region of the country (GOK and UNICEF 1992:81). Other causes of malnutrition and food shortages include lack of access to arable land, ethnic clashes, drought, and general poverty. Children are disproportionately affected when a country experiences chronic food shortages.

To conclude, it is clear that Kenyan children suffer from a variety of health problems that are not common in most economically developed countries. Diseases caused by unclean water and poor sanitation take the lives of many children each year. The growing AIDS epidemic will continue to kill more and more Kenyan children, at least in the foreseeable future.

Educational Decline

Since achieving political independence in 1963, Kenya has stressed the importance of educating its children. Until the late 1970s, the Kenyan government successfully encouraged more and more children to attend school and continued to spend a substantial amount of money on education. Educational enrollments were especially impressive during this period. Primary enrollment increased from 44 percent to 85 percent of eligible students for boys and from 25 percent to 76 percent for girls (see Figure 1, Plot 1). Moreover, secondary enrollment rates for both government-maintained schools and local nongovernment "self-help" schools also increased until the late 1970s (see Plots 2 and 3).[1] Enrollment rates for all types of schools vary widely by region; the percentage of eligible primary school students that attend school ranges from 18 to 100 depending on the province, and the percentage of eligible students that attend secondary school ranges from 4 to 42.

In the late 1970s, education in Kenya began to decline both in terms of enrollments and quality. This decline continues today, and the number of children without access to education has been increasing. Although the complete explanation for this situation is beyond the scope of this chapter (see Fuller and Bradshaw 1993), it is important to make

Plot 1 - Primary Enrollment Rate

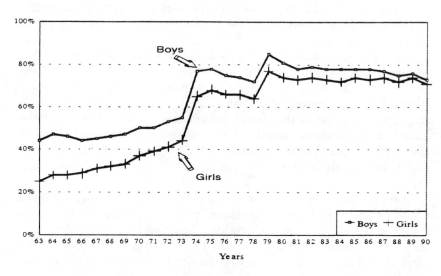

Plot 2 - Secondary Enrollment Rate (Girls Only)

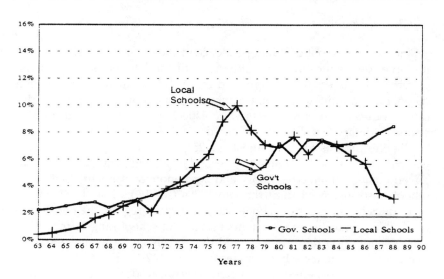

Figure 1. Kenya: School Enrollment Rates 1963-1990.

Plot 3 - Secondary Enrollment Rate (Boys Only)

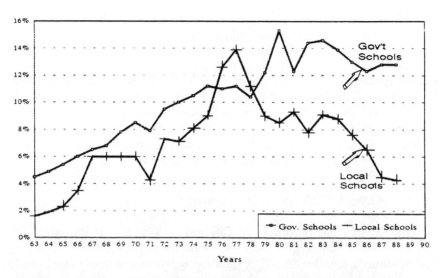

Figure 1 (continued)

several points. First, economic decline, external indebtedness, and structural adjustment programs have caused a decrease in the national quality of life and have made it increasingly difficult (and irrational) for parents to send their children to school. During difficult economic times, keeping children (especially girls) at home to work becomes a rational choice for parents. Second, although the Kenyan government continues to stress the importance of education as a symbol of modernity, it no longer possesses the capacity to further expand educational enrollments. Moreover, neither the government nor the private sector can provide enough meaningful jobs and other positions to educated citizens. All of these factors are slowing growth rates in enrollments and threatening to undermine the educational expansion that has been achieved since independence.

In addition to declining enrollments, fewer Kenyan children are having a *meaningful* educational experience. National test scores are falling, and school infrastructures are crumbling (Bradshaw and Fuller 1993; GOK and UNICEF 1992). The number of trained teachers has not kept pace with enrollments, teachers salaries have stagnated, and morale is low. Finally, because of increasing costs, many schools have been forced to cut back on textbooks, writing materials, and other resources that are fundamental to a quality learning experience. Education is declining in Kenya, whether we examine it from a "quantity" or "quality" stand-point.

Children are the losers when education declines. Quality education is associated with better nutrition, improved health, and upward mobility. Very important, education is also one of the ways in which girls and women can improve their position in society. And, as discussed below, when children are not in school they also become prime targets for exploitation by adults. Again, educational decline has not occurred in a vacuum; economic crisis takes money away from education and creates a climate that discourages further schooling. Unless Kenya's economic situation improves substantially, it is unlikely that the "quantity" or "quality" of education in the country will improve.

Growth of Homelessness and "Street Children"

When discussing the plight of children in Kenya, it is important to stress several demographic facts: 13.9 million Kenyans (59 percent of the population) are under age 20, 3.8 million Kenyans are under age 5, and an estimated 500,000 Kenyan children live primarily on the street (GOK and UNICEF 1992:14; Owuor 1993). Moreover, the number of street children is growing rapidly, underscoring the country's expanding poverty rate and level of family instability. This is among the most tragic events unfolding across the African continent.[2]

There have been few rigorous studies of street children in Kenya, but such children's means of survival are fairly well-known. First, it is virtually impossible to walk across downtown Nairobi without being confronted repeatedly by child beggars. Children as young as 2 years old will approach both Africans and foreigners, whom they will ask for money, even for as little as 1 shilling (65 Kenyan shillings are equal to U.S. $1). Some children work alone, but most work with a small group of other children or even with the child's entire family. A common scene is for a young girl (perhaps 12 years old) to beg for money with a young sibling on her back. At times, the young girl may claim that the child on her back is her own, which, on occasion, it may be. But, more often than not, the child is a younger brother or sister carried around in an effort to elicit sympathy from people being approached for money.

The method of approaching people varies. Children may simply approach strangers and ask for money, turning away when they are told no. Other children will walk with a person (especially foreign whites) for several blocks, stressing their chronic hunger. Some children even tug on the arms of people in an effort to "encourage" giving. Another approach occurs at stoplights, where children (either alone or in small groups) approach cars and ask the occupants for money. They move quickly to the next car when turned down, although some children move from the driver's window to the passenger side of the same car in an effort to find a sympathetic person. Although an occasional person in the car or on the street gives money to street beggars, the vast majority of people do not. Even those citizens who do give money often avoid all physical contact with the street child for fear of contracting some type of skin disease.

Second, most street children engage in some type of labor to survive. A large number of young boys are "parking boys," who wait on crowded urban streets for cars to approach. The child (or children) will "assist" the driver in pulling into a parking place and then will clean and "guard" the car while the driver is away. Street children hope that the driver will pay them for their efforts. Although some girls participate in this activity, the overwhelming majority of such children are boys. Other street children sell a variety of small items in the informal sector, including paper from trash containers, peanuts, candy, cigarettes, and other products. And, because of desperate economic conditions, some children increasingly steal watches, purses, and other items, especially in urban areas.

In addition, street children represent a large pool of easily exploited workers in various types of labor. Young boys are recruited for manual labor positions such as dishwashers and cleaners, especially in small informal-sector eating establishments known as kiosks. The boys wake very early to clean and work in the kitchen (e.g., peel potatoes), and, after working through the day and evening, they clean again after closing hours. It is very late before their working day ends. In exchange for this labor, the boys are paid a nominal wage, given food, and allowed to sleep on the kiosk floor. Clearly, these boys do not have the opportunity to attend school. Young girls often are recruited as "housegirls" (maids), where they work very long hours doing housework and caring for young children. Housegirls seldom have an opportunity to attend school and are paid very little or nothing for their labor; they often are given a room and food only. Moreover, housegirls are not infrequent victims of sexual abuse by men in the home. Kenyan laws on child labor are weak and rarely enforced (GOK and UNICEF 1992:112).

Third, one of the most alarming increases in child labor regards prostitution. The GOK and UNICEF (1992:132) state candidly:

> Recent surveys reveal that child prostitution is the leading form of child exploitation in Kenya today, particularly in urban centers. The majority of girls are from poor families—abandoned, neglected or orphaned children who are exposed to this lifestyle during their problematic young lives.

Although good estimates concerning the number of children engaged in prostitution are not available, there is a consensus that the numbers are growing for several reasons: (1) Kenya's deepening poverty is a breeding ground for sexual and other types of exploitation. More girls become involved in prostitution to survive and to generate additional income for their families. Increasingly boys are also turning to prostitution as a way to survive the streets. (2) The alarming increase in AIDS has caused men to look for younger and younger sexual partners in the belief that they will be free from the disease. This means that more and more children are contracting sexually transmitted diseases (STDs), including HIV. One estimate is that about 20 percent of children with AIDS are in the 5–14 age range, a group that has not contracted HIV at birth or through breast feeding. Much of this increase is due to growing prostitution among the very young in the country (GOK and UNICEF 1992:43; *Undugu* Society 1992:8–11). Some estimates indicate that 9 out of 10 street girls have been treated for sexually transmitted diseases and that 3 out of 10 are HIV positive (Owuor 1993).

To summarize, street children are compelled to beg, work, steal, and prostitute themselves in order to survive. The effects of this way of life are predictable and depressing. The physical toll is enormous. Street children suffer from high rates of disease, malnutrition, drug abuse (especially petrol and glue sniffing), and sexual abuse. Children without homes must also contend with rain, cold, lack of sanitation, and environmental hazards (Onyango 1989). In addition to disease and other adverse conditions, street children must face a general public that, although generally sympathetic, is growing increasingly frustrated with the aggressive tactics used by youngsters. Some children are slapped, pushed, or verbally abused by citizens on the street. A few children are also victims of random violence. Even the most concerned citizens often refuse to give money to street children and encourage them to move off the streets and back home. Unfortunately, the street is "home" for an increasing number of children.

Beyond the physical damage that accompanies street life, there is a substantial mental and emotional toll. Chronic malnutrition stunts mental development, as does the widespread drug abuse that characterizes street life. It is clear that "hard drugs" are now routinely used by some street children. In addition, street children seldom attend school for very long, precluding them from developing the basic skills necessary for life. All of these problems are compounded by the emotional stress and abuse that go along with begging, stealing, and prostitution. Even if street children were institutionalized for rehabilitation, they would still have to cope with the years of trauma, abuse, and sadness that many have endured. Street life in Kenya is extremely dangerous for children, "stealing" their childhood and producing circumstances that can end their lives.

REASONS FOR THE DETERIORATING CONDITION
OF CHILDREN

There is no single factor causing the declining quality of life among Kenya's children. Moreover, there is no magic formula to determine why children face increasingly difficult circumstances in the country. There are, however, a number of conditions and situations widely believed to cause or exacerbate the declining plight of Kenyan children.

Economic Stagnation

There is little question that economic performance and the distribution of income are integrally related to physical quality of life in a country. If a country has a growing economy and distributes resources equitably, then there will be more money for health, education, and the provision of basic services. Conversely, if a country has a contracting economy, or if it distributes resources inequitably, then there will be few resources available to improve the physical quality of life of the mass population. The biggest losers in this situation are children, who often have the lowest priority in difficult circumstances (UNICEF 1993).

In terms of economic growth, Kenya's situation has fluctuated since political independence in 1963. Between 1963 and 1980, the national economy was one of the healthiest in Africa, as the total gross domestic product (GDP) grew at an average annual rate of 6.8 percent and the industrial GDP expanded even faster at 9.7 percent (World Bank 1992:220). On balance, inflation and unemployment also remained relatively low during this period. The situation began to change significantly in Kenya and the rest of Africa during the 1980s. Between 1980 and 1990, Kenya's total economic growth slowed to 4.2 percent and its industrial expansion to 3.9 percent (World Bank 1992:220). Moreover, the situation has worsened in the last two or three years, with the economy slowing to near zero growth for the first time in Kenya's post-independence history (Makokha 1993). To make matters worse, inflation is skyrocketing at an annual rate that exceeds 40 percent, drastically reducing the standard of living of citizens already suffering in a stagnant economy. In real terms, the average income gross national product (GNP per capita) is about one-half of what it was in the late 1970s (Fuller and Bradshaw 1993).

Economic decline clearly affects children in specific ways. First, families have substantially less purchasing power today. This translates into less food, less medicine, less schooling, and fewer overall services for children. An increasing number of Kenyan families simply cannot afford even the basic necessities of life during this period of severe economic stagnation and austerity. Street children are a direct consequence of this climate. Second, the government and other national organizations do not have as much money for programs to assist children and other vulnerable groups. The Kenyan government is very explicit in stating that, with respect to health and other areas, "a greater role will have to be played by the private sector, self-help groups, and NGOs [nongovernmental organizations]" (GOK 1989:237). Moreover, health care will be more expensive, because "Government will introduce user charges and fees at graduated levels for hospital in-patient care and provide drugs at cost in public facilities" (GOK 1989:238). These measures, which have proven very controversial within Kenya, disproportionately affect children, because the young need frequent medical attention and access to other services.

We can learn more about this situation by looking closely at health clinics in Kenya. For example, the University of Nairobi health clinic, which is a government institution, used to provide very good care at virtually no cost to faculty, staff, and students. The national economic crisis has led to a sharp deterioration in clinic services. Clinic facilities are declining, and, perhaps worst of all, there is almost no medicine in the clinic. The few university personnel who possess sufficient resources simply by-pass the clinic and seek private medical attention elsewhere. Most people do not have this option, however, and they must go without proper medical attention and needed medication. This situation can be fatal for children who require immediate medical attention when they contract a disease. Unfortunately, the high inflation rate means that average citizens have even less opportunity than before to purchase medication and other services outside the clinic. Although the situation is bleak at the University of Nairobi clinic, it is even bleaker in urban slums and rural areas. About 40 percent of medical attention in rural areas must be provided by some type of nongovernment institution, which, again, often has very poor facilities and little medication (Bratton 1989; GOK and UNICEF 1992).

All of these factors reflect the economic reforms occurring across Africa, including Kenya. Such reforms have been discussed extensively elsewhere (e.g., Bradshaw et al. 1993) and will be described only briefly here. In response to Africa's mounting foreign debt and general economic crisis, the International Monetary Fund (IMF), the World Bank, and other global financial organizations are forcing countries to implement structural adjustment policies (SAPs) if they want additional loans or the freedom to renegotiate current debts. These SAPs are severe. To streamline the government and increase economic efficiency, the policies require (1) sharp government spending cuts, which reduce funding for health and various social services; (2) elimination of or reductions in government subsidies for food and other items, which drastically increase the cost of living; (3) reductions in government employment, which increase unemployment; (4) decontrol of prices and devaluation of the local currency, both of which increase prices for food and basic necessities.

Structural adjustment policies disproportionately harm poor citizens, especially children living in slums or depressed rural areas. This has led the GOK and UNICEF (1992:137) to note:

> During the difficult years when these structural adjustment reforms are being implemented, it will be necessary to design and implement safety nets for the most vulnerable groups, and particularly for women and children in poor and marginalized households. It is obvious that Government will not have the resources to finance these safety nets on its own. Substantial assistance from donor governments will be needed.

Without such "safety nets," it will be extremely difficult for many children to survive. The IMF, World Bank, and other organizations argue that, in the *long run*, structural adjustment will facilitate economic growth and physical quality of life for children. The early evidence does not support their case, largely because structural adjustments are implemented too quickly and without adequate attention to the specific features of individual countries (see, e.g., Bradshaw et al. 1993).

Finally, SAPs and general economic decline exacerbate the inequalities in wealth that already plague Kenya (see GOK and UNICEF 1992). Poverty, both relative and absolute, is growing quickly across Kenya, meaning that the small elite class gains a bigger share of the shrinking national income, while the majority of people get less. Most important, estimates show clearly that "the most vulnerable members of a poor family are inevitably the children and women" (GOK and UNICEF 1992:21). Many of the poorest children live in slum areas with their mother and several brothers and sisters.

Ethnic Clashes

Kenya is one of the most ethnically divided countries in Africa. Although the country has more than 32 ethnic groups (tribes), three groups account for about 50 percent of the population, namely, the

Kikuyu, the Luo, and the Luhya. The first president of Kenya, Jomo Kenyatta, was a Kikuyu who governed from 1963 until his death in 1978. During his reign, the Kikuyus derived enormous political and economic benefits through a patron-client network controlled by the president and his associates. After Kenyatta's death, his vice-president, Daniel arap Moi, assumed power and continues to govern today. President Moi is from one of Kenya's small tribes, the Kalenjin, whom he has strongly favored throughout his long tenure in office. In an attempt to win national support, President Moi has shrewdly "balanced" his cabinet and advisors with some representatives from major tribes. Otherwise, he is known to be very harsh on individuals, groups, and tribes suspected to be disloyal and critical to his regime in general.

President Moi's power was strengthened by the fact that his political party, the Kenya African National Union (KANU), was the only legal party in Kenya until 1991. This situation changed amid severe pressure from outside donors (e.g., the World Bank) and indigenous groups (political, religious, professional, and more) to initiate multiparty democracy. The introduction of multiparty democracy in December 1991 heightened ethnic tensions in the country.[3]

In fact, severe ethnic violence began in 1991, amid discussions of multiparty politics in Kenya. The KANU political leaders from Moi's Kalenjin base began to encourage small tribes to protect themselves against the "impending danger" of being governed by a large ethnic group. Three small groups in particular, the Kalenjin, the Maasai, and the Pokot, were encouraged to drive out "foreign" tribes—especially the Kikuyu, the Luhya, the Luo, and the Kisii—from a region in western Kenya. The resulting violence has been severe, as detailed by numerous groups such as the National Council of Churches of Kenya (NCCK).[4] One month after the clashes started, 67 houses had been burned to the ground and 1,700 people displaced. One month later, the toll stood at 4,500 homes destroyed, 22,490 people displaced, 12 schools closed, and 4,780 grain stores burned (over a year's supply of food) (NCCK 1992). The violence has continued for 18 months, up to the present day. The statistics are startling and resemble a warlike situation: over 1,000 dead and more than 200,000 displaced from their homes and land (Majtenyi 1993a; Press 1993). Kenya government officials dispute the 1,000 figure and place the number at about 365. Following this government claim, the *Daily Nation* ran a cartoon on May 7, 1993, that showed a very crowded grave yard with victims of the ethnic clashes. Two observers then commented to each other: "Do you mean there're only 365 graves here?" In addition to this loss of life, Kenya's agricultural production has been cut sharply, and the government is now begging for food aid from abroad. The government claims that the main problem is drought, when, in fact, the food shortages are largely a result of interrupted food production because of the ethnic clashes.

The ethnic clashes have severely affected the welfare of Kenya's children. Although precise numbers are not available, it is very clear that many children have died, either directly from the clashes or indirectly through the consequences of the clashes. Indeed, it is documented that "some of the children of displaced families in the various clash areas have died as a result of poor housing, a poor diet, and lack of adequate medical care" (Press, 1993:10). Thousands of children have become refugees, suffering from the usual circumstances that surround war: "Food shortages are common. Diseases such as tuberculosis, scabies and malaria spread quickly and frequently. ... Malnutrition is rampant especially amongst the children" (Majtenyi 1993b). These conditions, among others, have prompted some commentators to call child clash victims "the lost generation" (Majtenyi 1993b).

Education has also been severely disrupted in three specific ways. First, school enrollments have decreased. Again, although official statistics are not available, it is clear that thousands of children have lost their opportunity to attend school, at least for the foreseeable future. Enrollment is reduced, because (1) a number of schools have been burned to the ground; (2) many parents will not allow their children to go to school, because they fear attacks on the children while they are going to or returning from school; (3) many children and their families have simply left the area, because they fear attacks on their home.

Second, the ethnic clashes have created a climate of violence, fear, intimidation, and psychological trauma in the schools. Majtenyi (1993c) notes:

> Prior to the clashes, children of all ethnic groups would mix, play together and speak to each other in Kiswahili [the national language]. That behavior stopped immediately when the clashes began says a teacher at the school [who stated]: "During the clashes, the children sat in separate ethnic groups and spoke in their mother tongue. They refused to sit together and speak in Kiswahili."

Children of certain ethnic groups often are attacked and driven from the school. Furthermore, teachers have also been threatened or attacked. Teachers report that they are even afraid to discipline children from certain ethnic groups because of the possibility of reprisal (Majtenyi 1993c). The ethnic tension between students, teachers, and parents has undermined education in clash-ridden areas of the country. It will leave long-term psychological scars on the children that will be difficult to overcome.

Third, the clashes are also responsible for a drastic deterioration of quality in the schools operating in the threatened areas. Because many schools have been destroyed, children of all ages are placed together in makeshift classrooms that lack even the basic educational necessities. Moreover, many teachers—especially those from the "wrong" ethnic group—are fleeing the clash-ridden areas. It will be increasingly difficult to recruit quality teachers into the areas affected by the clashes.

To summarize, Kenya's ethnic clashes have had devastating consequences on children. Death, disease, malnutrition, ignorance, fear, and psychological trauma have resulted from the ongoing violence. The primary victims of war around the world are children; as noted by UNICEF (1992:50): "In the last decade alone, more than 1.5 million children have been killed in wars, more than 4 million have been physically disabled, more than 5 million have been forced into refugee camps and more than 12 million have lost their homes." Although Kenya has always been thought of as a "peaceful country" without civil wars and violent conflicts with other countries, it is clear that this perception is no longer valid. Political violence is a reality in parts of Kenya, as a version of ethnic cleansing continues.[5]

AIDS and Children

Kenya's first national conference on AIDS was held in Nairobi on April 21, 1993. Those in attendance included doctors, social scientists, AIDS sufferers, educators, journalists, and others. One of the most valuable aspects of the conference was a compilation of all known studies of AIDS in Kenya. The country has not yet had a series of national AIDS studies; but there have been a number of regional studies. These studies, combined with other information gathered by organizations such as the Kenyan government, UNICEF, and the World Health Organization (WHO), provide an early portrait of AIDS in Kenya.

It is no exaggeration to state that AIDS has reached crisis proportions in Kenya. The GOK and UNICEF (1992:41) report the facts:

> In Kenya, it is estimated that 8–9% of the general population is HIV-positive. In addition, 16–20% of all Kenyans carrying sexually transmitted diseases are expected to become HIV-positive. Officially, pediatric diagnoses suggest that 3% of all HIV carriers are children under five years old; unofficially, the proportion is believed to be 10%.

More alarming, other studies suggest that the AIDS epidemic is even worse in some areas of the country. A pilot study conducted in 1992 by the Moi University Faculty of Health Sciences and the Indiana University School of Medicine was especially revealing (see Menya and Mulli 1993). The study took blood samples from 140 pregnant women visiting a health clinic around the city of Eldoret, located in the western part of the country. The women were not considered a "high-risk" group, that is, they were not commercial sex workers. However, the women do live in an area of Kenya that has a relatively high rate of polygamy, contributing to their exposure to men who have multiple sexual partners. Nearly 40 percent of the women had at least one STD, and 14.5 were HIV-positive. It is estimated that 25 to 40 percent of children born to mothers who are HIV-positive will become HIV-positive themselves (GOK and UNICEF 1992:43).

The AIDS epidemic affects children in three primary ways. First, and most obvious, many of the children born to HIV-positive mothers will contract AIDS and die a very painful death. Most will die before age 5. Second, a large number of children will become AIDS orphans over the next few years. By 1996, 300,000 Kenyan children will be without a parent because of AIDS (GOK and UNICEF 1992:43; Owino 1993). This means that either extended families—many of which are becoming poorer—will have to adopt these children, or AIDS orphans will live on the street. As we have already seen, street children have higher rates of malnutrition, disease, and prostitution than children who live at home. Third, AIDS orphans will have to deal with the psychological trauma of watching parents die a difficult death and of beginning a "new life" without their parents. The Kenyan government and other organizations are in no position to enact an effective program for AIDS orphans.

Unfortunately, the effects of AIDS on children will continue to worsen during the 1990s. The reason for this bleak assessment is simple: The AIDS situation is growing worse across Kenya and the rest of Africa. Although more Kenyans know about the disease, there is little evidence to suggest that this knowledge is causing a majority of the population to change their sexual habits. There is still a high rate of multiple sexual partners in the country, and sexual activity begins at an earlier age. A study of sexual activity conducted in 1991 among young people aged 12–19 substantiates this point. More than 50 percent of the sample was sexually active, with the average age of first intercourse occurring between age 13 and 14. The vast majority of the sample—89 percent—had *never* used any form of contraception. The adult population does not fare much better. Only about 38 million condoms are used in Kenya per year, which is roughly six condoms per adult male. This is *far below* the number of acts of intercourse per year in the country. Because abstinence is not occurring and condom use is minimal, the spread of AIDS will likely continue unabated (GOK and UNICEF 1992:43).

The AIDS epidemic is a relatively new phenomenon, but it will have one of the greatest effects on modern Africa. It is killing many children and adults and *may* even *reverse* population growth on the continent. Moreover, the AIDS epidemic will severely alter the social structure of Kenyan society. Grandparents, extended families, and street friends must suddenly care for a whole new generation of children without parents. This situation cannot be remedied immediately, because there is no cure for AIDS; furthermore, preventative measures have not generally been accepted. To date, despite the enthusiastic AIDS prevention campaigns that have been launched by the Ministry of Health and some NGOs, critical aspects of social habits associated with the spread of the disease have not changed, partly because of cultural factors. For example, it is common in urban areas for some married men to habitually engage in extramarital affairs, thereby putting their wives—who frequently reside in the countryside—at risk of contracting AIDS. In some other communities, men continue to marry more than one wife as sanctioned by their cultural traditions, a practice that can facilitate the spread of AIDS. Worse still, Western AIDS-prevention techniques such as the use of condoms are yet to be assimilated into the local culture. This may take more time to change, because local churches (especially Catholic churches) object to the use of some preventative measures. Other factors that contribute to lack of preventative measures include ignorance, absence of devices (e.g., condoms), illiteracy, and apathy, especially among the very poor.

Tragically, the AIDS epidemic is an additional crisis that Kenya simply cannot afford. As noted earlier, children already are harmed by many intractable diseases, severe structural adjustment policies that are reducing expenditures on health and other services, and the stagnant national economy. The AIDS epidemic will make the situation even worse for children.

WHAT CAN BE DONE TO HELP CHILDREN IN KENYA?

The situation facing Kenyan children appears quite bleak, at least for the foreseeable future. Long-term solutions to the plight of children include national economic recovery, control of the AIDS epidemic, better overall health care, and additional resources for various development programs. As discussed, it is unlikely that these solutions will occur in the near future. In fact, it also is unlikely that any national short-term programs will be initiated, largely because of (1) Kenya's deteriorating position in the world economy; and (2) the Kenyan government's indifference to the situation.

Foreign donors are unlikely to give substantial *new* sums of capital to

Kenya, at least not as long as the present regime remains in power. The country has an expanding foreign debt, a stagnating economy, and a corrupt government, none of which is conducive to attracting new foreign investment or aid. Investors and donors (including NGOs) will not leave Kenya, but they probably will be more circumspect in their giving. This means that new programs—such as money for AIDS orphans—will be difficult to fund on a long-term basis. Until Kenya undertakes extensive economic and political reforms, foreign donors are unlikely to change their basic posture.

Under incredible pressure from the IMF, the Kenyan government *has* initiated *some* economic reforms (e.g., a sharp devaluation of the shilling), but the government has done little to discourage the corruption that continues to siphon off millions of U.S. dollars from development programs. Moreover, it continues to repress true democratic reform and free expression of opposition views. In addition to these shortcomings, the Kenyan government is rather indifferent to the nation's children. It has not yet initiated tangible programs to assist street children; it seldom speaks out on AIDS; it "steals" foreign assistance that could be used for development programs; and, perhaps most reprehensibly, it has been reluctant to stop the ethnic violence that is devastating the next generation of Kenyan children. Although the government cannot end child poverty and disease in Kenya, it *can* help coordinate and initiate programs that would alleviate the problem to some extent. Furthermore, it could initiate reforms that would attract outside aid specifically for programs to assist children.

With these points in mind, we believe that an agenda for assisting Kenyan children must have several specific objectives, none easy to achieve. First, the Kenyan government (current or future) must initiate substantial reforms, including an effort to curb corruption and implement more democracy. The government should also take some of the money previously used for corrupt activities and channel them into programs for children. The government must also end the ethnic violence. It has the power to achieve this last objective within a matter of days by: (1) using the police and military to intervene in clash areas; (2) telling KANU politicians to speak out against the violence; and (3) aggressively prosecuting those who continue to commit violence, regardless of their ethnic background.

Second, foreign donors and the international financial community need to give more aid *specifically for programs that assist children*. Such programs could be for health, education, or other needed services. Important, however, donors should *not* give the money to the national government for distribution; instead, they should distribute the money themselves or give it to a trusted NGO for distribution. Moreover, foreign donors should withhold nonhumanitarian aid from Kenya until the government stops the ethnic clashes and other forms of harassment. The IMF and other organizations have made future assistance contingent on economic reforms and a few political reforms, but they have not insisted on an end to ethnic violence. International donors have significant leverage on the Kenyan government, and they should use it to end violence whenever possible.

Third, NGOs must continue to work closely with local communities on programs to assist children. Kenya currently has more NGOs than any other sub-Saharan African country (over 400) that work on a variety of development projects. One of the most effective is the *Undugu* Society, a Kenya-based organization that works with boys and girls facing difficult circumstances, especially those living on the street. For over 20 years, the *Undugu* Society has initiated a variety of effective programs that work with local communities to assist children. The *Undugu* Society provides health and education programs for street children, mobilizes women's groups, operates training programs for youths who hope to work in the informal sector, sponsors agricultural projects, provides low-cost shelter, and implements other programs (*Undugu* Society of Kenya 1991, 1992). This NGO is relatively successful, because it (1) supplements its own income-generating projects with external money; (2) does not suffer from government interference; and (3) assumes a community-oriented approach to development.[6]

A fourth objective to assist children consists of community-level actions. Villages, slums, and other communities must work hard to provide as much assistance for children as possible, especially in conjunction with NGOs. Kenya has a long tradition of self-help within the *harambee* tradition, and it must be targeted increasingly for programs that assist children. The cooperation between the *Undugu* Society and various communities is a model that should be emulated throughout Kenya. Because the government cannot be relied on to facilitate development, it is essential for local communities to work hard with a variety of NGOs to assist children. This approach would create a number of small "success stories" among an otherwise bleak situation for Kenyan children.

CONCLUSION

On a macro level, the 1990s will be a devastating time for the African continent. Economies will stagnate further, health and education will decline, and the AIDS epidemic will continue to claim more victims. The outside world is also asking Africa to do something that is virtually unprecedented in recent history: democratize during a period of economic stagnation and underdevelopment. Although we applaud democratic efforts, we also caution against thinking of democracy as a panacea for the many intractable problems facing the continent. If past history is a good indicator, democracy may only be possible after overall development occurs.

Amid the bleak situation facing Africa, however, we can find local success stories because of efforts at the community level. Local communities are making a difference in the lives of children, especially when assisted by NGOs and other organizations. Western observers should not look at the tragic pictures coming from Africa and conclude that the situation is hopeless. It is not. Observers must look beneath the surface to find some of the local success stories that are occurring and that can occur in the future. These stories will not reverse the macro trend that shows a declining quality of life for the nation's children. Important, though, they will make a difference in the lives of some children who otherwise have very little hope.

ACKNOWLEDGMENTS

This article would not have been possible without the support of two organizations. York Bradshaw appreciates the support of the United States Information Agency (USIA), which funds a faculty exchange program between Indiana University and the University of Nairobi. He spent part of 1993 in Kenya. Claudia Buchmann appreciates the support of a Social Science Research Council (SSRC) Predissertation Fellowship. The fellowship provided 12 months of support for the study of East Africa, including six months of predissertation field research in Kenya during 1993.

NOTES

1. Kenya's first president, Jomo Kenyatta, encouraged community-based self-help efforts in education, health, and other areas. These self-help projects are known as *harambee* efforts, a Swahili term meaning "Let us all pull together." *Harambee* schools are locally based schools that provide an educational opportunity (especially at the secondary level) for many children who cannot gain admission to government-maintained institutions. *Harambee* schools are funded primarily by communities and their parents. However, local schools are expensive and of inferior quality relative to government schools.

2. The growth in the number of street children is certainly not unique to Africa. Street children are becoming more prevalent throughout the Third World. Some of Brazil's street children are even killed by government "hit squads," underscoring the lack of tolerance that its society has for these children.

3. President Moi and other representatives of small ethnic groups strongly opposed a multiparty system, because they feared that Kenyans would vote largely along ethnic lines, thereby favoring big ethnic groups. President Moi and his associates reasoned that he might loose the presidency to a person from the larger groups. To prevent this logical scenario from becoming a reality, a shrewd strategy was crafted by the president and his associates. They argued publicly that multiparty democracy in an ethnically divided society would foment inter-tribal violence, ultimately resembling Somalia or some other conflict-ridden situation. Soon after these statements, ethnic violence began in Kenya. It is well-known that the government encouraged and even started some of the ethnic violence, providing the Moi government with the perfect opportunity to stress that it was Kenya's only hope to avoid civil war. President Moi then campaigned hard for the vote of ethnic minorities.

4. This NCCK (1992) report was one of the first relatively comprehensive reports of the ethnic violence in Kenya. Its contents were based on information compiled by newspaper reporters and other observers on the scene. After the report was released, the government harshly condemned its contents and claimed that the NCCK was a tool of the opposition. (It is well-known that NCCK is dominated by church leaders critical to the present KANU regime). The government dispatched its own research team (a select committee from parliament) to the clash areas to compile the KANU response to the NCCK report. The KANU research team completed a report that nearly matched the NCCK document! This infuriated high-ranking KANU members, who had the KANU report rejected in parliament. The chairman of the select committee was highly censored by the same KANU people within and outside parliament for allegedly taking an "anti-KANU stand."

5. Fortunately, the outside world is finally being made aware of the ethnic clashes. Indeed, some members of parliament from the opposition parties in Kenya have even threatened to visit UN headquarters in New York to lobby for international intervention after noting the government's vested interest in perpetuating the clashes, its reluctance to stop the clashes despite its rhetorical promises, its failure to use its numerous forces impartially in protecting the lives of its citizens, and its reluctance to prosecute or even seriously investigate violence perpetrated in the clash areas against non-Kalenjin citizens.

6. Because of the continuing weakness of African governments, some observers placed great hope in the utility of NGOs (Bratton 1989). Some of these same observers now argue that NGOs also have limitations with respect to their ability to facilitate development. Like governments, some NGOs are inefficient, corrupt, and ineffective. Others, however, are relatively productive and capable of enhancing development in local areas. Foreign aid through NGOs should thus be given selectively.

REFERENCES

Bradshaw, Y. W. 1993. "State Limitations, Self-Help Secondary Schooling, and Development in Kenya." *Social Forces* 72:347-78.

Bradshaw, Y. W., R. Noonan, L. Gash, and C. B. Sershen. 1993. "Borrowing against the Future: Children and Third World Indebtedness." *Social Forces* 71:629–56.

Bratton, M. 1989. "The Politics of Government-NGO Relations in Africa." *World Development* 7:569–87.

Daily Nation. 1993. "Time to Focus on the Dying Child." Editorial (June 16):6.

Fuller, B., and Y. Bradshaw. 1993. "When Strong States Grow Fragile: The Rise and Fall of School Demand in Kenya." Under review.

Government of Kenya (GOK). 1989. *Development Plan, 1989–1993*. Nairobi: Government Printer.

GOK and UNICEF. 1992. *Children and Women in Kenya: A Situation Analysis, 1992*. Nairobi: Regal Press.

Majtenyi, C. 1993a. "Victims Will Suffer Mentally for Ever." *Daily Nation* (May 29):11.

———. 1993b. "The Lost Generation." *Daily Nation* (May 29):10.

———. 1993c. "Grim Future for Children Hit by Political Violence." *Daily Nation* (May 29):10.

Makokha, F. 1993. "Economy Records Shocking Decline." *Daily Nation* (June 4):1.

Menya, D., and F. Mulli. 1993. "High Prevalence of Sexually Transmitted Diseases and HIV Infection in Uasin Gishu District, Kenya: A Case for Coordination of Control Activities." Paper presented at National AIDS Conference, Nairobi, April 20.

National Council of Churches of Kenya. 1992. *The Cursed Arrow: A Report on Organized Violence Against Democracy in Kenya*. Nairobi: Church House.

Onyango, P. 1989. "Keynote Address: Child Abuse and Neglect." Pp. 11–26 in *Child Abuse and Neglect*, edited by Kenya Medical Women's Association. Nairobi: Initiative Ltd.

Owino, G. 1993. "Nation's AIDS Orphans on the Rise." *Daily Nation* (May 13):21.

Owuor, O. 1993. "500,000 Children Live on the Street." *Daily Nation* (June 3):1.

Press, M. R. 1993. "Tribal Clashes in Kenya Continue." *The Christian Science Monitor* (September):27.

Undugu Society. 1991. "Experiences in Community Development." Nairobi: Undugu Society.

———. 1992. *Street Contact, 1992*. Nairobi: Undugu Society.

UNICEF. 1992. *The State of the World's Children, 1992*. New York: Oxford University Press.

———. 1993. *The State of the World's Children, 1993*. New York: Oxford University Press.

World Bank. 1992. *World Development Report, 1992*. New York: Oxford University Press.

———. 1993. *World Development Report, 1993*. New York: Oxford University Press.

Chapter 3

When Parents Discuss the Price of Bread: Albanian Children and the Economic Crisis

Marion Kloep

One day in August 1992, a miner from Northern Albania took the rifle his father had left from the partisan war and shot his three children, his wife, and himself. This was his personal solution to his country's economic crisis.

Though an extreme example, this case suggests that an economic crisis's most dramatic effects, especially on children, are not produced by material shortage itself, but by the way people—principally adults— react to and try to cope with the crisis. Using the example of Albania, we are going to examine some direct and indirect effects of economic crisis on children.[1]

An economic crisis usually affects health, nutrition, and the educational system. Furthermore, it leads to inflation, unemployment, more intense competition for scarce resources, and economic hardship for large parts of the population. The extent of these effects mainly depends on how politicians handle the situation. They can give priority to different means of coping and take measures to reduce the impact on certain groups within the population.

Conditions for individual children can be aggravated or improved according to the coping strategies chosen by adults. Parents choose how to spend their money, how to distribute scarce resources within the family. Economic stress can bring a family together in an effort to survive, or it can lead to conflict and competition. Teachers can try to compensate for the lack of teaching materials by doubling their efforts and by finding new ways to teach, or they can resign themselves to the growing problems. Whereas some adults make efforts to protect children from the crisis, others take advantage of the situation and exploit children as cheap labor, prostitutes, or assistants in criminal acts. Further-more, children's own coping resources—such as their social and intel-lectual abilities and the emotional support they receive from adults other than their parents—can moderate the effects of economic crisis on children's well-being.

This chapter begins by examining the general impact of the ongoing crisis on the health, nutrition, and education of Albanian children and compare those findings to studies from other countries. Then, concen-trating mainly on families, we will take a closer look at how adults deal economically and emotionally with economic hardship and how this affects their psychological well-being. Finally, we investigate the impact of adults' coping strategies on children's lives.

My focus on the effects of adult behavior on children is unidirection-al, and oversimplifies the actual relationships. Of course, reciprocal effects exist as well: How children cope with their situation will influ-ence adults' behavior (Bell and Harper 1977; Patterson et al. 1990). Chil-dren's antisocial behavior, for example, may not only affect parents' well-being and coping behaviors but also aggravate the family's eco-nomic problems. Nevertheless, this chapter concentrates only on the general impact of economic crisis and adults' coping behavior on chil-dren, neglecting such interactive effects.

In addition to official statistics, we will use data from an ongoing lon-gitudinal study with 285 initially 12-year-old children from Tirana, the Albanian capital.[2] On two occasions, in the spring 1992 and 1993, they and their parents answered extensive questionnaires about their per-sonal experiences. Some children, their parents, and their teachers were also interviewed in an effort to obtain some qualitative information.

From descriptions of the situation in rural Albania, it is evident that these regions are considerably more affected by the crisis than the cap-ital. Unfortunately, conditions did not allow us to collect data in the countryside. Since family structure, child-rearing practices, general val-ues, and attitudes differ widely between cities and rural areas, our con-clusions refer only to the children of Tirana.

BACKGROUND: THE ECONOMIC SITUATION IN ALBANIA

For centuries, Albania has been Europe's poorest country. Five hun-dred years of Ottoman occupation left the country without industry, infrastructure, or an educational system. After World War II, the new Communist government tried to transform the devastated country into a modern industrial nation. Apart from considerable achievements in education and health, economic progress was slow and came to a stand-still by the end of the 1980s. When the socialist bloc in Europe disintegrated in 1990, the Albanian economy virtually collapsed. Neither the Communist government nor the elected pluralistic government that followed could stop the decline. Today, an unemployment rate of about 50 percent (*Zeri i Popullit* 1993b), an inflation rate of 500 percent (Commission of the European Communities 1993), and permanent emigration by educated young men put Albania in the position of a Third World country.

CHILDREN'S HEALTH

In a study prepared for UNICEF (Jolly and Cornia 1984), the impact of a worldwide recession on children's welfare was explored in 15 countries (Tanzania, Sri Lanka, India, Zambia, Nigeria, Brazil, South Korea, Chile, Costa Rica, Cuba, Panama, Columbia, Venezuela, Italy, and the United States). A clear relationship was found between a fall in earnings or government cuts and a rise in the infant and child mortality rate. In all countries surveyed, except Cuba and South Korea, mortality rates rose or at least stagnated in areas characterized by high unemployment or declines in real wages. Furthermore, deteriorations in children's health occurred in India, Sri Lanka, Chile, and the United States. Diseases such as typhoid fever, hepatitis, and tuberculosis rose among the children of low-income and unemployed workers.

In Albania, the child mortality rate declined constantly between 1960 and 1990. In 1960, 8.3 percent of children died before the age of 1; this percentage had fallen to 2.8 by 1990. By 1992, the trend was reversed: Today, the infant mortality rate has reached 4 percent again (*Statistical Yearbook of Albania* 1991; personal communication with Ministry of Public Health 1993).

Health conditions in general are deteriorating. Many hospitals, particularly in rural areas, have closed. The open hospitals almost totally lack medicine and equipment. In some maternity wards, for example, there are two pregnant women for each bed, and newspapers are used instead of sheets. Furthermore, the best qualified staff have left the country to find work abroad. Previously free of charge, health services now must be purchased. Given the economic situation, many parents hesitate to contact a doctor if their children become ill. Families who have connections abroad try to import the most necessary medicines (and even syringes, in fear of infection from the unsterilized syringes used in hospitals).

NUTRITION

Economic crisis usually is accompanied by reductions in food supply (Cornia 1984). Because nearly all food-producing industry has closed and many fields lie fallow, Albania suffers from a considerable food shortage.

Nutrition is maintained mainly by foreign aid. Market prices for the available food have risen to astronomic heights. In 1993, no less than 36 percent of the parents in our sample stated that it was difficult or impossible to give their families good food every day. This is 16 percent more than in 1992, although at that time, shops were empty and large queues a common sight. Moreover, 37 percent reported that they had cut down on expenses for food. In 1991, UNICEF (Grant 1992) reported that more than 20 percent of the Albanian children suffered from malnutrition.

Since then, the situation has become worse. Albania's patriarchal traditions are reflected in the way families distribute the burdens of poverty: Asked, "Who eats best in your family?" 42 percent of the children name the children, 29 percent the father, and only 4 percent the mother (Kloep and Tarifa 1993a). In interviews, parents confirmed that their main concern was to feed their children properly. Our data reflect their efforts: In 1992, when there was hardly any food available in the shops, 22 percent of the children reported that it had been a week or more since they last ate fruit; in 1993, the percentage fell to 4 percent. As the price of apples, oranges, or bananas varies between US $1 and $2 per kilo, and an average monthly family income (if both parents are employed) is around $60, proper nutrition for children can only be achieved by parents making considerable sacrifices. Again, these data refer to the capital; in rural areas, the situation is known to be much worse.

EDUCATION

Usually, cuts in education precede those in health services during economic recessions (Cornia 1984). So, too, in Albania. Since 1990, about 700 Albanian schools have closed, and secondary school enrollment has dropped from 85 to 42 percent. Mainly in rural areas, but even in the cities, a growing number of children have to contribute to the family economy by working in the fields or selling in the streets, instead of going to school. Moreover, a considerable number of teachers have emigrated or have left the schools to find better-paying jobs or start private businesses. Physical conditions in the schools are almost intolerable: broken windows, no heating, toilets that do not function. In winter, children have to sit dressed in coats and jackets that hardly protect them against the cold. There are no textbooks, and not all children can afford such essential materials as paper and pens.

Until a few years ago, teachers could compensate for the difficult economic situation by working harder. Though dissatisfied with their wages, they showed admirable enthusiasm for teaching and a high commitment to their work: Comparative survey data from six different countries (Japan, USA, Great Britain, West Germany, Singapore, and Albania) showed Albanian teachers ranking highest in work commitment and satisfaction (Kloep and Tarifa 1992). Two years later, asking the same questions, we found significant reductions in these indicators. Cooperation with parents has diminished, and students are less motivated. Consequently, in 1993, pupils reported doing significantly less well in school and more truancy.

UNEMPLOYMENT AND ECONOMIC HARDSHIP

Up to now we have concentrated on the effects of economic crisis on the larger society. This section focuses on the impact of the national economic crisis on the family.

Both in 1992 and 1993, we asked the parents in our sample to rate their economic circumstances "today" and "two years ago." In 1992, 46 percent said their situation had gotten worse, and only 23 percent felt it had improved; The corresponding figures for 1993 were 22 and 66 percent, respectively. The percentage who regard their situation as improved is higher than the figure of 47 percent obtained in a nationwide study conducted by the International Organization of Migration (1993); this probably reflects the fact that our data come from the more prosperous capital. The relative improvement from 1992 to 1993 is, among other things, caused by the fact that unemployed people can now start private businesses, which sometimes give them more income than their former jobs. Another important factor improving some families' income is the money received from family members who work abroad.

The monthly family income of our sample ranges from $10 to $300. Obviously, in Albania, as in most other countries, the economic crisis does not affect all citizens equally. Although many people suffer from income losses or unemployment, some can take advantage of the situation and start a business of their own, legally or illegally importing and selling goods, renting apartments, or engaging in the black market. Such people, particularly if they have access to foreign currency, can make a fortune in a short time. The emerging income inequalities are likely to have an additional adverse effect on families' psychological well-being. Not only do families who cannot improve their situation feel like failures, but also they daily face the extravagant life-styles of other people. For example, whereas over 90 percent of the parents questioned regard it as simply impossible to buy a car or travel abroad, some 4 percent— almost all of them with access to foreign currency—find it easy to afford these things. For Albanians, this inequality is a new experience: Until recently, people have been poor, but all have been more or less equally poor. Several of our respondents refer to this:

> How is it possible that in only one or two years, 2 percent of the population have become millionaires, while we have to send our husbands and sons abroad to be able to afford food?

> Before, we had little, but all of us had something. Now some drink champagne, while others can't even pay the water bill.

The reactions of adults, particularly fathers, determine how this new social competition affects children's well-being. Many fathers who had the chance to travel abroad spent several months' wages on yuppie toys and status symbols, such as mobile telephones, VCRs, and parabolic antennas, whereas their wives did not know how to maintain their families.

Furthermore, during decades of money abundance relative to goods supply, many people never learned elementary economic skills, such as managing a personal budget. Parents have spent a month's wage on one visit to restaurant, only realizing afterward that there was no money left for lunch the next day. A highly educated person was shocked after receiving a $50 phone bill, which he was unable to pay.

The combination of poverty and income inequality is known to be a strong predictor of delinquency (e.g., Danziger 1976; Berk et al. 1980; Blau and Blau 1982). Thus, in Albania, crime rates are escalating.

The number of murders, for example, increased 130 percent between 1990 and 1992 (*Zeri i Popullit* 1993a). Children are affected in two different ways: as potential victims, and as misled collaborators of adolescent and adult criminal gangs.

Some years ago, the streets of Tirana were pretty safe, even in the evenings. Children could play peacefully wherever they wanted, and they were free to explore their environment. Now, in the middle of the day, groups of youngsters or adults may attack children on their way home and steal their clothes. Young girls have been attacked, gang-raped, and even killed. According to mass media reports, children have been kidnapped and sold abroad. Such things concern both parents and children. Criminals and hooligans top the list of children's fears (Tarifa and Kloep 1993).

Asked in interviews, what had changed during the last two years, children often answered: "We can't go out in the streets" or "There are so many bad people outside." No less than 32 percent of our children report that they have been victims of at least one assault during the past year. Children are kept at home as soon as it gets dark, and they do not dare take their favorite toys out or wear their new shoes in the street.

On the other hand, bad conditions in school, no hope for a future job, and economic hardship make it more profitable for some children to leave school to join gangs and indulge in criminal activities. Groups of amazingly young children besiege the tourist hotels, begging and stealing whatever they can get.

Children's behavior problems in early adolescence are strong predictors of delinquency in adulthood. Trivial antisocial acts such as stealing, lying, or truancy (measured at age 12 to 14) are quite predictive of later delinquency (Loeber 1985). Our data show a significant increase in the frequency of antisocial behavior, such as stealing, truancy, seeing friends who are disliked by one's parents, damaging public goods, and smoking. Only one child reported using drugs. Interviews with children revealed that at least some parents are losing control over their preadolescent offspring: "One thing we have learned during the last two years is to lie. Our parents believe that we are in school, but we meet in the park. We pretend to do our homework, but we write love letters, or we read *Erosi* [a journal with slightly erotic contents] on the toilet."

On a sunny Monday morning, for example, one-half of our subjects were absent from school. "It seems that they are sick," explained a slightly embarrassed teacher. Parents and teachers react helplessly, with either resignation or repression. One father who just had learned that his son had been caught stealing, reported that he had, of course, severely beaten him. Some schools lock the entrance doors to prevent pupils from leaving during the lessons. But how effective is this measure when there is no glass in the windows?

ECONOMIC HARDSHIP AND PARENTS' PSYCHOLOGICAL WELL-BEING

Economic hardship, particularly unemployment, are among the most stressful life events, leading to psychosomatic symptoms and lowered psychological well-being (e.g., Mills et al. 1992; Schlozman and Verba

1978), especially in middle-aged adults who are responsible for children (Warr 1978).

Thirty percent of the parents in our sample report being unemployed. Some have, for the time being, solved their economic problems by starting small businesses, sometimes with considerable success. They often see their future with optimism. However, for others, the situation is quite different. Women have few opportunities to start a business of their own; patriarchal traditions still forbid them, for example, to sell goods in the streets. Another group negatively affected are former Communist Party members. Among them are many intellectuals and highly educated specialists who lost their jobs for political reasons. They are discriminated against in the labor market, and they cannot get licenses to start private businesses. In these groups, bitterness and despair seem to be common.

> I will never get a job again. I have worked for 27 years, and I have done so with pleasure. Now I stay at home, cooking, cleaning, talking to the walls? I do not know what to do. Even if I get the chance to emigrate—what life would that be? My family, my friends, my home are here. What to do with my parents? But neither is there a future for me here. They do not let me work. Your life might be complicated—but my life is over! And I am only 39 years old.

Unemployment thus has different effects on different groups of people, mainly depending on their opportunities to deal with it. The impact of family income on parents' psychological well-being, however, is more clear-cut and more obvious in the 1993 data, than in 1992. Low income is a significant predictor of self-reported bad moods, sleeping problems, anxiety, and depression, as well as marital disharmony. From the interviews, it appears that the effects of economic hardship on people's psychological well-being are more problematic the better off they were before. Those who enjoyed certain small privileges under the former political system find it more difficult to adjust to the prevailing conditions. For them, economic hardship also implies a considerable loss of status.

Research on the impact of economic hardship and unemployment on psychological well-being usually shows men to be more affected than women, probably because of their role as breadwinners. However, with growing participation of women in the labor market, gender differences have declined (Horwitz 1984; Mills et al. 1992), and single mothers are as severely affected by economic problems as men (McLoyd and Wilson 1990). This is of particular importance for Albania, as the number of female-headed families is growing constantly because of the emigration of men. By 1993, more than 400,000 men had left the country to look for work abroad.

In our sample, 14 percent of the children lived in families where at least one of the parents had left the country, and over 40 percent of the parents report that they have tried to emigrate or are considering doing so. Thus, this study found no significant differences between men and women regarding the effects of economic hardship on their psychological well-being.

LINKING PARENTS' WELL-BEING TO CHILDREN'S LIVES

Few studies have found a direct relationship between economic hardship and children's psychological well-being (e.g., Takeuchi et al. 1991). However, work by Elder and his colleagues (Elder et al. 1985, 1992; Skinner et al. 1992) reveals that parents' behavior mediates the relationship between hardship and well-being. According to these studies, economic hardship, particularly if it leads to coping behavior that implies a form of loss (e.g., cutbacks on expenses, borrowing, selling property), affects parents' social behavior. Often the father, afraid of losing authority if he can no longer serve as breadwinner, reacts to economic problems with heightened irritability and aggressiveness toward his wife and children. This results in marital disharmony (Elder et al. 1990, 1992; Schlozman and Verba 1978; Skinner et al. 1992) and parents rejecting their children (Elder et al. 1985, 1992; Flanagan 1990; Lempers et al. 1989; Skinner et al. 1992). Conflicts in the family, in turn, have a direct impact on children's psychological well-being: Harsh parental discipline and hostility (again, particularly by the father), as well as conflicts between parents, have been shown to be related to psychological distress (Elder et al. 1985, 1992) and antisocial and aggressive behavior in children, and later in adults (Elder et al. 1992; Farrington 1983; Hallstrom 1983; Lempers et al. 1989; McCord 1990; Skinner et al. 1992).

All of these studies were conducted in Western industrial societies, mainly the United States. There is some reason to expect different results in Albania. In this traditional society, patriarchal structures prevail even in the cities, family bonds are strong, and marriage is sacred. Thus, we assumed that the economic crisis would usually bring family members together to support each other and thereby reduce conflict among them.

This was not the case. The results of various regression analyses done with the data from our 1992 survey closely parallel the findings of previous studies. We measured adjustments to economic adversity by summarizing parents' reports of how often they had to cut down their expenditures on food, clothing, and leisure and how often they had to borrow money, sell property, or use their savings in order to cope with their economic situation (following a suggestion by Elder et al. 1992).

This measure correlated significantly with marital disharmony (as reported by the parents) and the frequency of father-child conflicts (as reported by the children). In contrast, the frequency of mother-child conflicts was not correlated with these adjustments to economic adversity, perhaps because economic problems tend to affect women less than men (as discussed). What is more, frequent father-child conflicts seem to lead to higher rates of antisocial behavior in children (such as stealing, begging, drinking alcohol, etc.), interestingly for girls to a much higher degree than for boys. Similarly, the impact of adjustments to economic adversity, mediated by the frequency of father-child conflict, has a significant effect on psychological depression for girls only (Kloep and Tarifa 1993b).

In a patriarchal society such as Albania, the pressure on men to support their families and to legitimate their status through economic power is even higher than in Western countries. To lose employment or be unable to make enough money to meet his family's needs presents a serious threat to an Albanian man's status and authority. So he has to find other ways to exercise and to maintain his power, often by adopting a demanding, exploitative attitude toward his wife and his children.

Furthermore, as the family is the father's only source of security in times of instability, he cannot tolerate any changes in the traditional way of life. Along with the economic crisis, Albania is undergoing great social transformations. Western influences have had their impact, particularly on the young, who now demand more freedom from their parents and have begun to indulge in activities previously regarded as decadent and immoral. Children no longer want their parents to control their choices of friends, books, and music. Particularly girls, who were kept under strict parental control much more than boys, have started to antagonize their parents and demand certain rights. For a father, already shaken in his position as the unquestioned head of the family, a daughter's rebellion must represent an enormous provocation, threatening his status not only as a parent but also as a man. This may be the reason for the stronger association found between adjustments to economic adversity—an obvious sign of a father's inability to maintain the family's living standard—and the frequency of father-daughter (compared to father-son) conflict. In this struggle for power, the father's weakened position and his hostile reaction to his daughter's behavior may, in turn, lead some girls to further provocations. From TV and foreign visitors, they have learned about the rights of females and adolescents in other countries, and they experience their fathers' growing efforts to keep them under control as deeply unjust. Thus, instead of submitting to their fathers' demands, as generations of Albanian girls have been forced to do, some react with naughty, "unfemale" behavior. More than one-half of the 13-year-old girls in our sample admit that they were meeting friends whom their parents had forbidden them to see, about the same number have at least sometimes been absent from school without permission, and 20 percent have tried cigarettes and strong liquor—something many adult Albanian women never would do. On the other hand, Albanian girls have strong, affectionate ties to their families, and must pay a high price for their rebellion. There is a high correlation between frequency of father-daughter conflict and girls' depression scores.

Boys, on the other hand, not only enjoy greater tolerance from their fathers but also have other coping possibilities. If annoyed by their hostile fathers, they simply stay away from home and receive emotional support from their friends. Boys in our sample report spending more time outside their homes, having more friends, and receiving more social support from their peers than girls do.

However, not all fathers react to the crisis with heightened irritability toward their families. In our sample, 18 out of 48 fathers who reported more adjustments to economic adversity (more than 0.5 standard deviations above the sample mean) rarely quarrel with their children (more than 0.5 standard deviations under the mean of children's ratings). Obviously, several different factors may account for the way parents behave. Research has shown, for example, that adjustments to economic adversity or unemployment lead to marital disharmony mainly in marriages that already were troubled (Bleich and Witte 1992; Moen et al. 1982) and that unattractive girls have to suffer more from their father's negativism than attractive ones (Elder et al. 1985).

In a similar way, conflicts with fathers do not necessarily lead to depression and antisocial behavior in girls. Seven out of 22 girls who reported frequent conflicts with their fathers had relatively low depression scores, and seven different girls from the same group reported comparatively low frequencies of antisocial behavior. Again, this shows the importance of a multifactorial, dynamic approach in studying the impact of macrosocial events on individuals. In Albania, grandparents seem to play a notable role in moderating the effects of economic hardship. Very often, they share the household with one of their married children, usually a son. More often than not, the grandfather has the most authority in the extended family, and thus great influence on family members' behavior. Not only can grandparents help moderate a father's behavior toward his children, but also they can buffer the effects of harsh parental attitudes by giving children emotional support. This is reflected in children's answers when asked to list the six persons whom they loved most: 64 percent named at least one of their grandparents, often in the third or fourth place. Furthermore, four of those seven girls, who in spite of frequent father-daughter conflict remained remarkably undepressed, reported that they received considerable emotional support from their grandparents. The same is true for four of the seven girls who showed a low frequency of antisocial behavior (the other three had no grandparents).

HOW CHILDREN EXPERIENCE ECONOMIC CRISIS

Most of Tirana's children are not directly affected by the economic crisis. Seventeen percent of the children rate their families as "rich" or "very rich," and only 2 percent rate them as "poor" or "very poor," and many are not aware of the serious problems their parents face. But the number of children perceiving the situation more realistically is growing.

Parental overprotecting, which is a central feature of the paternalistic style prevailing in Albanian families, results not only in strong efforts to feed and dress the children properly but also in shielding them from adult worries and preoccupations. Although some children mentioned discussing economic problems with their parents, further questioning revealed that, in these cases, the main topic was whether there was money to buy some trendy clothes or to go to a disco. The price of bread is not discussed with children.

On the other hand, parents complain about their children's lack of understanding:

> You see, my husband had to emigrate to Greece to try to find work. I myself am unemployed, and in some months social assistance will be reduced to 10 dollars a month. I really don't know how I will manage to feed the children and pay the rent for the flat. And all they do is complain, all they want is fun, all that is on their mind is sex and disco and entertainment. You see, we adults can abstain from things. Of course, we suffer from seeing all these beautiful things in the shops that we can never afford. But we are reasonable enough to understand. Children they are different. They see chewing gum, fruits, and lemonade in tins, and they want to have them, and they want them now. It is so hard to say no, and often I can't.

Yet, not all children remain in happy ignorance. For some parents, economic problems have become so overwhelming that they must send their children to work. In Tirana, the only way for children to make some money is to sell cigarettes, refreshments, or sweets in the streets, either alone or together with their parents. Many children do this after school, but the number of children who have to give up school for full-time work is growing. Boys as young as 10 or 11 leave at six in the morning to go to the central market to buy cigarettes, which they try to sell in the streets until late in the evening. The job is risky; all the children we met reported having been assaulted and robbed by armed teenage gangs. The police do not protect them, thus they often work in groups. Although they report being sent to work by and delivering all money to their parents, it is obvious that many are organized by professional criminals. Not only do these children lose their opportunity for an education (which, according to the new Albanian Charter of Rights, is one of their fundamental rights), but also they are very much at risk of drifting into organized criminality. They can earn up to $80 a month, which is more than their parents can get in a normal job, if they have one. In contrast to the majority of Albanian children, they are neither controlled nor protected by their parents or other adults. Often, they come from female-headed families, living with a divorced mother and several siblings, and are the family's main breadwinner. Most of these children named their main concerns as making enough money and the fear of being robbed or killed.

His greatest dream, a small boy confessed, was to possess enough money one day to buy a car. For between 100 and 200 street children in Tirana, childhood is over at the age of 11.

OUTLOOK

Many Albanian children are growing up in misery, without an adequate education, the emotional support that once distinguished the Albanian family, or hope for the future. This will only halt if adults decide to give priority to solving children's problems. Obviously, a first policy recommendation must be for direct efforts to improve Albania's economic situation (Dooley and Catalano 1980). Albania cannot do this on its own, and the children's fate is not only Albania's responsibility. Over 30 percent of the Albanian population is under 15 years old, and in 20 years, these children will form the core of Albanian society. As Europe moves toward integration, European countries should not be insensitive to the needs of the next generation in a neighboring country. Second, the public sector needs to take appropriate measures, such as encouraging programs that, in the long run, offer the greatest public benefits at the lowest public costs (Dooley and Catalano 1980). These could, for example, include maintaining schools and health centers, tax measures to improve income distribution, or state interventions to reduce unemployment. The examples of South Korea and Cuba show that it is possible to offset the negative effects of recession by appropriate policy measures, in spite of reduced resources (Cornia 1984). During the worldwide recession of 1979–83, South Korea implemented special measures against unemployment and for children's education, particularly for the poorest 10 percent of the population (Suh 1984). Almost all of the country's children were in primary school during a period when South Korea's per capita gross national product (GNP) was lower than that of most developing countries today. During the same period, the Cuban government also decided to maintain its expenditures on education and health, although the public sector budget was being reduced by 10 percent (Ennew and Milne 1989; Gutierrez et al. 1984). A decade later, after the collapse of trade relations with the former socialist bloc, Cuba faces economic problems similar to Albania's. Having lost about 70 percent of its export income and seen a two-third reduction of oil imports, Cuba faces the most serious economic crisis in its modern history. Despite this, the government again decided not to cut expenses on health and education. From elementary school to the university level, the authorities guarantee students functioning schools, uninterrupted schooling, and necessary instruction materials. Children below age 7 still receive a daily ration of milk. All food is rationed and available at low prices to guarantee a minimum level of nutrition for everyone. Thus, the stress put on parents is considerably reduced, particularly as the authorities are quite creative in finding ways to keep unemployment low and minimizing its effects.

However, Albanian children (like most children in the world) have no lobby in parliament. Since the last elections, even women, who might have protected children's interests, have nearly disappeared from politics (Tarifa 1993). Politicians are occupied with passing laws on privatization, discussing the pros and cons of legalizing pornography and accusing each other of corruption. Politicians who have ideas for solving the country's problems propose developing the infrastructure and stimulating foreign investments in order to consolidate the Albanian economy, hoping that this will solve social problems in the long run. Concerning education, however, this strategy has proven quite ineffective. In Japan and South Korea, for example, basic investments in people, such as guaranteeing universal primary education, preceded economic takeoff (Grant 1992). None of the politicians we talked to gave priority to children's circumstances or had specific plans for improving them. The higher the politician's position, the more words and the fewer answers in his response. Maybe the helplessness of politicians explains why, in this formerly atheist country, most of the children, their parents, and politicians—including the president—put the greatest hope for the solution to their problems in God.

Finally, at the family level, some form of counseling for parents and children is needed (Dooley and Catalano 1980). Because families react differently to economic problems, individual counseling, family therapy, and marriage therapy are required. Particularly, fathers and daughters seem to need support to overcome the stress caused by economic problems and changing family structures. Traditional family structures, particularly the extended family, should be preserved. In addition, emerging women's groups should be encouraged to defend girls' and women's positions in the changing patriarchal society. Albania faces several serious problems. It has to overcome the difficulties of the transition to a market economy, face the danger of war and civil war, and rebuild its devastated economy. An unusual amount of wisdom is needed to adopt a long-term view and give priority to children's needs. Yet, children have only one opportunity to grow; chances lost in the early years are lost forever, and this loss affects not only individual children but the society's future.

CONCLUSION

Investigating the living conditions of children in Tirana, the Albanian capital, we found that this country's economic crisis has direct effects on the physical well-being of children (e.g., insufficient nutrition and health services) and that it also disrupts their parents' lives and thereby affects children's psychological well-being. These findings reaffirm research results from other countries with quite different cultures and histories. In spite of the immense sociocultural differences, such as between Albania and the United States, for example, in both countries, individual differences in coping behavior and coping resources account for the well-being of children during an economic crisis. But this finding tells only half the truth. Whether in Albania or the United States, not all children exposed to poverty, disease, and family instability become criminals or develop psychological problems.

Even under the worst conditions of health and nutrition, some children survive. A longitudinal study of immigrant children in Hawaii found that about 10 percent of children in the high-risk group developed, against all odds, into competent and autonomous young adults who "worked well, played well, loved well, and expected well" (Werner and Smith 1989:153). Variables that affected their resiliency included the number of children in the family, the number and type of alternate caretakers available to the mother within the household, the amount of attention given to the child in infancy, the cohesiveness of the family, and the presence of an informal multigenerational network of kin and friends during adolescence.

Our own findings suggest that, in addition to the way people cope with economic problems, variables such as family network, social support, and educational style play significant mediating roles in reducing the effects of an economic crisis. Further research should concentrate on "survivors," on those who make their way in spite of adverse conditions. We need to know more about which conditions create appropriate coping resources in adults and in children.

On the other hand, more knowledge about what children need to overcome adverse conditions will not, in itself, lead to the necessary policy changes. In many cases, it may be impossible to create the necessary coping resources—for example to broaden a child's social network or to give a child a supportive sibling. Particularly in competitive societies, enhancing some people's coping skills may only work to the disadvantage of others. If the number of jobs is limited, for example, training in job-seeking skills may give trainees a competitive advantage, but it cannot solve the basic problem.

Furthermore, concentrating too heavily on individual reactions to economic crisis distracts our attention away from the conditions that create the crisis and implies ultimately the admission that social scientists have renounced their hope of changing the world.

NOTES

1. My collaborator on this study was Fatos Tarifa of the University of Tirana, Albania.

2. In spring 1992, we distributed 287 questionnaires to sixth- and seventh-grade children in five schools in central Tirana. At that time, the children's mean age was 11.9. Two hundred fifty children also received a questionnaire for their parents to complete at home. We did not specify which parent should complete the questionnaire. Not all subjects completed the questionnaire, and some questionnaires had to be discarded. Altogether, we received completed questionnaires from 189 children and their parents.

In spring 1993, we collected more data. This time, we gave the children a questionnaire for each parent, and we offered $1 for returning the parents' questionnaire. We were able to collect 1993 data from 164 of the families who had responded in 1992. In addition, we received 59 questionnaires from parents who had not responded in 1992 (although their children had), as well as data from 42 new children and their parents.

The 1992 children's questionnaire consisted of 89 questions, most featuring five-point rating scales. These questions sought to measure social support received by children, family conflict, the children's perceptions of economic conditions, antisocial behavior, fears about the future, psychological depression, and social skills. In 1993, we discarded the scale measuring social skills and added some items to the antisocial behavior scale, as well as new items measuring values and attitudes.

The 1992 parents' questionnaire consisted of 37 questions aimed at measuring family conflicts, marital harmony, economic conditions, coping strategies, and psychological well-being. The 1993 questionnaire contained some additional items about values and attitudes.

REFERENCES

Bell, R. Q., and L. V. Harper (eds.). 1977. *Child Effects on Adults*. Hillsdale, NJ: Erlbaum.

Berk, R. A., K. J. Lenihan, and P. H. Rossi. 1980. "Crime and Poverty: Some Experimental Evidence from Ex-offenders." *American Sociological Review* 45:766–86.

Blau, J. R., and P. M. Blau. 1982. "The Cost of Inequality: Metropolitan Structure and Violent Crime." *American Sociological Review* 47:114–29.

Bleich, C., and E. H. Witte. 1992. "Zu Veranderungen in der Paarbeziehung bei Erwerbslosigkeit des Mannes." *Kölner Zeitschrift für Soziologie und Sozial Psychologie* 44:731–46.

Commission of the European Communities. 1993. *Central and Eastern Eurobarometer* No. 3 (February).

Cornia, G. A. 1984. "A Summary and Interpretation of the Evidence." Pp. 211–21 in *The Impact of World Recession on Children*, edited by R. Jolly and G. A. Cornia. Elmsford, NY: Pergamon Press.

Danziger, S. 1976. "Explaining Urban Crime Rates." *Criminology* 14:291–96.

Dooley, D., and R. Catalano. 1980. "Economic Change as a Cause of Behavioral Disorder." *Psychological Bulletin* 87:450–68.

Elder, G. H., Jr., T. Van Nguyen, and A. Caspi. 1985. "Linking Family Hardship to Children's Lives." *Child Development* 56:361–75.

Elder, G. H., F. O. Lorenz, K. J. Conger, R. L. Simons, L. B. Whitbeck, S. Huck, and J. N. Melby. 1990. "Linking Economic Hardship to Marital Quality and Instability." *Journal of Marriage and the Family* 52:643–56.

Elder, G. H., Jr., R. D. Conger, E. M. Foster, and M. Ardelt. 1992. "Families under Economic Pressure." *Journal of Family Issues* 13:5–37.

Ennew, J., and B. Milne. 1989. *The Next Generation: Lives of Third World Children*. London: Zed Books.

Farrington, D. P. 1983. "Offending from 10 to 25 Years of Age." Pp. 17–37 in *Prospective Studies of Crime and Delinquency*, edited by K. T. Van Dusen and S. A. Mednick. Boston: Kluwer-Nijhoff.

Flanagan, C. A. 1990. "Families and Schools in Hard Times." *New Directions in Child Development* 46:7–26.

Grant, James P. 1992. *The State of the World's Children*. New York: Oxford University Press.

Gutierrez, J. M., J. C. Fabian, J. C. Manriquez, and R. Hertenberg. 1984. "The Recent Worldwide Economic Crisis and the Welfare of Children: The Case of Cuba." Pp. 77–90 in *The Impact of World Recession on Children*, edited by R. Jolly and G. A. Cornia. Elmsford, NY: Pergamon Press.

Hallstrom, T. 1983. "Early Life Experiences That Relate to Later Aggression by Women." Pp. 345–74 in *Prospective Studies of Crime and Delinquency*, edited by K. T. Van Dusen and S. A. Mednick. Boston: Kluwer-Nijhoff.

Horwitz, A. V. 1984. "The Economy and Social Pathology." *Annual Review of Sociology* 10:95–119.

International Organization of Migration. 1993. *Albania—Migrant Profile Project Country File*. Brussels: Unpublished report (January).

Jolly, R., and G. A. Cornia (eds.). 1984. *The Impact of World Recession on Children*. Elmsford, NY: Pergamon Press.

Kloep, M., and F. Tarifa. 1992. *Working Conditions and Workstyles among Albanian Teachers*. Unpublished paper, Mid-Sweden University at Österlund.

_____. 1993a. "Albanian Children in the Winds of Change." Pp. 85–116 in *Human Resource Development*, edited by L. E. Wolvin. *Rapport 6*.

_____. 1993b. "Linking Economic Hardship to Families' Lives and Children's Psychological Well-being." *Childhood 1*, in press.

Lempers, J. D., D. Clark-Lempers, and R. L. Simons. 1989. "Economic Hardship, Parenting, and Distress in Adolescence." *Child Development* 60:25–39.

Loeber, R. 1985. "Patterns and Development of Antisocial Child Behavior." *Annals of Child Development* 2:77–116.

McCord, J. 1990. "Problem Behaviors." Pp. 414–430 in *At the Threshold: The Developing Adolescent*, edited by S. S. Feldman and G. R. Elliott. Cambridge, MA: Harvard University Press.

McLoyd, V., and L. Wilson. 1990. "Maternal Behavior, Social Support, and Economic Conditions as Predictors of Distress in Children." *New Directions in Child Development* 46:49–69.

Moen, P., E. L. Kain, and G. H. Elder, Jr. 1982. "Economic Conditions and Family Life: Contemporary and Historical Perspectives." In *Economics and the Family*, edited by R. Nelson and F. Skidmore. Washington, DC: National Academy.

Mills, R. J., H. G., Grasmick, C. S., Morgan, and D. A. Wenk. 1992. "The Effects of Gender, Family Satisfaction, and Economic Strain on Psychological Well-being." *Family Relations* 41:440–46.

Patterson, G. R., L. Bank, and M. Stoolmiller. 1990. "The Preadolescent's Contributions to Disrupted Family Process." Pp. 107–33 in *From Childhood to Adolescence*, edited by R. Montemayor, G. R. Adams, and T. P. Gullotta. Newbury Park, CA: Sage.

Schlozman, K. L., and S. Verba. 1978. "The New Unemployment: Does It Hurt?" *Public Policy* 26:333–58.

Skinner, M. L., G. H. Elder, Jr., and R. D. Conger. 1992. "Linking Economic Hardship to Adolescent Aggression." *Journal of Youth and Adolescence* 12:259–76.

Statistical Yearbook of Albania. 1991. Tirana: Ministria e ekonomise, drejtoria e statistikes.

Suh, S. M. 1984. "Effects of the Current World Recession on the Welfare of Children: The Case of Korea. Pp. 159–68 in *The Impact of World Recession on Children,* edited by R. Jolly and G. A. Cornia. Elmsford, NY: Pergamon Press.

Takeuchi, D. T., D. R. Williams, and R. K. Adair. 1991. "Economic Stress in the Family and Children's Emotional and Behavioral Problems." *Journal of Marriage and the Family* 53:1031–41.

Tarifa, F. 1993. "Disappearing from Politics: Social Change and Women in Albania." In *Women in the Politics of Post-Communist Eastern Europe,* edited by M. Ruschemeyer. Armonk, NY: M. E. Sharpe.

Tarifa, F., and M. Kloep. 1993. *War vs. Ghosts: Children's Fears in Different Societies.* In preparation.

Werner, E. E., and R. S. Smith. 1981. *Vulnerable, but Invincible: A Longitudinal Study of Resilient Children and Youth.* New York: McGraw-Hill. (Reprint Adams, Bannister, Cox 1989).

Warr, P. 1978. "A Study of Psychological Well-being." *British Journal of Psychology* 69:111–21.

Zeri i Popullit. 1993a. (March 7).

Zeri i Popullit. 1993b. (March 17).

Part III

PREGNANCY AND INFANCY

Chapter 4

Little Strangers:
Pregnancy Conduct and the Twentieth-Century
Rhetoric of Endangerment

Carol Brooks Gardner

Recently, students of social problems have analyzed social problems as moral discourses employing different types of rhetoric (Best 1990; Ibarra and Kitsuse 1990, 1993). This use of discourse and its associated vocabulary describes the argumentation over a wide range of conditions deemed "social problems" (Best 1990; Ibarra and Kitsuse 1990, 1993). Various social problems involving children as victims are among those recently examined (Best 1990; John Johnson 1989; Kitzinger 1988). However, social constructionists have thus far given little attention to "victimization" rhetoric regarding unborn children. Examining the social construction of endangerment to the fetus and embryo can help us understand the social controls that operate on pregnant women—and on their husbands and partners—as well as on women contemplating or planning pregnancy.

My analysis of popular advice on pregnancy suggests that those social controls are fetus-centered; they are oriented—through the rhetoric of fetal endangerment—toward structuring and reifying the period of pregnancy and anticipatorily socializing the pregnant woman to regard her fetus's concerns as more important than her own. The rhetoric of fetal endangerment at once signifies the importance of activities and attitudes that will give every chance to the fetus and the impunity with which any of a pregnant woman's activities and attitudes that do not concern the fetus must be discarded.

Although this article concentrates on the modern rhetoric of fetal endangerment, a full examination of social problems rhetorics surrounding pregnancy would no doubt uncover other claims. Besides the rhetoric of fetal endangerment, for example, there is a woman-centered rhetoric that might be summarized as "childbearer's liberation," which urges a woman to be more self-interested during pregnancy and aims to demythologize the "pregnancy paranoia" promulgated through fetus-centered rhetoric. This second, seemingly liberated rhetoric, achieved a vogue during the 1970s and early 1980s but now typically pales in comparison to the fetus-centered rhetoric's myriad injunctions and prescriptions. These injunctions and prescriptions require a pregnant woman's circumspect attention in restraining her personal impulses, desires, interests, and activities.[1]

FETAL ENDANGERMENT AND RECENT CLAIMSMAKING

Although not an exclusively modern concern, fetal harm, resulting in the presumed warping of a child to be born, is a concern with modern dimensions that have been reflected in fiction and film. It did not take the scientifically engineered horrors of the unending *It's Alive* movie series or the morally hybrid birth of *Rosemary's Baby* to worry prospective parents, although fiction and film often depict melodramatic situations where the wrongs of parents or the parents' generation have been visited on hapless embryos and often on the societies into which those embryos have been born. In this generally circular trajectory, parents or "society" (often in the form of mad scientists or irresponsible environmentalists) irresponsibly create or injure a fetus that, when born, returns the harm—an intuitively fit retribution and one that gives parents, as well as others, added incentive for closely toeing the line.[2]

Because pregnancy is an opaque condition, involving an especially long period when results, good or bad, are not directly evident, it is a fruitful ground for the forces of informal social control. A pregnant woman can be advised to refrain from certain behaviors lest she harm her unborn child; however, the outcome of any precautions she takes up may well be obscure for nine months, perhaps even after. It is in part the obscure character of pregnancy that allows the expansion of claims about stimuli that "create" fetal harm on to relatively minor causes.

By the term *condition-category*, social constructionists Ibarra and Kitsuse (1990, 1993) refer to what claimsmakers understand a social problem is "about." Following this usage, I am interested the condition-categories of benign and endangering behavior during pregnancy. I focus in particular on some ways in which rhetorical arguments about fetal endangerment have been articulated in the past 10 years—that is, the period 1983–93—as well as on the scope and character of those arguments. Using limited documentary sources mainly from one mass-distribution magazine, *American Baby*, I demonstrate that, in the United States, a woman's behavior during pregnancy becomes subject to many measures of control that emphasize the indirect consequences of her actions, thoughts, and feelings on the malleable fetus. These control efforts require the pregnant woman—and the pregnant woman alone—to self-impose restraints, with the alleged future good of the child to be born at stake. Rarely is it argued that others, such as family members or professionals, are responsible for helping her; often she is reminded of her duties in thinking of the good of these others or in minding what they say.

Some claimsmakers argue that the pregnant woman has the good or health of the entire nation or the human race in her control, and this magnified import justifies greater restrictions. With this great power, a woman has correspondingly great responsibility, responsibility that is difficult to exercise because of the nature of pregnancy. As modern as these concerns are, they have a considerable world history and a quite detailed U.S. history reflected in popular advice and even medical writings.

PREGNANCY, PERCEIVED DEFECTS, AND HISTORY

For centuries, the physical state and the social situation of pregnancy have been used to explain physical and mental traits considered undesirable in children (Thompsson 1896). In past centuries, children with diabilities were considered reliable evidence of divine pleasure or displeasure or simply predictors of future events. But modernism has shifted responsibility from gods to parents. Much popular (even at times medical) advice literature is reminiscent of advice literature of the previous century, which advised progressive nineteenth-century Americans to understand that "children are made by their parents, not sent, with all their imperfections on their head, from heaven" (Evans 1875:83). Parents, especially mothers, should cease to hinder "the progress of the human race in so many ways" (ibid.). They should devote themselves to preparing for the future—in fact, to devote themselves to preparing children who are themselves capable of preparing for the future (Evans 1875:108).

Today, we usually label the "avoidable" traits that caught the attention of the nineteenth century as disabilities. In fact, it is significant that we now avoid the term "disability" or "disabled" when we speak of women's conduct during pregnancy. Customarily, contemporary rhetoric speaks of the injured fetus or embryo, yet often halts at stigmatizing (or even considering) the child or, eventually, the adult with a disability.[3] But the traits that erring mothers are even now believed to visit on the malleable fetus include flaws of temperament, mental aptitudes and gifts, as well as minor physical characteristics such as birthmarks, minor allergies, an unhealthy constitution, and personal unattractiveness. Taken together, these qualities are an obverse signifying the many requirements that the "perfect" child is now expected to have, the need for parental efforts to imbue these qualities, and the mother's ultimate responsibility for effecting them. (Sometimes fathers are also faulted, typically for transmitting genetic disease or for having been [typically involuntarily] exposed to toxic agents.)

The American rhetoric of fetal endangerment, therefore, goes back at least to the nineteenth century. I examine that rhetoric in one particular recent period, 1983–93, looking at a mass-distribution magazine devoted to pregnant women and new mothers. I argue that the rhetoric of fetal endangerment has a scope and character that fits well with the American idea of ameliorative progressivism—the idea that dangers (what we often label as social problems these days) may be avoided through expert knowledge and careful conduct. At the same time, activities during pregnancy allow a woman to argue that she is engaging in responsible nurturing toward a being whose particular wants, desires, and quirks she cannot reliably be expected to know just yet. In this sense, all such maternal behavior is done with an eye toward fetal-maternal interaction.

Among other things, then, fetal endangerment is a social problem that comes equipped with its own achievable solution, one that befits U.S. patterns of behavior. Knowing how to behave responsibly can color much of the woman's time and activity during her nine months of pregnancy. Part of the way in which women can "train" themselves to be pregnant is to seek and absorb the knowledge of experts, especially experts in print. There are a number of advice books for expectant women (e.g., Curtis and Coroles 1985; Hales and Creasy 1982; Scher and Dix 1983; Thomas and Browder 1987), much fewer for men (e.g., Marshall 1992), and, in the last decade, many works to help parents through a "pregnancy loss" (e.g., Berezin 1982; Berg 1981; Davidson 1979; DeFrain 1986; R. Friedman and Gradstein 1982; James Johnson et al. 1985). But recommendations to expectant parents often come in the form of late-breaking, scientific news, and for this purpose a magazine for expectant pregnancy can be useful. *American Baby* is one of three magazines I have come across that contain a fair amount of material on pregnancy; of the three, it has the widest distribution, is the cheapest, and is targeted toward the middle middle class.

METHODOLOGY

Before characterizing the features of fetus-centered rhetoric of fetal endangerment, I will discuss the magazine from which the sample articles were taken and assess its advantages and drawbacks as a literary source.

American Baby is a mass-circulation magazine that reaches about 1,300,000 readers with each monthly issue. Each issue has two versions, one for expectant mothers and one for new mothers, each with approximately equal distribution. (I analyze only the expectant mother version.) An additional 100,000 copies of the pregnancy version are distributed free in obstetrician-gynecologists' waiting rooms—where I first met the publication myself, when pregnant with my daughter some 12 years ago. Like many readers, I "converted": when my daughter was born, I became a paid subscriber. I imagine many expectant women convert for the same reasons I did. *American Baby* is geared toward women of middle income. Readers' median age is 28, and median family income is $33,700. Forty-five percent of these women are first-time mothers, so that what they learn from *American Baby* can be argued to have an especially salient effect on them. During their pregnancy, 45 percent are employed full- or part-time, and 84 percent are currently married. Subscription price is a modest $10 yer year.

Visually, *American Baby* is attractive and cheerful, containing photographs and drawings of babies of a variety of ethnic backgrounds, and there are a number of expert columnists (sociologist Pepper Schwartz does a frequent column on sex and pregnancy, for example), as well as a section of coupons intended to help women buy baby-care products for their anticipated child. In short, *American Baby* seems an ideal exemplar of advice given to a certain stratum of U.S. women by popular experts and some "accredited experts" as well. In reading 10 years' worth of issues, I have taken care to select information from a variety of columns, articles, and features within the magazines.

Of course, it is impossible to know if these articles stimulate feelings or behavior in their readers, or, indeed, if the particular articles I have cited have ever been read at all. Yet, there are good reasons for using these sources. First, specialized magazines such as *American Baby* are among the few venues for the collected and organized expression of beliefs and advice about pregnancy, both popular and scientificized.

In such a circumscribed chapter as this one it is impossible to conclude that the sources or the genre faithfully repeat, report, or distort rhetorics actually used in everyday life. When, therefore, I write about individuals who "make claims" or about "claimsmaking" in general, I write with license. In so writing, I often imply that the rhetoric of fetal endangerment I describe has a life beyond the printed pages of *American Baby*. In fact, I do not attempt to prove that this is so. However, other work (Best 1990; Gardner 1993), as well as my own extensive observations of and interviews with pregnant women now in progress, are consistent with the themes I identify. For the middle-class readership at which it is targeted, *American Baby* seems to present remarkably representative views. Like other sources, it suggests that advice given to pregnant women centers on activities and ingestible substances during pregnancy.

ACTIVITY AND THE TIME TO ABUSE IT: A FETUS-CENTERED FETAL ENDANGERMENT RHETORIC

Legitimate Activity and Pregnancy

Nineteenth-century and early twentieth-century writing on activities during pregnancy amounted to counseling a woman to remain quiet and at home. Nowadays, this is rarely advised explicitly (however, for exceptions to the modern trend, see the forthright Eberlein [1989] and Stein [1984]). Activities, even those inside the home, and the pregnant woman still seem to exist in an uncomfortable relationship. Although most pregnant women work outside the home as well as within it, and certainly many of *American Baby*'s readers are among these, pregnant women are advised simultaneously to avoid any activities that might strain the fetus and to engage in activities that are mundane or boring or blot out thought.

Sometimes detailed agendas requiring otherwise prosaic activities are justified by a vision of the nine months of pregnancy stretching without landmark before a woman (see, e.g., Gardephe 1985c). If a woman accepts the prospect of pregnancy as an undifferentiated vista, it is reasonable that she also will be prone to adopt views of activities of pregnancy—eating, for instance—as strongly occurring on a time schedule: As she eats her healthy meals, for example, she can be advised to visualize how these foods are helping build a healthy fetus at each stage of its development (Gardephe 1985c). Pregnant women often are advised to spend long hours cleaning up (though not strenuously), researching pediatricians, and "getting organized" for the birth. They rarely are told to spend a day at the research laboratory or a night at the opera.

In addition, any pregnant woman not demonstrably engaged in paid work is suspected of laziness. Even women ordered by doctors to complete bed rest (as few are these days) are told to maintain their activity level. They should, for example, dedicate themselves to keeping "your eyes on the prize" by thinking positively, moving cheerfully from room to room to brighten their spirits, phone catalogue-shopping, and decorating their "space" with attractive objects "on the same level as your head on a pillow" (Lieberman 1993). If they work outside the home, perhaps a loaner Fax or modem can be arranged. In short, even if a woman is confined to bed for nine months, she is still to fulfill role requirements, whether as future mother, attractive wife, current housekeeper, or worker at an outside job.

Some activities are said to be prudent now, because they will be impossible for a new mother to manage, although they are quite possible for a pregnant woman. Generally, these involve "getting organized":

> The months before your baby arrives offer an opportunity—maybe your last for some time—to get organized. Put your bills, receipts, and other paperwork in order so you won't waste precious time searching for them later. . . . Next time you're put on hold on the phone, use those minutes to weed out old, never-used numbers in your Rolodex. Mark with a paper clip where you leave off after each call. (*American Baby* 1983)

Of course, not all prospective mothers have partners to help them engage in these cleanup tasks (*American Baby* 1983; Gardephe 1985a, 1993b). Interestingly, however, participation in mundane activities such as these is virtually never recommended for a father or other partner: These individuals are, presumably, already engaged in defensible activities, whereas pregnant women "have nothing better to do." What they do need to do, however, is to accept the child, now fetus, and to demonstrate their devotion to it through interested information gathering that attempts to discover—insofar as that is possible—what the child is up to and what it may look like.

Ingestion as Conscious Activity

Articles from the last decade identify two principal causes of harm to a fetus: first, imprudent exertion, such as too-ambitious exercise, activity at work, or even sexual intercourse; and, second—and by far most common—unwise ingestion of food, drink, or other substances. Ingestion has long had a special moral valence for women, pregnant or not (Bell 1987; Millman 1980). At the same time, diverse cultures surround pregnant women with food myths and taboos (Gregor 1985), perhaps superstitious remnants of the notion that what goes into a pregnant woman's body becomes a fetus. Popular recent U.S. guides to pregnancy have centered on food and substance proscriptions for some time now (e.g., Apgar and Beck 1972). Almost every week's reading brings some new evidence of the understanding that an irresponsibly ingesting woman abuses a fetus, then a child, if not with alcohol or cigarettes, then certainly with drugs (the most recent to cross my desk while writing this article was "New Mother Charged with Neglecting Child" [*Indianapolis Star* 1993]).

Yet, by far the most severe cause of harm today is ingestion—a health-based version of the nineteenth-century's fears about the consequences of improper thoughts and unwomanly behavior for the pregnant woman (Gardner 1993). In the nineteenth century, the popular and even the scientific literature was willing to indict explicitly pregnant women who had failed to live up to their gender roles. For example, if the pregnant woman who worked outside the home or failed to be enchanted with marriage or motherhood gave birth to a child with a disability, this result was used to cudgel her for her unwomanly thoughts or actions. Although gender conduct is not so indicted as once it was, nevertheless responsibility for ingestion devolves mainly on the future mother (as an expectant woman is seen). As she watches what she ingests and guards what she does, she serves an important function for society, because "we express our wishes for tomorrow by the way we raise our children today" (Arnott 1991)—and pregnancy has become part of the extended timeline of childhood.

It is somewhat unusual to think of ingestion as a conscious activity, given that it is one needed to sustain life and thus unavoidable. During pregnancy, however, what can usually be accomplished without great thought is to be constantly on a woman's mind; some advice books are little more than lists of foods and drinks, vitamin supplements, and over-the-counter and prescription drugs (e.g., Gots and Gots 1981). Women are to compare ingestibles they choose with the lists in what amount to reference books. The catalogue of ingestibles—and of other activities—women are to approach with prudence is impressive. Together, this catalogue suggests that, were a woman to try and conscientiously take every instance of potential harm into account while pregnant, she would need to consider the impact of virtually every thought and deed and certainly every bite of food, sip of drink, and each potentially harmful substance.

As a woman reads popular, even scientific, sources, she discovers that basically no ingestible is reliably safe, so that even eating—which might seem the most humble, even automatic of required actions—is difficult to perform without meticulous consideration, much less to number among her pleasures. At the same time, she has a wealth of detail about common substances to learn and relearn. What seems innocuous for nonpregnant women (several cups of tea or coffee, a cigarette of two, a beer, sodas, mild recreational marijuana use) becomes a possible killer of the fetus. Scientific studies published in 1985, which have only now come under question, suggested that consuming several sodas a day made a fetus at risk for growth retardation, microcephaly, or death by miscarriage (Hinchley 1993). A typical popular advice article on any ingestible still advises women of the direst results that can eventuate ("death, stroke, brain damage") but avoids advising her just how much is safe to ingest, recommending she consult a medical expert as her best bet (Heins 1992). According to another article, even "light drinking" (which, uncharacteristically, *is* defined, here as four drinks per month) can cause a fetus to become a child "deficient in preacademic, as well as math and reading skills ... [and] showing attention and behavioral problems" (Winthrop 1992). By educating herself about ingestibles and faithfully putting what she learns into practice when pregnant, it seems that a mother-to-be can affect a child's educability.

Suspicion of the familiar and the need for rereducation are not the only hallmarks of pregnancy advice that might disorient or perplex a pregnant woman. Another is that old habits, patterns, and ingestibles must often be rigorously examined anew: a woman who believes she has heretofore understood calcium requirements may simply be told that she must now think of "providing for baby" in a way that will enrich her or his entire life, too.

Another hallmark of popular advice articles is to make a pregnant woman in some measure responsible for other members of her family, notably her husband. In advice writings, pregnant women are not merely eating for two: they are often eating for three, a nice symbolic touch that suggests a unity of the members of the nuclear family but also makes the woman responsible for her spouse as well as her fetus. For example, one writer suggests that a woman's newly adopted concern about calcium should also be "shared with her husband," thus providing yet another family member with "lifelong" benefits, for men suffer from colon cancer and high blood pressure more than do women and risks for these ailments can be decreased by high calcium intake (Henslin 1992). At times, ingestion becomes a window on the development of the pregnant child, allowing a woman to imagine the progress of fetal development much as feeding a new baby is said to allow the new mother a chance to assess and evaluate her baby's progress daily (Gardephe 1993b). It is a window she will be accustomed to opening, thanks to the emphasis on information gathering that exists during pregnancy.

Getting to Know the Hidden: Information Gathering about the Fetus

One legitimate activity for the pregnant woman is a conscientious information gathering, a sort of first step in becoming acquainted with the child presumed to be on the way. In general, any activity that takes a woman's attention off her nonfetal interests is to be applauded and encouraged.

At the most basic level, women are encouraged to amass all evidence of and about the physical fetus that they can: they are, for example, to familiarize themselves with the fetus's schedule of developmental milestones (much as they will be urged to do for their infants and children) and observe quickening, movement and kicking schedules, turning, and so on. Taking advantage of quite recent technology, women are advised to keep hard copies or videotapes of amniocentesis readings, X rays, and sonograms; even parents of stillborn fetuses are encouraged to take photographs of their fetuses (James Johnson et al. 1985).[4] Commonly, popular press articles encourage prospective mothers to visualize their eventual children, imagining whether they are girls or boys, as well as whether the baby will "look like me" (Gardephe 1992; Heins 1992). A wide variety of "pregnancy diaries" are available, many advertised in *American Baby* (see the advertisement for the "Countdown to Baby" calendar, adorned with "facts to learn (300 in all) about what's happening now to your baby and you" [*American Baby*, July 1983]). These often encourage a woman to write her daily thoughts and feelings concerning the fetus that she imagines within her, as well as measurable changes of her weight—a reflection of the fetus's growth—and other physical changes.

Mental and Emotional Harness: Against Worry,
in Favor of Acceptance

I hesitate to note injunctions toward mental and emotional self-control as simply another activity recommended during pregnancy. Yet, recommendations about maintaining the proper attitude and eschewing anxiety occur again and again. It seems to me that much of the other advice about activities is complexly related to the pregnant woman's mental and emotional self-management. Thus, writers have long presumed that the anticipated experience of pain, which we still understand childbirth to include, will color preparation for that experience (Scarry 1985). Advice in the U.S. about pregnancy has long contained a rock-solid conviction that women's labile emotions during pregnancy can cause anything from death of a fetus to the birth of an "anxious" child, and this assumption continues. Where earlier times saw the woman—hence the fetus—as subject to overwhelming fears and cravings, we now charge pregnant women with creating harmed fetuses, then flawed children, because of mental or emotional weakness while pregnant.

Adopting a rhetoric of fetal endangerment, no matter its details, is facilitated and supported by folk beliefs and biological "knowledge" about women and pregnancy. Even authoritative sources still warn that pregnant women may experience an unpredictable range of emotional and behavioral extremes that can easily harm the fetus (see, for example, the constantly "updated" but little-changing U.S. Department of Health, Education, and Welfare pamphlet [1973]). Pregnancy may cause women to become ecstatic or depressed, and these states make women capable of more than ordinary emotional reactions that can affect their children.

For the most part, advice writing invokes trivial thought processes that aptly complement the trivial activities recommended for a pregnant woman. During pregnancy, women are often told to avoid "thinking too much," "being anxious," "worrying," or "introspecting" for a variety of reasons. Advisors of the recent past even went so far as to counsel a pregnant woman to avoid reflecting on her pregnancy and "cultivate a certain oblivion" toward it (Eastman 1963:73; see also p. 72). Today, the litany is to advise a woman to shun thought that will lead to worry (e.g., Gardephe 1985c), even though this seems a difficult thing to do, given the extent of the prescriptions and proscriptions we have for pregnant women. Advice writers link thought with worry and worry with lack of acceptance of the pregnancy itself, and it is the pregnant woman's responsibility alone that rejects the temptation to spend nine months "wallow[ing] in self-pity" and come to "accept the pregnancy with a positive attitude," as a slightly earlier work put it (E. Miller 1976:24). The popular advice literature, in sum, suspects ratiocination of admitting doubt about her role as a pregnant woman. Any chink in a pregnant woman's devotion to the fetus is deeply suspect, perhaps because—as fetal effects are magnified—magnified maternal effects could have a poor effect on the child once born.

Legitimate Concern with Appearance: The Pregnant Appearance and Its Connotations

Yet another legitimate activity is maintaining one's appearance while pregnant. Much of this appearance maintenance is said to be for a woman's husband—and perhaps can be understood functionally as a way in which to ensure that the marriage bond remains strong—but much of the advice on appearance maintenance is also written with attention to the woman's emotional health: A fat or sloppy pregnant woman, these articles say, is a depressed or anxious, a resistant pregnant woman. Rather than attending to the root cause of depression or anxiety, advisors recommend diets, exercise, and slimming clothing.

The pregnant appearance in public context has traditionally been thought symbolically to introduce sexuality into precincts where it has no business, such as school, places of commercial business, and restaurants. Historically, the workplace was no place for a pregnant woman who had begun to "show." Even advice writers of only 30 years past held that, although employers were "very liberal-minded about such matters, there are naturally certain positions which cannot be held after the pregancy becomes apparent. If this is a factor, plans should be made to discontinue work before the end of the fifth month" (Eastman 1963:82). The same author advised pregnant women to regard their "abdominal rotundity [as] a handicap," but that it was "possible to look attractive at this time as at any other." This continued allure was due to a pregnant woman's compensatory "special radiance" and maternity clothing "so ingeniously contrived these days that they resemble an optical illusion in their ability to beguile the eye in regard to your real contour" (Eastman 1963:73). Then, as now, a pregnant woman was expected to devote considerable energy to maintaining prepregnant appearance standards.

Our standards for appearance for pregnant women compare them to an ideal of never- and nonpregnant women. The greatest compliment a woman can receive while pregnant is that she looks just like her prepregnant self, albeit with a small embryonic bolus traveling somewhere in front. Similarly, we do not cherish—indeed, we have created plastic surgery to outwit—the physical evidence that a woman has been pregnant. A woman is advised to keep to an ideal timetable: For example, she should return, after delivery, to her prepregnant appearance as quickly and precisely as possible, preferably without drooping breasts, scarred abdomen, stretch marks, or weight change.

Pregnant women are encouraged to perform activities that concern the physical home. In addition to these, we see, are activities in service of symbolic family relationships, namely, a maintenance of prepregnant appearance, accomplished so that the fetus is safe and the husband is pleased (Gardephe 1993a).[5] She should not forget her obligations to stay attractive and fit—perhaps by purchasing and following one of the many pregnancy workout videotapes now available (see the review given in Spielvogel [1990], for example). A woman may even want to "prepare" for pregnancy by adopting and mastering good eating habits *before* she becomes pregnant, "psyching up to slim down." She may also decide to join a group of fellow pregnant dieters or keep a faithful food diary of her avoidance triumphs (Spielvogel 1990).

Students of Pregnancy

Another legitimate activity is to become a student of pregnancy. A woman may be advised to study many topics while pregnant, such as the stages of pregnancy and labor options. Of immediate concern to a woman may be preparation for delivering a baby. Selecting a pediatrician (Eden 1992), through an extensive series of visits to many different doctors if need be, and learning about labor are two topics the practical woman should study (Lieberman 1993). Even a bed-resting woman can manage these, through phone calls to physicians or hiring a private tutor or watching videos to learn about labor. Somewhat more surprisingly, *before* a baby arrives, a mother may be advised to educate herself about the first few months of her child's life, the local school system, and her own family history or to revamp her home with an eye to the safety of the child who will live there (Gardephe 1993b; see also J. Miller 1991).

Of course, all these activities bespeak a woman's concern for the health of the future child she envisions. Sometimes, however, advice seems to encourage overpreparation. A woman may be told, for example, that she should envision the child's friendships with other neighborhood children. To best prepare her fetus to have friends and herself to be friendly with the mothers of other children, she should now— while pregnant—take neighborhood walks, preparing herself to smile in a friendly manner and introduce herself (and, presumably, allude in some way to her fetus as well). Such measures will pay off later (Arnott 1991)—and they testify to her visualization both of her social child and of her life as a responsible mother.

Developing the Rhetoric of Fetal Endangerment

Up until the 1930s and 1940s, activities of many sorts—even those that seemed relatively harmless—were seen as potential direct causes of harm to the fetus. Women still are often enjoined to have pregnancies that would leave them bored, even sequestered at home, and robbed of many pleasures, including satisfying dining and complex, questioning thought.

Even when activities are not specifically linked with fetal endangerment, however, there are many suggestions and requirements for the modification of a woman's activities—modifications that might, in fact, occupy much of a woman's pregnancy and become to seem as necessary for the good of the fetus as any drug avoidance. Pregnancy conduct advice is of a piece, and cautions about fetal endangerment exist in the fuller context of advice about looking good, getting organized, and getting to know one's fetus by conscientious information gathering. In fact, although modern pregnancy conduct advice with regard to fetal health pertains most to ingestion, there is some aspect of every other activity advised that reflects on fetal health, too.

Furthermore, pregnancy advice claimsmakers invoke an expanded retrospective timeline, sometimes cautioning prospective mothers to monitor their behavior for years in advance of actually becoming pregnant, as when they speak of slimming down or setting aside poor eating habits in service of becoming pregnancy- and fetus-ready. Thus, nonpregnant women are also subject to measures to ensure fetal health. For women, an expanded timeline would result, if put into practice, in pregnancy careers reaching far beyond the actual nine months of gestation. Indeed, some writers suggest periods of one, or two, or even three years of "preparation" for pregnancy: gynecological assessments, fertility workups, weight loss when needed, an exercise program that will increase a mother's chances of passing through pregnancy and childbirth easily, and attainment of job status that will facilitate a stress-free pregnancy or a pregnancy with job benefits (Gardephe 1992). Pregnancy thereby becomes a long-range and deeply involving process, one that speaks at every turn and twist of the pregnant woman's devotion to her fetus and of the fetus itself as a profoundly social being toward whom one must behave responsibly—preparing a woman, perhaps, for the responsible way in which she is to behave toward the child she will bear. It is significant, however, that prospective fathers have not been similarly targeted: Ignoring men in pregnancy advice literature diminishes their roles in the lives of their born children, too.

In the nineteenth and early twentieth centuries, advice manuals and medical experts often forbade the pregnant woman from venturing outside her house, because it was always possible that there she would see a fearsome creature such as a dog, wolf, or "deformed" stranger. If she did, her child would surely be marked—as a woman was informed by cautionary tales of women who foolishly went outside or, more foolishly still, worked outside the home or traveled. This general proscription against going out of the house can be seen as reinforcing the growing "cult of true womanhood," which demanded that a wife remain at home, not only to care for the family, but also to cultivate talents of decorating—hence celebrating—the home (Welter 1966). We share with the nineteenth century a fear of women's emotions during pregnancy, although we express our fears in terms of current science. Nineteenth-century proscriptions for pregnant women's behavior effectively restricted pregnant women to menial activity in the house, ostensibly to shield them from some shocking sight that would mark the fetus. It is important to realize that the result of our modern advice on restricting activities would—if taken to heart and put into practice—be less different from previous days than we might like to think. In sum, we still subscribe to married domesticity: We simply say that it is for the good of the fetus.

Assumptions about pregnant women's emotions often tacitly guide concerns about activities and ingestibles. Activities proposed for women often presume that they are fearful worriers without the capacity to structure their time or complete any pursuit more complex than tidying a house. Left alone, they will succumb to worry or anxiety (e.g., Stern 1992). Instructions to pregnant women about activities that focus on the child they do not yet know may well help them form a bond with that unknown child, but they also "overprescribe" activities, far more than necessary. By so doing, they presume that a future mother must be artificially stimulated to form a relationship with and care for her future child; apparently, no time is too soon to start, nor any activity too trivial, for an expectant mother. Added to trivial activities prescribed are new ways of performing old activities that a pregnant woman may well imagine she has mastered, from rising when seated to reaching for a quart of milk (Endler 1991; for a medicalized series of rationales, see E. Friedman 1978).

In particular, advice on ingestibles is customarily confusing, contradictory, and often overstated, "just to be on the safe side." It is quite true that being on the safe side cannot possibly result in harm to a fetus; it can, however, considerably add to the burden of a pregnant woman's behavioral requirements. Should a pregnant woman take an aspirin? an acetaminophen? an ibuprofen? And if one is all right, will two be safe? Does she eat enough green, leafy vegetables? If she ate more, would that be better, or would it result in a dangerous superabundance of vitamins? Of the many types of soft drinks—sugared or with sugar substitutes, clear or brown, caffeinated or not—which are safe for drink, and how much? Concerns such as these can stimulate the anxiety that most writers say they hope to erase in pregnant women. In turn, this anxiety production itself is mocked in descriptions of the pregnant woman consumed with anxiety, gulled by the myths and superstitions of pregnancy (Gardephe and Ettlinger 1993; Montague 1993). Perhaps women's anxiety reflects the magnitude of what popular writing holds them responsible for—and the vagueness of the advice given.

RHETORICS OF ENDANGERMENT AND THE PRICE
OF DISAGREEMENT

All rhetorics of endangerment share similar features. The twentieth-century rhetoric regarding pregnancy's dangers typically warns of magnified effects, and this has become especially evident in the last decade. Endangerment supposedly results when relatively small events in the experience or conduct of a parent—most often the mother—are subsequently writ large in fetal effects. Eventually, it may be said, the damaged fetus will grow to childhood in a nation replete with others of its kind. This rhetoric can incorporate a highly melodramatic claimsmaking style (Ibarra and Kitsuse 1993). However, hyperbole in popular written claimsmaking style has decreased since the nineteenth century: the last century's horror stories with illustratory casts of wrongdoers have been replaced by dryly scienticized anonymity. It is difficult to judge which variety is, at bottom, more anxiety provoking for a pregnant woman.

Certainly, there are ways in which the rhetoric of fetal endangerment befits the physical state of pregnancy; certainly too, the rhetoric of fetal endangerment is now the dominant one with regard to pregnancy. For all that a rhetoric of endangerment fits or is encouraged by the physical condition of pregnancy, it is noteworthy that some other rhetoric is *not* the dominant one. It speaks to what we are willing to suffer—or, rather, what we are willing for pregnant (and even nonpregnant) women to suffer—in order to ensure, we think, healthy, attractive, and intelligent future members of society.

The limits of the contemporary rhetoric of fetal endangerment are significant. Every rhetoric names responsible parties, and the responsible party overwhelmingly named in the rhetoric of fetal endangerment is the pregnant woman. It is she, for the most part, who controls events in her womb, and she also is given a wealth of other tasks to perform, among them paying attention to official experts and maintaining a bond with her husband. In fact, pregnant women are not just students of pregnancy. They are, more precisely, students of and defenders of the family with children and largely responsible for the success of such families. In this, our current rhetoric of fetal endangerment does not obviate, yet does not emphasize, the possible responsibility of others such as physicians, relatives, the scientific community, fate or laws of genetic averages, or agencies such as the March of Dimes that minister to and educate about harmed fetuses. In short, this rhetoric points out whose interests may be risked or overlooked when weighed against who else's: a pregnant woman's may be overlooked when compared to a fetus's. In its details, the rhetoric shows what exactly can be sacrificed, namely, a pregnant woman's peace of mind, activity pattern, fit body, career, and preferred diet can all easily be sacrificed for the good of the future child.

We must see developments on other fronts—legal, for example, as well as popular ideas about abortion—as consistent with this popular advice rhetoric, even in its most *soi-disant* liberal moments.

Thus, the fetus-centered rhetoric of endangerment necessarily implies a good deal of control on the pregnant woman's part; simply, it argues that some small act of ingestion or some minor activity can mark a fetus with physical or emotional harm, much as the nineteenth century believed that "maternal impressions" were ready and reliable records of what a pregnant woman saw, ate, wished for, and feared (Gardner 1993). The rhetoric of fetal endangerment lends itself handily to vivid cautionary tales of women who behave inappropriately while pregnant or experience inappropriate emotions and subsequently have children symbolically marked as reminders of unmet expectations. Claimsmakers carrying tales of this kind can arguably recommend powerful negative sanctions for prospective parents.

Rhetorics of endangerment characterize moral discourses associated with particular types of social problems. These rhetorics can be easily applied to perceived problems "that can be expressed as threats to the health and safety of the human body" (Ibarra and Kitsuse 1993:39). Thus, rhetorics of endangerment presume that individuals have a right to good health and safety, that the less endangered have a duty to protect the more vulnerable, that good health and safety are reasonable grounds on which to evaluate individuals, that ill health and mental disability are at one extreme on a continuum that features small "marks" and "flaws" at the midpoint of the continuum and an apparently attainable bodily and mental perfection at the opposite extreme, and that all causal dangers can in fact be avoided by human effort and perfection thus attained. Rhetorics of endangerment are often distinguished, because they target the effect of a condition or practice on others (and not the immorality of the condition or practice itself). Among other functions, our current rhetoric of fetal endangerment reinforces and elaborates traditional twentieth-century gender norms: obsession with eating, appearance, guilt about shirking work and activity, and traditional restrictions on women, including emotional restrictions.

Why would a pregnant woman be motivated to adhere to the many suggestions of our present rhetoric of fetal endangerment? The price of disagreeing with this moral idiom is high, typically higher than the price for disagreeing with, for example, the rhetoric of maternal entitlement that flourished during the 1970s. The pregnant woman who shunned or failed at maternal entitlement was usually guilty of little more than presenting herself as a woman less devoted to self-realization and individualism than was thought fashionable: She risked no one's life. The pregnant woman who disagrees with our rhetoric of fetal endangerment is in a very different position, however. She must take a position against

aiding the most helpless children, those yet to be born. She must argue
with the wisdom of thinking of the future good of the nation—indeed,
the world. She must support her own right to put her personal satisfaction of seemingly petty wants and desires against the physical and mental health of a fetus soon to be child. Finally, she must do all this while
knowingly contradicting those "expert" enough to write articles, even
volumes, detailing the subtle and blatant damage that can result.

At risk in our late-twentieth-century discourse, too, is the malleable
embryo or fetus within the body of the pregnant woman. A pregnant
woman's emotional state, eating habits, thoughts, and activities are
believed to endanger directly an embryo or fetus, soon—it is optimisti-
cally assumed—to be a child. Important for students of social interaction, the rhetoric of fetal endangerment features everyday behavior,
face-to-face interaction, and mundane activity: a certain activity taken
up or avoided, a certain food ingested, careful attention paid to clothing
and appearance during pregnancy, the responsible way a pregnant
woman teaches her husband about his nutritional needs while meeting
hers. All these prescriptions for involvement suggest that it is social
interaction that molds pregnancy and, conversely, that pregnancy outcomes can be managed and directed by interactional means. (These
interactional measures contrast, for example, with a scienticized genet-
ics-dependent idea that pregnancy outcomes are largely foreordained by
chromosomal makeup; hence, the individual can do little to control
them.) Thus, the rhetoric of fetal endangerment elevates the everyday
measures it prescribes to potent forces that create future interactants.

Having problematized certain physical and mental traits or conditions
apparent in children, claimsmakers use this rhetoric to evaluate and
judge the prospective mother, fetus, and child. To say that a child has
an "attention problem" and is failing in school may indict the caffeinated-
soda–drinking mother while ignoring the rest of the family, the school
and the teacher, as well as all other interaction a mother has with that
child. Through the exercise of this rhetoric, the thoughts, feelings, and
actions of a future parent—most often, of a pregnant woman—are
deemed acceptable or unacceptable because of their alleged effect on the
fetus. In addition, the rhetorical idiom implicitly judges a child's physical and mental disability, as well as a child's undesirable personality
traits and physical appearance: The rhetoric of fetal endangerment does
not simply warn pregnant women of unacceptable or harmful acts; it
also creates and sustains categories of unacceptable and undesirable
children, among them children with disabilities. This rhetoric of fetal
endangerment therefore participates in the expansion and refinement of
distinctions among disabilities and in the medicalization of disabilities
that began in the nineteenth century (Blaxter 1976; Haj 1970; Liachowitz

1988). The "successful" outcome of a pregnancy is not merely a live birth. Rather, all women are presumed capable of conceiving and delivering a "perfect" child, barring the knowledge of severe genetic defects or the defects of teratogens such as Thalidomide;[6] therefore, children with shortcomings, large or small, can be read as evidence of parental moral failure during pregnancy.[7]

In previous centuries, disabilities marked divine or supernatural communications that often concerned the entire community, not merely the parents and child. In such births, what we would call a disability was interpreted as a vital communication. The association of pregnancy with grand, high-prestige, or supernatural individuals or events can signal symbolically the fetus's worth or, on the contrary, stand in ironic counterpoint to it. But this is common: in our own time, advice writers spoke of World War II Victory pregnancies that would produce "Victory babies," who would be "the kind of citizen[s] who will justify our faith in the democratic freedoms we fight to win" (Whipple 1944:3). Thus, it is not just that the mother has much reponsibility put on her—but so does the fetus, which is obligated, as any mature over-21 citizen, to be worthy of democracy. In the same way, observers reported pregnant patients during the 1960s who chose all-natural diets in order to avoid any connection with the Establishment for their child, or who chose vegan diets while pregnant in order to avoid producing a fetus, then a child, with violent tendencies (Colman and Colman 1971:18; Yntema 1980:72–80).

It is, in fact, worthwhile to speculate about the effects of our rhetoric of fetal endangerment on the child that is born. Certainly, this rhetoric facilitates reactions to children as either responsible or not responsible for their own perceived flaws (as, for a time, "crack babies" had almost every failing related to maternal drug use). Thus, the rhetoric of endangerment crystalizes beliefs about what is an undesirable disability and also fosters judgments about and enables evaluation of physical attractiveness and personality. In addition, knowing that one's future had been determined before birth could help the individual make sense of the disability that she or he regards as a misfortune. Advice literature is one setting where writers elaborate a moral discourse, and the information *American Baby* provides its readers is consistent with the information of many other popular articles and books. Recent books, including *Caring for Your Unborn Child* and *The Genetic Connection: How to Protect Your Family Against Hereditary Disease*, suggest that advice for today's parents is an amalgam of popular and scientific genres. These works regard the reproductive process not as making do with the child that one receives but, rather, as the creation of a satisfactory fetus (thus implicitly affirming the idea that pregnancy can be directed by everyday

actions and thoughts). Currently, a pregnant woman's conduct and feelings are labeled direct agents for the future child's physical well-being
and mental stability.

Rhetorics of endangerment in general fit certain conditions better than
others, as all rhetorics fit some conditions and categories better than others (Ibarra and Kitsuse 1993). There are features of pregnancy that make
it particularly suited for a rhetoric of endangerment. First, as a status
passage, pregnancy is a state that many cultures have found anxiety
provoking. Tensions of gender relations can be further exacerbated by a
second factor, the physical reticence of the fetus—there is no certainty
that the fetus is free of problems. In addition to the privacy of fetal
developments during pregnancy, there is a third factor, prolonged gestation. This makes pregnancy suited to a system of blame in which
seemingly small misdeeds (eating a particular food or fleeting anger at
one's husband) can have large effects—especially if the pregnant woman
is proscribed from committing a wide enough range of misdeeds. The
same conditions facilitate the rhetoric of fetal endangerment: A well-
worked-out plan of action and hopes for success would be welcome
during a tense status passage, and the complex injunctions signal the
importance of the parents' transition in status (Davis-Floyd 1992; Gennep 1969; Raphael 1988). The reticence of the fetus makes it equally easy
to argue that much has gone right; and the extended period of gestation
provides nine months' experience from which to choose in claiming that
one has successfully "created" one's child.

Finally, it is appropriate to note that the constructionist analysis of
pregnancy and fetal development I have used goes beyond biological,
physiological, psychological, and other sociological conceptions of pregnancy. To analyze the rhetoric of fetal endangerment in pregnancy is,
first, to understand how some actors and some casts are chosen as relevant in blame-attribution—mothers regularly, though not fathers. It is
also to understand that some casts and events are relegated to the side-
lines when fault is found—as were environmental conditions in the
nineteenth century, though not today. Second, constructionist analysis
levels "scientific" proofs and arguments with folk proofs and arguments, proposing that both are capable of being exploited by societal
interest groups.

ACKNOWLEDGMENTS

I am grateful for the suggestions of William Gronfein and for the research
assistance of Wendy Hancock-Becher, Shari Hanesworth, Karen Hurt, Melody
Owen Stiles, and Brian E. Withem. Candace West supplied a guiding spirit for

considering pregnancy phenomena, and Erving Goffman supplied a guiding spirit somewhat more distant in time but nonetheless vibrant in memory. I am grateful to both these people for reminding me that pregnancy is, among other things, concerned with interaction, even when some of the interactants are unavailable for direct examination because of circumstances beyond their control and even when the burden of keeping the lines of communication open tends to reside with one gender more than another.

I also acknowledge financial support from the Faculty Development Office of Indiana University for part of the period in which I did research for this chapter. Finally, without the help of Mary Jo Romeo of *American Baby* Magazine—who supplied the magazine's official mission, marketing statements, and subscriber statistics—this article could not have been written; my thanks to her, too.

NOTES

1. Elsewhere, I have described this other, more woman-centered rhetoric of fetal endangerment in detail, noting that it places maternal "rights" foremost. This rhetoric is now often heard when women discuss continuing conduct during pregnancy that they believe may harm the fetus (Gardner, 1993). In contrast to the fetus-centered rhetoric, this woman-centered understanding of fetal endangerment concentrates on maternal rights to health and "normal" nonpregnant activity. Both rhetorics, of course, presume that fetal health—even character—can be shaped by parents during pregnancy. My own recent interviews show that, although concerns about fetal character have largely faded from the contemporary popular advice literature, they remain vivid for women I have interviewed.

Referring to a rhetoric as "fetus-" or "woman-centered" is in some ways shortsighted. Changes in fetal health undoubtedly affect the mother who cares for the injured child that is born, and the pregnant woman who is so centered on her fetus that she forgets her own health will, in time, harm her fetus or be unable to care for it. Often, I am persuaded that the understanding of the new women's health movement—namely, that a woman and a fetus are a new creature themselves, unlike either alone—is most accurate.

By focusing in this article on diet and activities advised for pregnant women, I have, incidentally, ignored another set of circumstances discussed less often in popular and scientific writings but arguably of greater danger to pregnant women than to their fetuses, namely, medical procedures such as X rays and such interventions as vaccinations (Shore 1978).

2. Typical recent works of fiction and films include popular horror novelist Stephen King's *Firestarter* (1980), in which a couple, duped by a cynical scientist into taking an untested experimental drug, have a daughter skilled in spontaneous combustion; and the movie *The Unborn* (U.S.; 1991), in which a malevolent obstetrician-gynecologist genetically engineers evil embryos given to eating their way out of their mothers. On the popularity of the child-endangerment tale in general among horror writers, see Best (1990:113–118).

In this chapter I focus primarily on the period 1983–93. However, a somewhat older version of pregnancy horror features the uterine invasion of superior alien forces, as in the two movies derived from John Wyndham's novel *The Midwich*

Cuckoos (1957): *The Village of the Damned* (British; 1960) and *The Children of the Damned* (British; 1964).

3. Compare the nineteenth-century rhetoric of fetal endangerment, that relished expounding on the lifelong harm a mother's momentary lapse might do the child to be born and morbidly expatiating on the disability itself (see Gardner 1993).

4. Similarly, Baker (1989) treats socialization "with" the dead as a form of relationship formation, although necessarily retrospective, one of remembrance.

5. In the same way, the importance of sex to a husband is often discussed in tandem with the safety of sex for a fetus, obliging a woman to manage at least two complex relationship agendas without necessarily considering her own wishes (see Schwartz 1993).

6. In fact, genetics screening and careful avoidance of teratogens are believed to relieve prospective parents of these possibilities, reducing or eliminating otherwise depressing odds.

7. This rhetoric takes as given the desirability of a "healthy, normal" newborn free of various "anomalies" that, in other cultures or times, might be received, accepted, and perhaps even sought after, as auspicious portents or distinguishing traits. Thus, before the nineteenth century, nonhuman agencies were widely felt to intervene in fetal life. Sometimes God or nature expressed a complicated message directed to an entire nation through the birth of a "marked" child or a child with a disability, as when such a birth was said to herald a change in monarchs or victory or defeat in war (Thompsson 1896:8–10). In such births, what we would call a disability was interpreted as a vital communication.

REFERENCES

American Baby Magazine. 1983. "Crib Notes." December:45.

Arnott, N. 1991. "Mom to Mom." *American Baby* March:48.

Apgar, V., and J. Beck. 1972. *Is My Baby All Right? A Guide to Birth Defects.* New York: Trident.

Baker, P. M. 1989. "Socialization after Death: The Might of the Living Dead." Pp. 45–57 in *Growing Old in America,* edited by B. B. Hess and E. B. Markson. New Brunswick, NJ: Transaction Books.

Bell, R. M. 1987. *Holy Anorexia.* Chicago: University of Chicago Press.

Berezin, N. 1982. *After a Loss in Pregnancy.* New York: Simon & Schuster.

Berg, B. 1981. *Nothing to Cry About.* New York: Seaview.

Best, J. 1990. *Threatened Children: Rhetoric and Concern about Child-Victims.* Chicago: University of Chicago Press.

Blaxter, M. 1976. *The Meaning of Disability.* London: Heinemann.

Colman, A., and L. L. Colman. 1971. *Pregnancy: The Psychological Experience.* New York: Herder and Herder.

Curtis, L. R., and Y. Coroles. 1985. *Pregnant and Lovin' It.* New York: The Body Press.

Davidson, G. 1979. *Understanding the Death of the Wished-For Child.* Springfield, IL: OGR Service Corporation.

Davis-Floyd, R. 1992. *Birth as an American Rite of Passage.* Berkeley: University of California Press.

DeFrain, J. (ed.). 1986. *Stillborn: The Invisible Death.* Lexington, MA: Lexington Books.

Eastman, N. J. 1963. *Expectant Motherhood.* Boston: Little, Brown.

Eberlein, T. 1989. "Speaking with . . . The Outspoken Penelope Leach." *American Baby* March:78, 80.

Eden, A. 1992. "Visit with a Pediatrician." *American Baby* January:10, 37.

Endler, C. 1991. "Save Your Back!" *American Baby* December:53, 56.

Evans, E. E. 1875. *The Abuse of Maternity.* Philadelphia: J. B. Lippincott.

Friedman, E. A. 1978. "The Physiological Aspects of Pregnancy." Pp. 55–71 in *The Woman Patient,* edited by M. Notman and C. Nadelson. New York: Plenum.

Friedman, R., and B. Gradstein. 1982. *Surviving Pregnancy Loss.* Boston: Little, Brown.

Gardephe, C. D. 1985a. "Before Baby Comes, Get Organized!" *American Baby* March:20.

_____. 1985b. "Feeding the Growing Baby." *American Baby* March:20.

_____. 1985c. "The Waiting Game." *American Baby* March:20.

_____. 1992. "Will It Be a Boy?" *American Baby* October:26.

_____. 1993a. "Baby Fat." *American Baby* May:26, 29–30.

_____. 1993b. "Exercise Is Essential." *American Baby* May:28.

Gardephe, C. D., and Steven Ettlinger. 1993. *Don't Pick Up the Baby or You'll Spoil the Child and Other Old Wives' Tales about Pregnancy and Parenting.* New York: Chronicle.

Gardner, C. B. 1993. "The 19th-Century Rhetoric of Fetal Endangerment." Unpublished paper.

Gennep, A. van. 1969/1909. *Les Rites de Passage.* New York: Johnson Reprint Corporation.

Gots, R. E., and S. Gots. 1981. *Caring for Your Unborn Child.* New York: Harcourt, Brace.

Gregor, T. 1985. *Anxious Pleasures: The Sexual Lives of an Amazonian People.* Chicago: University of Chicago Press.

Haj, F. 1970. *Disability in Antiquity.* New York: Philosophical Library.

Hales, D., and R. K. Creasy. 1982. *New Hope for Problem Pregnancies: Helping Babies Before They're Born.* New York: Harper & Row.

Heins, H. 1992. "Your Healthy Pregnancy: 'Will My Baby Look Like Me?'" *American Baby* March:14, A12.

Henslin, J.-A. 1992. "Calcium: The White Stuff." *American Baby* September:50–52, 70.

Hinchley, T. 1993. "Study Says a Few Cups of Coffee a Day Pose No Danger to a Fetus." *New York Times* February 3:A16.

Ibarra, P. R., and J. I. Kitsuse. 1990. "Reconstructing the Rhetoric of Social Problems Discourse." Paper presented at Society for the Study of Social Problems, Washington, DC.

_____. 1993. "Vernacular Constituents of Moral Discourse: An Interactionist Proposal for the Study of Social Problems." Pp. 25–58 in *Reconsidering Social Constructionism,* edited by J. A. Holstein and G. Miller. Hawthorne, NY: Aldine de Gruyter.

Indianapolis Star. 1993. "New Mother Charged with Neglecting Child." August 5:C3.

Johnson, James D., et al. 1985. *A Most Important Picture.* Omaha: Centering Corporation.

Johnson, John M. 1989. "Horror Stories and the Construction of Child Abuse." Pp. 5–17 in *Images of Issues: Typifying Contemporary Social Problems,* edited by J. Best. Hawthorne, NY: Aldine de Gruyter.

King, S. 1980. *Firestarter.* New York: Viking.

Kitzinger, J. 1988. "Defending Innocence: Ideologies of Childhood." *Feminist Review* 28:77–87.

Liachowitz, C. 1988. *Disability as a Social Construct.* Philadelphia: University of Pennsylvania Press.

Lieberman, C., 1993. "Making the Best of Bed Rest." *American Baby* May:62, 64, 66, 87.

Marshall, C. 1992. *The Expectant Father.* New York: St. Martin's Press.

Miller, E. M. 1976. *I Am a Mother.* Old Tappan, NJ: Spire.

Miller, J. 1991. *The Perfectly Safe Home.* New York: Simon & Schuster.

Millman, M. 1980. *Such a Pretty Face.* New York: Norton.

Montague, D. 1993. "About Men: The Beat Goes On." *The New York Times Magazine* September 26:20, 22.

Raphael, R. 1988. *The Men from the Boys: Rites of Passage in Male America.* Lincoln: University of Nebraska Press.

Scarry, E. 1985. *The Body in Pain: The Making and Unmaking of the World.* New York: Oxford University Press.

Scher, J., and C. Dix. 1983. *Will My Baby Be Normal? Everything You Need to Know about Pregnancy.* New York: Dial.

Schwartz, P. 1993. "Talking about Sex." *American Baby* June:14, 31.

Shore, E. G. 1978. "Prenatal Influences on Child Health and Development." Pp. 21–32 in *The Woman Patient,* edited by M. Notman and C. Nadelson. New York: Plenum.

Spielvogel, C. 1990. "Six Great Videos." *American Baby* November:46, 48–49.

Stein, H. 1984. "The Case for Staying Home." *Esquire* June:44–47, 53.

Stern, E. S. 1992. "Pregnant Feelings." *American Baby* March:18.

Thomas, E., and S. Browder. 1987. *Born Dancing: How Intuitive Parents Understand Their Baby's Unspoken Language and Natural Rhythms.* New York: Harper & Row.

Thompsson, C. J. S. 1896. *The Mystery and Lore of Monsters.* New York: Citadel.

U.S. Department of Health, Education, and Welfare. 1973. "Prenatal Care." Washington, D.C.: Children's Bureau Publication No. 4.

Welter, B. 1966. "The Cult of True Womanhood, 1820–1860." *American Quarterly* 18:44–62.

Whipple, D. V. 1944. *Our American Babies.* New York: M. Barrows.

Winthrop, A. 1992. "Alcohol and Pregnancy." *American Baby* July:6.

Wyndham, J. 1957. *The Midwich Cuckoos.* New York: Dell.

Yntema, S. 1980. *Vegetarian Baby.* Ithaca, NY: McBooks.

Chapter 5

"Crack Babies" and the Politics of Reproduction and Nurturance

Jacquelyn Litt and Maureen McNeil

The term "crack baby" acquired currency and resonance during recent years in the United States. The term refers to infants and children who were exposed to crack cocaine during their mothers' pregnancies.[1] Yet, the term "crack baby" also stands as a metaphor for a range of medical, social, and political difficulties in contemporary society—physically disabled and socially disadvantaged children, increasing numbers of women taking "street drugs,"[2] and the seemingly endless cycle of poverty in urban centers. The mass media creates these associations in their accounts of "crack babies," linking pregnant women's crack cocaine use to these most pressing social problems.

Increased prosecutions against pregnant women using illegal drugs reflect a new concern that women's drug use threatens not only the woman herself but also her child and ultimately her community's future. In 1990, "Drug Czar" William Bennett called for the establishment of orphanages and youth camps as refuges for children exposed to "systematic child abuse" in drug-infested homes. He stated, "no one is a stronger proponent of family. But when it reaches a level of systematic child abuse, we have got to do something" (New York Times 1990b:8). Federally funded research, such as the 1993 project by the National Institute of Child Health to study the effects of cocaine use on women and children, also reflects a new emphasis on curtailing pregnant women's drug use. The Journal of Recovery and Addiction (July/August 1991) advertises a film entitled "Drug Babies: The Epidemic of the 90s" for sale to "women's programs, pregnant teen programs, perinatal education, and . . . health care professionals." From all of these quarters—legal, medical, and political—we have the making of a moral crusade to save the "crack baby" from the "pregnant addict." In the wake of this surge of concern, social critiques (Dunlap 1992; Humphries 1993) and scientific reappraisals of the fears associated with "crack babies" have begun to emerge (Koren et al. 1989; *Science* 1992; Zuckerman and Frank 1992). Hence, it is appropriate to explore the imagery associated with this term and to consider what has been at stake in the labeling and associated panic around the "crack baby."

The term itself is striking. It is terse and deterministic; the fate of these children is attributed to one factor—their mothers' use of crack cocaine. They become *essentially* designated by this single aspect of their formation and environment; they *are* "crack babies." Indeed, The *Washington Post* recast the term "crack babies" and its meaning by entitling their 1991 series on the topic "Crack's Children," in effect erasing the mother entirely and presuming hostility and indifference to her situation (Norris 1991a, b, c). Both the *Post*'s title and the commonplace "crack baby" are extremely evocative labels. Juxtaposing maternal corruption, even invisibility, with childhood innocence evokes horror and condemnation. And as we will see, the fate of these babies appears fixed from birth, indeed, prior to birth.

In this essay we travel beneath and around these evocative and powerful characterizations to understand precisely what animates the so-called problem of the "crack baby." We argue that the problem of "crack babies"—the very idea of the category "crack babies"—emerges from a particular packaging of contemporary social problems rather than from a discretely identifiable medical condition. We see in the fashionable construction of the "crack baby" a simultaneous creation of the "crack mother" and argue that fears about these children are being mobilized on the basis of suspicions about their mothers. Detective Sergeant Van Hemert of Muskegon County, Michigan, expresses the oppositional nature of the mother-child relationship that we find dominates the current discourse on "crack babies": "If the mother wants to smoke crack and kill herself, I don't care. Let her die, but don't take that poor baby with her" (quoted in Hoffman 1990).

IDENTIFYING THE PROBLEM

A generation of babies affected by the drug (crack cocaine) is on the way. How will society cope?

Dorris (1990:8)

The range of potential "signs" of damage associated with crack cocaine use during pregnancy is extensive. Early research attributed respiratory and urinary tract difficulties and even sudden infant death syndrome (SIDS) to cocaine exposure in the womb (Chasnoff 1988; Chasnoff et al. 1986). A summary of recent research cites studies of prenatal cocaine exposure that have linked it to a range of "adverse maternal, fetal, and natal outcomes" or "toxic effects" that "include an increased incidence of spontaneous abortion, fetal death, prematurity, abruptio placentae, and congenital malformations." It goes on to identify decreased fetal growth, "small-for-gestational-age births," and adverse neurological development as further problems emerging from such exposure (Handler et al. 1991:818; see also Chasnoff et al. 1986).

These references to "congenital malformations" and "adverse neurological development" are vague and broad. The popular media often represent these signs as an extensive set of concrete symptoms and, more commonly, ominous prognoses. For example, Zuckerman and Frank (1992) cite a 1990 article in *Rolling Stone* that claimed that these babies were "like no others, brain damaged in ways yet unknown, oblivious to affection." *Time* exclaimed that "even one 'hit' of crack can irreparably damage a fetus or breast-fed baby" (Langone 1988:85). A recent front-page story in the *New York Times*, which ostensibly reported challenges to pessimistic prognoses for these children, typifies the latitude taken in accounts about the impact of "crack" on children. This report claimed that cocaine:

> lingers in an infant's system for nearly a week after birth, . . . causing the newborn to be jittery, irritable and given to stretches of high-pitched crying. But beyond that, the experts say, the most common affliction of cocaine-exposed children is a central nervous system disorder in which they are quickly overwhelmed by the sensations of everyday life. (Treaster 1993:B4)

"Jittery, irritable" babies or children "overwhelmed by the sensations of everyday life" are common occurrences, and it would appear impossible to establish these conditions as due to such a specific cause as in utero exposure to crack cocaine. The *New York Times* article continues to list other widespread phenomena that have been attributed to such exposure: children not beginning to talk and walk when they should; children throwing tantrums and darting around the classrooms; and children periodically drifting into daydreams.

Behind this imagery and the broad range of signs used to measure the putative impact of crack cocaine on babies, the medical profile of these problems is contested and now shows signs of optimism. Generalizations about its medical impact often derive from medical research that is not always focused exclusively on crack cocaine. Indeed, it was only in 1992 that *Index Medicus* began to have a distinctive listing for crack cocaine. In regard to "crack babies," Zuckerman and Frank refer to the "absence of any credible scientific data regarding the sequelae of prenatal exposure beyond the newborn period" (1992:337). Even the evidence from this newborn period has been described as "too inadequate and inconsistent to allow any clear predictions about the effects of prenatal exposure to cocaine on children's development and behavior" (Zuckerman and Frank 1992:337). The *New York Times* reports that medical experts' "worst fears" about "crack babies" are not being realized:

> While up to a third appear to have been seriously damaged, 20 to 40 percent seem unscathed. . . . Those who have been harmed by cocaine need not be written off as a lost generation, but can be greatly improved with therapy and other special attention. Not all recover fully, but many do. (Treaster 1993:A1)

Questions have also been raised about bias in the representation of research findings (Koren et al. 1989), about the inconsistency in those findings (Gieringer 1990; Kusserow 1990), and about the difficulty of isolating the effects of crack cocaine use from those caused by the use of other drugs and environmental factors (Humphries 1993:33–35).

The reported problems of "crack babies" are multidimensional and go beyond the medical domain. They include the burden so-called crack children place on adoptive parents, biological grandparents, school teachers, and hospital staff, as well as on society in general. A number of reports point to the increased demand on public expenditures that "crack babies" will require as they enter and go through the public school and social service systems. A 1990 report by the Department of Health and Human Services observed that in the eight cities surveyed, 8,974 babies were born to mothers addicted to crack. According to DHHS calculations, hospital delivery and prenatal and foster care through age 5 would cost $500 million; costs for preparing these children for school could go higher than $1.5 billion (*New York Times* 1990a:8). As these children enter schools, administrators report drains on school resources. *Juvenile Justice Digest* (1990:18) reports: "Five years after crack cocaine swept into Florida, the region's schools are bracing for an influx of children with developmental problems caused by their exposure to cocaine while in the womb." It is not only these "crack children" who will be harmed; according to a report in the *Washington Post:* "all the children who were not exposed to crack in the womb will suffer as their teachers become preoccupied with the crack-affected youngsters' overwhelming problems" (Norris 1991b:A8).

These frantic appraisals are matched in other quarters, where "crack babies" are said to be deluging foster care and hospital services. A special population of "crack babies" has been labeled "boarder babies"—

defined by the *Washington Post* as "children left by crack addicted mothers and left for hospitals to rear or place in foster homes." Between 1985 and 1990, the demand for foster care in Washington, D.C., increased more than 80 percent, a demand attributed to the increasing numbers of pregnant women using crack cocaine (Norris 1991a:A1). Grandmothers also have been called into service; many now raise the children of their crack-addicted daughters (Norris 1991c:A1).

Phrases such as "an influx of children," "a lost generation," and "a generation of crack babies" appear in these accounts, conjuring up an image of and fears associated with an epidemic. Yet, just as the medical press now questions earlier claims about the permanence of medical and educational handicaps, the magnitude of these other problems is by no means established (see Humphries 1992:32–33). In the early stages of the panic about "crack babies," the figure of 375,000 drug-affected births per year (Chasnoff, 1988) became a familiar reference point, repeated in virtually every press report about the problem. However, this was a composite figure that did not distinguish crack cocaine from other forms of cocaine or from other illegal drugs and was based on studies of urban hospitals, where rates of drug use and testing might be particularly high. Humphries (1992) reviews the estimates and suggests that the widely circulated figure of 375,000 drug-affected births may be inflated. She cites a key source text for the Bush administration (Kusserow 1990) as providing the figure of 100,000 "crack baby" births each year. More recently, Ira J. Chasnoff, President of the National Association for Perinatal Addiction Research and Education, modified his earlier estimation of 375,000 annual births, stating that, in total, "more than 500,000 children have been exposed to cocaine and other drugs, and that perhaps 300,000 have suffered some damage" (Treaster 1993:B4). His later statement is clearly much more tentative than earlier claims about the extent of exposure and damage.

These revisions in the popular and medical discourses indicate that fears about "crack babies" and the significance of the label itself are rooted less in consistent medical findings than in a moral panic around children and mothers in the inner city. Reinarman and Levine (1989:570, fn 4) analyze the wider drug scare that emerged in the late 1980s, noting that "the attention given to crack and drugs did not arise from evidence about victims alone, if at all, but from the news producing and vote-getting procedures of the media and politicians respectively, and also from a scapegoating or blame the victim tendency in the American political culture." In the remainder of this chapter, we pursue the analysis of this panic, suggesting that it is linked to a series of interrelated and powerful social concerns around poverty and motherhood. An adversarial relationship between a putatively dangerous mother and an innocent, vulnerable fetus or child structures the discourse on "crack babies," as it does a number of related controversies regarding repro- duction: abortion, reproductive technologies, genetic counseling, and fetal protection policies (Litt and McNeil 1992; Petchesky 1987; Rothman 1989). It is poor, black, inner-city mothers who appear as the character- istic adversaries in this particular drama around crack cocaine; corre- spondingly, although illegal drug use cuts across all class and race lines, women of color and poor women are more likely to be arrested and prosecuted for allegedly harming their fetus (Paltrow 1992). The par- ticular packaging and treatment of the problem minimize any claim these mothers might make for social resources for themselves and their children.

A NEW BIO-UNDERCLASS?

The early, albeit contested, emphasis on the neurological damage that "crack babies" suffer may signal a new political landscape, where pub- lic resentment might well shift away from the so-called "welfare queen" to a new "bio-underclass" (Humphries 1993). Humphries explains that "what was once thought of as a cultural problem, the transmission of welfare dependency from mother to daughter, became [in the context of the drug scare] at once a biological matter" (1993:42). The attention given to another newly identified medical condition, fetal alcohol syn- drome (FAS), could be seen as part of this trend (McNeil and Litt 1992). Michael Dorris who in 1989 won the National Book Critics Circle Award for his autobiographical account of raising an adopted son with FAS quotes Dr. Philip May, a nationally recognized expert on Native Amer- ican alcohol use: "If we have a lot of drinking mothers, we may some- day have whole societies with lower average intelligence" (quoted in Dorris 1989:183). It is perhaps significant that Michael Dorris, who played a key role in bringing FAS to public attention, has been con- sulted and quoted extensively in media coverage about crack children. In *Newsweek*, Dorris (1990:8) concluded an essay on "A Desperate Crack Legacy" with an apocalyptic warning: "And we worry about the very fabric of society when hundreds or thousands of others with [my son's] problems, or worse, become teenagers, become adults, in the year 2000." The discourse on crack cocaine resembles that on FAS; both mobilize a moral panic around children that is based on biological harm to the fetus.

The term *crack baby*, then, symbolizes biological determinism and is compatible with a more general trend to see identities and life trajectories as set from birth. The contemporary obsession with genetic deter-minations and the ubiquitous search for "causal genes" for alcoholism, homosexuality, and so on are part of this wider pattern. In the context of increasing attribution of features of our individual being to genetic traits, the fears associated with "crack babies" are very much of these times.

The enthusiasm for genetic explanations runs parallel to a more dif-fused concern for identifying groups associated with "biologic vulnera-bility" (Zuckerman and Frank 1992:337), and "crack babies" are seen as one such group. The media attention given to "crack babies" is domi-nated by expectations of permanent neurological damage (medical find-ings notwithstanding) that may create generations of impaired, depen-dent people. We would add that targeting socially and economically disadvantaged groups (specifically black and Latino urban communities in relation to "crack babies" and Native American communities in rela-tion to FAS) through biomedical designations is also a way of sidestep-ping thorny social and political issues. Communities can be blamed for their social disadvantage by designating them through medical labels. Curiously, medical designations are often used in ways that eliminate social responsibility; disease replaces irresponsibility as the underpin-ning of "deviant" behavior (Conrad 1992). Yet, in the cases of FAS and "crack babies," moral stigma toward mothers is not suspended but presumed.

The failure to suspend moral censure may in fact be related to the association between this putatively new "bio-underclass" and the wider panic about the so-called urban underclass, a topic that has received enormous attention in the academic and popular presses (Jencks and Peterson, 1991; Katz 1990, 1993; Wilson 1987). A historian of poverty refers to the term *underclass* as itself a "convenient metaphor," evoking "three widely shared perceptions: novelty, complexity, and danger. Conditions within inner cities are unprecedented; they cannot be reduced to a single factor; and they menace the rest of us" (Katz 1993:3). The alleged "bio-underclass" of "crack babies" biologizes the scenarios of urban poverty elaborated by scholars of the urban underclass; per-manent and concentrated pockets of poverty, and social isolation, are created and recreated here through biological damage.

This biological version of the urban underclass rests on a gendered construction of the transmission of poverty; it rests, in fact, on the iden-tification of women as the "vectors of transmission," (Treichler 1988) lit-erally reproducing poverty from one generation to the next. Blaming mothers, particularly black mothers, for the reproduction of poverty has a long history in U.S. public policy, social science, and media reporting (Collins 1990). Among the most important statements, Daniel Patrick

Moynihan's *The Negro Family: The Case for National Action* (1965) laid the responsibility for the problem of black poverty largely at the feet of the contemporary "black matriarch." The recent responses to the problems of "crack babies" also associate poverty with bad mothering, although much of the current coverage mobilizes fears about the black mother's sexuality and irresponsibility, rather than her power. The word *matriarch* virtually never appears in the current discourse, in part, we would suggest, because there has been some effort to disassociate current analysis from the furor raised over the Moynihan Report.

Moreover, recent representations of black mothers register some of the new circumstances of their lives, including their increasing involvement in the drug scene and their participation in street cultures. Comparing the representations in the Moynihan Report with more recent images, the contrast is between a powerful matriarch who wields her power within the extended black family network and who emasculates and alienates her male partner, on the one hand, and on the other, of a younger figure, much more publicly visible, selling drugs, heterosexually active, and neglecting her fetus and child. Although the assumption of a "culture of poverty" continues to underlie assumptions about irresponsible black mothers, it is now her biological legacy that is targeted for much of the blame. Of course, what remains with this change of imagery is the continuing pathologization of black women and the mobilization of fears about their threats to social order.

We see this mobilization of fears about biological damage in the celebration of middle-class biological motherhood embedded in the new reproductive technologies. Barbara Katz Rothman has observed a general tendency in the contemporary Western world to think about children as "products—the quality of whom can be controlled" (1989:13). The development and extended use of "new reproductive technologies," including genetic counseling, genetic engineering, and fetal surgery, can be seen as part of this more general trend. These developments involve major economic and social investments in biological improvements. At the moment, they are predominantly used by more privileged parents and would-be parents seeking to control and improve their heritage.

Juxtaposed with these developments, the panics over "crack babies" and FAS are about controlling biological heritage, albeit in a different way. They focus on the lower end of the social spectrum. The predominant images of "crack babies" in both popular articles and the medical press concern the urban poor, often black women. Hence, the bifurcation of the biological damage to "the crack baby" and the biological perfectibility of the highly medically monitored baby expresses social expectations about reproduction in contemporary society. Privileged consumers use more of their own resources and draw on social resources to facilitate their reproduction. Meanwhile, the panic around "crack babies" expresses strong fears about, and moral indignation toward, reproduction among the urban poor. In stark terms, the reproduction of the relatively privileged becomes identified with scientific achievement, whereas the reproduction of the underprivileged is linked to biological degeneration. The former becomes the occasion for social investment (and celebration); the latter reflects attempts to limit social expenditure.

Biological damage is not the only legacy of the crack mother and not the only threat to her children. As we will explore, a great deal of media and research attention has gone toward elaborating the psychological and social deprivations that "crack babies" suffer at the hands of negligent mothers. Not surprisingly, these discussions contain themes that parallel those we elaborated with regard to the alleged emergence of a new "bio-underclass": invisibility and hostility toward the mothers of "crack children" and celebration of the capacities of white, middle-class mothers to provide for children.

THE POLITICS OF NURTURANCE

Anthropologist Faye Ginsburg (1989) sees the abortion debate as centered around a "politics of nurturance." The "choices" offered to more and more women to control their reproduction have rendered traditional categories of biological inevitability unstable. Pregnancy—and thus biological motherhood—are now seen as achievements, albeit contested ones, rather than "natural" outcomes of a biological process. The "crucible" test of female identity and femaleness, Ginsburg claims, resides no longer in biological or essential femininity but in a woman's *"stance toward* her body and pregnancy in particular" (emphasis in original:60). Measuring mothers by their capacity to provide (both biologically and socially) for the child is precisely what underlies the discourse around "crack babies." What are these mothers providing for their children? Are the provisions adequate or, indeed, dangerous? And if not the mother, who shall provide for these children? The problem of provision is linked to "family values": abstinence, morality, and discipline, all "values" that crack mothers allegedly lack.

In their elaborations of the harms inflicted on "crack babies" in their own homes, medical, media, and academic accounts show remarkable continuity, outlining a trajectory of maternal neglect during early childrearing, leading toward the production of another generation of crack users. Paralleling the reproduction scenario embedded in the constructions of a bio-underclass, the discourse categorizes children as an at-risk category and their mothers as ultimately failing to provide the necessary elements for growth and development. Indeed, the reported disruptions to the *biological* trajectory of the fetus that dominate so many accounts about "pregnant addicts" are analogous to the reported disruptions to the *social* trajectory of child development. Dr. Barry Zuckerman, head of the Division of Developmental and Behavioral Pediatrics at Boston City Hospital, enumerated for *Time* the problems that these children find at home:

> It is bad enough that the drug assaults children in the womb, but the injury is too often compounded after birth by an environment of neglect, poverty and violence. I sometimes believe that babies are better protected before they are born than they are after. (quoted in Toufexis 1990)

Media representations, often structured around a series of "experts'" testimony, construct a vivid portrait of this neglectful mother. Mothers appear simply "unmotivated," one pediatrician reported:

> We could see the speech delay, social delays. But it wasn't because of the crack. This child had little human interaction. With these babies, we are finding they are not being talked to, stimulated, because mom is too busy taking care of her business, drugs and whatever. *She is not into mothering.* (Williams 1990— emphasis added)

And again:

> The true horror coming to life at D.C. General may not be the obvious abuse and abandonment of crack babies but the desperate, empty lives later forced on them when their mothers or grandmothers take them out of the hospital. (Williams 1990)

In yet another construction of this mother, an article in the *New York Times* declared that "crack can overwhelm one of the strongest forces in nature, the parental instinct" (Hinds 1990). The "crack mother" is constructed as an anti-mother: unmotivated, selfish, abusing, abandoning, even unnatural.

A recent series in the *New York Times*, "Children of the Shadows" (1993), features the lives of 10 young people (primarily teenagers), all of whom live in urban neighborhoods dominated by "temptations," "chaos," and "danger." The children appear in these narratives as either succumbing to these temptations and dangers, as overcoming them, or, often, as doing both. The plots in these newspaper narratives center around the pressing question of whether children can be motivated to leave behind or stand above the degeneracy of the urban ghetto and on the question who has and who will save the children from these dangers. Fathers are virtually absent; mothers are present but, although occasionally angelic, most often negligent. According to these accounts, the children's prospects depend on how their families function; and although many children find safety and acquire middle-class motives from church or school personnel, it is around the family—and its ability to secure these connections to school and church—that the child's life depends.

What is striking about this collection of narratives is the unitary portrayal of children at risk—in profound, life-threatening danger. Urban settings appear as uniformly dangerous and chaotic, and only rarely can children find protection in their own homes. Unlike the conventional ideal where the home serves as a "haven in a heartless world," the private domain of maternal activity is represented here as steeped in the chaos and dangers of public life. Most often it is the drug-addicted mother who appears as the dangerous figure. Jerina, a young woman featured in the series, was "abandoned by her mother (a drug abuser), struggling for months to survive in cheap motels, ramshackle apartments and in the backseat of a car . . . and [finally] offered safe haven by a young English teacher at school" (Gross 1993:A1). Another mother is present but apparently unable to negotiate the demands of raising a child "through the minefields" of childhood:

> What is absent [in Crystal's] life is a quiet steady voice of encouragement, a single figure to lead Crystal through the minefields of a childhood in Bensonhurst. Pressures abound, applied by teachers, parents and even friends, but Crystal seems without a touchstone to guide her and give her a sense of her potential. (Manegold 1993:A1)

Indeed, the model of the mother as absent and desperate was held up in another case as providing the motivation for a child to reach beyond despair. Jerina states "what makes you have a determined attitude like I do is something real bad has to happen. My mother wasn't there, and that's as bad as it gets" (Gross 1993:A1). The absence of her father warrants less attention and censure than the drug addiction and abandonment of the mother.[3]

The apparent failure of mothers to provide for and protect their children from the dangers of the urban ghetto also appears in academic ethnographic accounts. Eloise Dunlap, an African-American researcher on crack dealing and poverty in New York City, conceptualizes the family as a primary transmitter of drug abuse and other dysfunctional behaviors. She introduces an essay analyzing six "single-parent, drug-dependent, inner-city African-American families" by underscoring the family's impact: "For many children of the inner city, life's basic outcomes are determined at a very early age. Born into drug-dependent families, they inherit a lifestyle that swiftly forecloses alternative opportunities" (Dunlap 1992:181). Dunlap is keenly sensitive to the economic disadvantages these women and their extended families face and traces the destructive impact that drugs have on family life. Yet, her analysis remains within the normative tradition; she focuses the case studies on the households of six women, ultimately hinging the children's fate on the mothers' capacity to provide stable households. She concludes:

> African-American females who traditionally have played a vital role in keeping families intact are being psychologically, emotionally, and financially overwhelmed. Provision of food, clothes, and shelter becomes secondary to the needs of addicted mothers to acquire crack. In many instances, these women were, and their children are, grossly neglected. (Dunlap 1992:203)

Kinship support systems in this African-American community are "overwhelmed" by the large numbers of children requiring care.

In another ethnographic essay, Bourgois and Dunlap (1993) report that six pregnant women they met "deny" the damage that crack does to the fetus, and many believed that their pregnancies "were progressing healthily" and that they were "taking care of themselves and protecting their fetuses" (112). They report that many of the pregnant women "tr[y] to take care of the baby by eating 'good,' which translates into eating a little more than before and drinking juices and milk. It seems that this attitude is one that permeates most of the crack women who get pregnant" (112). Yet Bourgois and Dunlap seem to trivialize this maternal caretaking, remarking that "among the mothers, there is a great deal of straightforward denial about the damage crack does to their bodies" (1993:111).

According to Bourgois and Dunlap (1993) it is "female emancipation" that interferes with maternal nurturance and responsibility:

> Why are so many more young girls addicted to crack than ever were to heroin? . . . Greater female involvement in crack addiction is one of the ways the growing emancipation of women that is taking place throughout all aspects of America [sic] culture is expressing itself concretely in the crack-using street scene. Women—especially the emerging generation that is most at risk for crack addiction—are no longer as obliged to stay at home and maintain the family as they were a generation ago. They no longer so readily sacrifice public life for their children and spouse. A vis-

ible documentation of this is the presence in crack houses of pregnant women and of mothers accompanied by infant children and toddlers. (122; see also Bourgois 1989).

How are we to interpret this? It is difficult to know precisely what Bourgois and Dunlap had in mind in their definition of "emancipation": the relatively higher rates of employment among black women relative to black men; the rise in female single-headed families; women's participation in the informal economy, and so on. Wherever the reference points, their argument links maternal irresponsibility and neglect to recent female emancipation. Rather than seeing the state of these women as an indication of their *lack of emancipation*, they see *emancipation as the cause of their degradation*. Children are portrayed as the innocent victims of their mothers' willing negligence. Effectively, this eliminates any strategy for tackling the drug problem that would involve giving these women more autonomy and access to resources. Furthermore, it casts a shadow over all recent struggles for women's emancipation as running the risk of the sort of degradation that Bourgois and Dunlap describe. The emancipation of women is seen as limiting the possibilities for mothers' effective caretaking.

Against this backdrop of the nonnurturant, neglectful mother is the implicit standard of the good, providing mother. Indeed, representations of the negligent "crack mother" depend on a familiar, accessible image of the normative mother, and it is this latter image that constructs all others as marginal and deviant (Kaplan 1992). In the news media, this comparison is most explicit in stories explaining adoptive mothers' perspectives on "crack babies."

Certainly one of the clearest juxtapositions of the negligent (biological) mother with the normative (adoptive) mother appeared in an adopted mother's anonymous account published in the op-ed page of the *New York Times*, entitled "Why Should I Give My Baby Back?" "Jane Doe" begins by explaining her decision to adopt a "crack baby," elaborating on the differences between her stance toward motherhood and the one she presumes the baby's biological family holds:

> As work on a corporate project wound down, I made the call. I was ready to take home a "boarder baby." [One year later] No grandma has come to fetch him. No aunts, no uncles, no cousins. No mother. No one had even come to see him. Teams of social workers do tireless outreach work, and every few months I am told that they have found someone who "wants him." Translation: They have contacted some overburdened relative who is tempted by the monthly payments to take yet another unwanted child. But these families never request a visit, and each is ultimately rejected as unsuitable. (Doe 1990)

"Jane Doe's" identification of herself as "corporate" is part of the oppositional model she draws between her capacity to provide for the child
compared to the biological extended family's. Attributing lack of motivation and bad will, she dismisses the possible reasons for their failure
to claim and care for the child. After the biological mother failed to
show up for an arranged meeting, Jane Doe recalled her pain and her
own "ferocious" desire to protect this baby, ignoring the possible reasons why the biological mother did not show: "The pain of these
episodes is indescribable. To be a mother, to have that ferocious instinct
of protectiveness and to be rendered impotent is truly hell" (Doe 1990).

Her "ferocious instinct" sets the standard for mothering and is in
sharp contrast to the purported apathy and neglect of the biological
mother. Jane Doe appropriates the child and sets herself up (together
with her adopted child) as yet another victim of the negligent crack
mother.

Media accounts often present the adoptive mother's perspectives: It is
her voice that rings from the popular press and presents her as the nurturing, "motivated," good mother. It is the adoptive mother with whom
we are encouraged to identify and whose struggles, frustrations, and
terrors with these damaged "crack babies" we are invited to share:

> You know how babies stand on your lap? She'd hurt me. Her feet were
> extended, digging into my legs. I'd be holding her, cuddling her, and all
> of a sudden she'd clamp down and bite me. When I'd change her diaper,
> she'd kick me in the stomach. Do you know what it's like to hold a child
> you love and have her bite you? (Blakeslee 1990:8)

Another article in the *Washington Post*, "Suffering the Sins of Mothers: A
Generation Born to Crack Addicts Places New Burdens on Parents,
Social Services" (Norris 1991a), refers to the frustrations the adoptive
parents encounter, a theme that dominates media accounts:

> For now, it is primarily [adoptive] parents who must wrestle with these
> children's special problems. Thousands of parents like the DiLellas are
> discovering that old-fashioned discipline and tender loving care can be
> inadequate measures for dealing with children who are so physically and
> emotional impaired. (Norris 1991a:1)

In these portraits of adoptive mothers, we see the fantasies of "children as products" (Rothman 1989) once again. As in the presumptions
of child development more generally, these narratives on adoption presume a kind of omnipotence and control on the part of parents; qualities that perhaps only middle-class parents can feel about their parenting. Much like Dorris's account of his fantasies about raising a child

with "FAS" (see McNeil and Litt 1992), these accounts reveal the frustration of middle-class senses of entitlement and of the horror of those who expect efficacy and control.

Reports of "crack babies" mobilize sympathy for the struggling adoptive mother, who is generally white and middle-class and who is trying to undo the influence of the "bad" mother who is often black and part of the underclass. Media representations of crack divide 'good' and 'bad' mothers along class and race lines; this is part of a broader politics of reproduction and nurturance and of racial and class divisiveness. These representations mark white middle-class women as suitable mothers while they condemn poor and often black mothers for their maternal deficiencies.[4]

What worries us about this and similar representations is that women's social and economic difficulties are denied and the causes of drug addiction are collapsed into "female emancipation." The conclusion readers are encouraged to draw from such studies is that the solution to the crack problem is to curtail the freedom of women involved with the drug and possibly to curtail women's freedom more generally in the urban environment—and to do so in the name of children.

CONCLUSION

What guides the discussions of "crack babies" is a presumption of child saving, a presumption embedded in media, social science, medical, and social service involvements in the problem of crack cocaine. Various experts effectively "speak for" (Haraway 1991:312) "crack babies," forcefully silencing their biological mothers. Haraway calls this representational practice of "speaking for" a "magical operation . . . forever authorizing the ventriloquist." She continues: "pregnant women . . . are the *least able* to 'speak for' objects like . . . fetuses because they get discursively reconstituted as beings with opposing interests. . . . The *only* actor left is the spokesperson, the one who represents" (312). Thus, the provision of concern with "crack babies" not only silences the biological mothers but also gives authority to the experts themselves.

It is out of this authority and the oppositional model of mother and child that some experts create what we see as a particularly punitive response to pregnant women using crack cocaine. This dynamic emerges most clearly in the push towards criminal sanctions against crack-addicted mothers rather than toward the establishment of economic, health, and rehabilitation support for these women and their children.[5]

There is a severe shortage of prenatal and drug rehabilitation care for pregnant drug addicts. Sixteen percent of all women receive no prenatal care, increasing to 30 percent for Hispanic women, 27 percent for black women, and 33 percent for unmarried women (Dorris 1990). According to a survey undertaken by the House Select Committee on Children, Youth, and Families, two-thirds of all hospitals studied had no drug treatment programs available for pregnant patients, and none of the hospitals reported special programs that would provide both drug treatment and prenatal care (Fink 1990; Humphries et al. 1992).

A recent New York City study of drug-treatment facilities confirmed that programs for pregnant addicts are basically unavailable: 54 percent exclude women outright; 67 percent exclude pregnant women on Medicaid; 87 percent have no services for crack-addicted women on Medicaid; and of the few that accept pregnant women, only 44 percent offer prenatal care. And 54 percent of addicted mothers who are not in drug-treatment programs will have to give their children up to foster care by their babies' first birthdays (Fink 1990).

Instead of rehabilitation and support, women receive attention from the criminal justice system, which effectively separates these children from their biological mothers. "Crack mothers" attract a kind of police and prosecutory brutality that differs little from the physical beatings that have received wide public attention and scorn. Aggressive prosecutors have brought fetal endangerment charges against women, mainly against women of color.[6]

By April of 1992, 167 women in 24 states (primarily in Florida and South Carolina) had been arrested on criminal charges for behavior during pregnancy, or because they became pregnant while addicted to drugs (Paltrow 1992). Charges are based on drug-trafficking laws (transmission in the sixty to ninety seconds after birth through the umbilical cord) and child abuse or infant neglect. The latter method of prosection more often results in convictions, although many are overturned in appeal because most states do not include prenatal conduct under existing child abuse statutes (Humphries et al. 1992). Both methods of prosecution have been largely unsuccessful; with vigorous legal defenses, most convictions have been overturned (Paltrow 1992). It has become the task of some members of the legal community to provide women with this vigorous representation.

These child-saving efforts are organized around identifying certain categories of women as reproductive and maternal risks. In an interesting analysis of the American welfare system, Deborah A. Stone sketched the increasing importance of identifying groups "at risk" and the cultivation of individual responsibility as ways of restricting the expansion of welfare provision. Stone (1989:630) outlines the historical trajectory of American welfare provision that has led in this direction: "In the context of cost-containment and efficiency goals, the at-risk status is converted into a form of dangerousness, not just to self but to others." Media coverage designates crack mothers as "at risk" and embodying this "dangerousness." The reference to "crack babies," and by implication "crack mothers," as potentially increasing the burden on society as a whole is, as we have seen, a familiar element in reporting on crack cocaine. As the American public groans under the burden of health care costs, as welfare provisions are cut back and refashioned, and as minimalist taxation is in public favor, the imperative to restrict claims on the public purse is powerful. Within what Stone calls "the context of cost-containment and efficiency goals," coverage of the "crack baby" problem maximizes attention to the burdens that these women create for a starved federal budget and minimizes any claim on social resources they might make on behalf of their children.

ACKNOWLEDGMENTS

Craig Hosay provided invaluable guidance which sharpened the conceptual focus of the paper. Robert Horowitz of the American Bar Association Center on Children and the Law explained the use of criminal sanctions against pregnant women. Katherine Jones provided skillful editing which improved the paper.

NOTES

1. Concentrated alkaloid crystals of pure cocaine crack cocaine is smoked and sells for as little as $3 a vial. One expert described crack cocaine as "the junk-food of the drug business—cheap and readily available" (Fink 1990).

2. The number of women regularly using crack cocaine is noticeably higher than for other addictive drugs, and health officials report seeing more female than male crack cocaine users (Fink 1990). Fink reports that crack may be responsible for women "joining the ranks of the addicted in unprecedented numbers" (1990:460). A range of associated problems accompany women's dependence on crack cocaine: prostitution, violence, AIDS, and other sexually transmitted diseases. For further discussion, see Litt and McNeil (1992), Humphries (1993), and Ratner (1993).

3. The concern about the fate of black men and their capacity to father is apparent in both academic and popular culture. There has been a recent space of academic books on black masculinity (Anderson 1990; Duneier 1992; Majors and Billson 1992), emphasizing class differences among black men and the importance of attending to the difficulties black males face in the urban environment. These, combined with popular movies such as *Boyz N the Hood* can easily be read as a poignant and powerful plea for the restoration of black father-

hood as the key to survival of the African-American community. Like the discourse on "crack babies," the discourse on black masculinity/fatherhood erases the woman and presumes an indifference to her welfare apart from her children. See Haraway (1992:334) for a discussion of the misogyny inherent in this formulation and hooks (1990) for an analysis of feminism and representations of black masculinity.

4.   The overrepresentation of white adoptive parents in these accounts does not correspond to the recent patterns and policies that favor the adoption of black children by black parents.

5.   In an interesting essay, Maher examines how welfare controls of mothers intersect with sanctions administered by the criminal justice system. Welfare controls, she argues, "function as an independent and gender-specific form of punishment and regulation" (1993:158).

6.   Humphries et al. (1992) report a Florida study that found that women of low socioeconomic status were more likely to be tested for drug use during pregnancy and that black women were 10 times more likely to be tested than white women.

REFERENCES

Anderson, E. 1990. *Street Wise: Race, Class, and Change in an Urban Community.* Chicago: University of Chicago Press.

Blakeslee, S. 1990. "Child-Rearing is Stormy When Drugs Cloud Birth." *New York Times* May 19:1.

Bourgois, P., and E. Dunlap. 1989. "In Search of Horatio Alger: Culture and Ideology in the Crack Economy." *Contemporary Drug Problems* Winter:619–49.

_____. 1993. "Exorcising Sex-for-Crack: An Ethnographic Perspective from Harlem." Pp. 97–132 in *Crack Pipe as Pimp: An Ethnographic Investigation of Sex-for-Crack Exchanges,* edited by Mitchell S. Ratner. New York: Lexington Books.

Chasnoff, I. J. 1988. "Newborn Infants with Drug Withdrawal Symptoms." *Pediatrics in Review* 9:273–77.

Chasnoff, I. J., K. Burns, W. J. Burns, and S. H. Schnoll. 1986. "Prenatal Drug Exposure: Effects on Neonatal and Infant Growth and Development." *Neurobehavioral Toxicology and Teratology* 8:357–62.

Collins, P. H. 1990. *Black Feminist Thought: Knowledge, Consciousness, and the Politics of Empowerment.* London: Harper Collins.

Conrad, P. 1992. "Medicalization and Social Control." *Annual Review of Sociology* 18:209–32.

Doe, J. 1990. "Why Should I Give My Baby Back." *New York Times* December 22:27.

Dorris, M. 1989 *The Broken Cord.* New York: Harper & Row.

_____. 1990. "A Desperate Crack Legacy." *Newsweek* June 25:8.

Duneier, M. 1992. *Slim's Table: Race, Respectability, and Masculinity.* Chicago: University of Chicago Press.

Dunlap, E. 1992. "The Impact of Drugs on Family Life and Kin Networks in the

Inner-City African-American Single-Parent Household." Pp. 181–207 in *Drugs, Crime, and Social Isolation: Barriers to Urban Opportunity*, edited by Adele Harrell and George E. Peterson. Washington, DC: Urban Institute Press.

Fink, J. R. 1990. "Effects of Crack and Cocaine on Infants: A Brief Review of the Literature." *Clearinghouse Review* 24:460–66.

Gieringer, D. 1990. "How Many Crack Babies?" *Drug Policy Letter* March/April:4.

Ginsburg, F. D. 1989. *Contested Lives: The Abortion Debate in an American Community*. Berkeley: University of California Press.

Gross, J. 1993. "Views of Wretchedness by Children Born to It." *New York Times* September 25:A14.

Handler, A., N. Kistin, F. Davis, and C. Ferre. 1991. "Cocaine Use during Pregnancy: Perinatal Outcome." *American Journal of Epidemiology* 133:818–25.

Haraway, D. 1992. "The Promises of Monsters: A Regenerative Politics for Inappropriate/d Others." Pp. 295–337 in *Cultural Studies*, edited by L. Grossberg, C. Nelson, and P. Treichler. London: Routledge.

Hinds, M. D. 1990. "The Instincts of Parenthood Become Part of Crack's Toll." *New York Times* March17:8.

Hoffman, J. 1990. "Pregnant, Addicted, and Guilty?" *New York Times* August 19:32.

hooks, b. 1990. *Yearning: Race, Gender, and Cultural Politics*. Boston: South End Press.

Humphries, D. 1992. "The Rise and Fall of Crack Mothers." Paper presented at the annual meeting of the American Society of Criminology, New Orleans.

_____. 1993. "Crack Mothers, Drug Wars, and the Politics of Resentment." Pp. 31–48 in *Political Crime in Contemporary America: A Critical Approach*, edited by Kenneth D. Tunnell. New York: Garland.

Humphries, D., J. Dawson, V. Cronin, P. Keating, C. Wisniewski, and J. Eichfeld. 1992. "Mothers and Children, Drugs and Crack: Reactions to Maternal Drug Dependency." Pp. 203–21 *The Criminalization of a Woman's Body*, edited by C. Feinman. New York: Harrington Park Press.

Jencks, C. and P. E. Peterson. (eds.). 1991. *The Urban Underclass*. Washington, DC: Brookings Institution.

Journal of Recovery and Addiction. July–August 1991.

Juvenile Justice Digest. 1990. "South Florida Schools Brace for Influx of Crack Babies." May 16:18.

Kaplan, E. A. 1992. *Motherhood and Representation: The Mother in Popular Culture and Melodrama*. New York: Routledge.

Katz, M. B. 1990. *The Undeserving Poor: From the War on Poverty to the War on Welfare*. New York: Pantheon.

_____. 1993. "The Urban Underclass as a Metaphor of Social Transformation." Pp. 3–23 in *The Underclass Debate: Views from History*, edited by M. B. Katz. Princeton: Princeton University Press.

Koren, G., K. Graham, H. Shear, and T. Einarson. 1989. "Bias against the Null Hypothesis: The Reproductive Hazards of Crack Cocaine." *The Lancet* 8677 December:1440–42.

Kusserow, R. 1990. *Crack Babies.* U.S. Department of Health and Human Services.

Langone, J. 1988. "Crack Comes to the Nursery." *Time* 132September 19:85.

Litt, J., and M. McNeil. 1992. "Who are the Mothers of Crack Babies?: Silence and Blame in Dominant Representations of Maternal Crack Addiction." Paper presented at the annual meeting of the Sociologists for Women in Society, Pittsburgh.

Maher, L. 1993. "Punishment and Welfare: Crack Cocaine and the Regulation of Mothering." Pp. 157–92 in *The Criminalization of a Woman's Body*, edited by C. Feinman. New York: Harrington Park Press.

Majors, R., and J. M. Billson. 1992. *Cool Pose: The Dilemmas of Black Manhood in America.* New York: Lexington Books.

Manegold, C. S. 1993. "To Crystal, 12, School Serves No Purpose." *New York Times* April 8:A1.

McNeil, M., and J. Litt. 1992. "More Medicalizing of Mothers: Fetal Alcohol Syndrome in the USA and Related Developments." Pp. 112–32 in *Private Risks and Public Dangers*, edited by S. Scott, G. H. Williams, S. D. Platt, and H. A. Thomas. London: Avebury.

Moynihan, D. P. 1965. *The Negro Family: The Case for National Action.* Washington, DC: Office of Policy Planning and Research, U.S. Department of Labor.

New York Times. 1990a. "Study of Addicted Babies Hints Vast Cost." March 17:8.

_____. 1990b. "Call to Remove Addicts' Children." April 28:8.

_____. 1993. "Children of the Shadows." April:4–25.

Norris, M. L. 1991a. "Suffering the Sins of the Mothers: A Generation Born to Crack Addicts Places New Burdens on Parents, Social Services." *Washington Post* June 30:1.

_____. 1991b. "And the Children Shall Need: Drug-Induced Disabilities Will Tax School Resources." *Washington Post* July 1:1.

_____. 1991c. "Grandmothers Who Fill Void Carved by Drugs." *Washington Post* August 30:1

Paltrow, L. M. 1992. "Criminal Prosecutions Against Pregnant Women." Reproductive Freedom Project. New York: American Civil Liberties Union Foundation.

Petchesky, R. 1987. "Foetal Images: The Power of Visual Culture in the Politics of Reproduction." Pp. 57–80 in *Reproductive Technologies: Gender, Motherhood, and Medicine*, edited by M. Stanworth. Minneapolis: University of Minnesota Press.

Ratner, M. S. (ed.). 1993. *Crack Pipe as Pimp: An Ethnographic Investigation of Sex-for-Crack Exchanges.* New York: Lexington Books.

Reinarman, C., and H. G. Levine. 1989. "Crack in Context: Politics and Media in the Making of a Drug Scare." *Contemporary Drug Problems* 16:535–77.

Rothman, B. K. 1989. *Recreating Motherhood: Ideology and Technology in a Patriarchal Society.* New York: Norton.

Science. 1992. "Reopening the `Crack Baby' Question." 257:867.

Stone, D. 1989. "At Risk in the Welfare State." *Social Research* 56:591–633.

Toufexis, A. 1990. "Innocent Victims." *Time* 137 May 13:56–60.

Treaster, J. B. 1993. "For Children of Cocaine, Fresh Reasons for Hope." *New York Times* February 16:A1.

Treichler, P. A. 1988. "AIDS, Gender, and Biomedical Discourse: Current Contests for Meaning." Pp. 190–266 in *AIDS: The Burden of History*, edited by E. Fee and D. M. Fox. Berkeley: University of California Press.

Williams, J. 1990. "The Real Tragedy of Crack Babies: They Can Survive Drugs, but Can They Survive Their Homes?" *Washington Post* December 30:C5.

Wilson, W. J. 1987. *The Truly Disadvantaged: The Inner City, The Underclass, and Public Policy*. Chicago: University of Chicago Press.

Zuckerman, B., and D. A. Frank. 1992. "'Crack Kids?': 'Not Broken'." *Pediatrics* 82 February:337–39.

Part IV

FAMILIES AND CHILDREN

Chapter 6

Ritual, Magic, and Educational Toys: Symbolic Aspects of Toy Selection

Shan Nelson-Rowe

Most social research on toys addresses those toys considered problematic in one way or another. Guns and other "war toys" are linked to violence and aggression in children (Brown 1990; Buettner 1981; Carlson-Paige and Levin 1987; Masters 1990; Sutton-Smith 1988). Dolls and "domestic role play" toys receive criticism for their perpetuation of traditional gender role behavior (Cox 1977; Motz 1983; Pursell 1979; Wilkinson 1987). Video games and toys tied in with television programming are criticized for their negative effects on children's imaginations and for the crassly commercialized nature of the play they promote (Kinder 1991; Kline 1989; Kunkel 1988; Provenzo 1991; Winn 1977). By contrast, "educational toys" get little critical attention from sociologists.

This essay offers a cultural analysis of the meanings given to educational toys by parents of preschool and kindergarten children. Briefly stated, my thesis is that parents imbue toys with magical qualities and that toy buying has ritual importance. The ritual character of toy selection arises from parental beliefs, fostered by the mass media and popular culture, about the dangers facing contemporary children and the uncertain nature of childrearing. These perceived dangers include child snatching, illicit drugs, poor schools, and an uncertain economic future. In response to the anxiety about these dangers, parents buy "educational toys" in order to ritually communicate their commitment to protecting their children from harm and securing a positive future for them. By doing so, parents construct an identity as good parents.

DATA AND METHODS

I use two kinds of data to analyze the cultural meaning and significance of educational toys in the lives of parents. First, I analyze seven
toy catalogues (see Appendix A) for the claims they make about the
educational qualities of the toys offered for sale. These catalogues were
collected between Christmas 1991 and 1992 and represent toy merchants
whose advertising copy suggests they specialize in educational toys.
Some catalogue covers convey their educational agenda by using such
phrases as "toys that teach," or "learn and play." Similarly, some
include statements to the reader about the educational purpose of their
toys. One, for example, refers to its "affordable toys and educational
games" (*Lilly's Kids*:2). Another describes "a whole new way of thinking
about learning, playtime, and toys" (*Early Learning Centre*: inside front
cover).

These catalogues, as I will discuss in more detail, are also distin-
guishable by what they exclude as much as by what they include. In
contrast to major retailers such as Toys R' Us, the catalogue merchants
analyzed offer few action figures, fashion dolls, guns, video games, or
other products heavily advertised on or tied into children's television.
The few tie-ins that are included are from public television programs,
such as *Sesame Street*, which are known as educational programs. In
short, these catalogues promote toys and play that are purportedly good
for children in addition to being fun.

In-depth interviews with 26 middle- and upper-middle class parents
of preschool and kindergarten children provide the second source of
data. Subjects were selected through an open invitation to parents of
children at two daycare centers and consisted of 18 mothers and 8
fathers. With a mean age of just over 38 years, all but two of the subjects were currently married, and all but five had a four-year college
degree or higher. More than three-quarters had gross family incomes
above $75,000, and all but four owned their homes.

I conducted all the interviews between September and November
1991, using a loosely structured questionnaire that included both fixed
response and open-ended questions. Individual interviews lasted from
15 to 45 minutes, and covered the following topics: the kinds of toys
parents prefer and dislike for their children, what effects they believe
these toys have on their children, what the term educational toy means
to the parents, and related issues. The interviews also explored the concerns parents have about their children's welfare in the present and the
future.

The catalogue and interview data are not strictly representative of any
larger population of educational toy merchants or parents. Nevertheless,

the richly detailed data can yield insights into the previously unexplored territory of the symbolic meanings of toys and provide a basis for more far-reaching cultural studies of toys.

WHAT IS AN EDUCATIONAL TOY?

One approach to answering this question begins by asking what is educational and then by examining toys to see if they foster education. Here, beliefs about education provide the basis for an analysis of toys. Psychologists and educators usually take this path when analyzing educational toys. A second, more sociological way of answering the question begins by asking what toys categorized as educational have in common, and what this says about cultural beliefs about learning. Here the focus of analysis shifts to those cultural beliefs that the first approach leaves largely unexamined. What, then, is an educational toy? Following the second approach I view educational toys as those play objects that, in the minds of the people who make, sell, and buy them, promote culturally valued learning.

The catalogues and interviews suggest that educational toys are seen as fostering two sorts of learning: general skills, traits and values, and specific intellectual skills. The first area of learning includes such broad skill categories as hand-eye coordination, fine-motor skills, and concentration, as well as such general traits as creativity, imagination, and discovery. It also includes social skills such as sharing and cooperation. The second category includes specific skills such as reading, writing, and mathematics, as well as knowledge of colors, time, and science. The celebration of types of learning by toy merchants and parents alike suggests that although fun may be an important element in play, other "educational" attributes of toys bear consideration when selecting playthings for children.

General Learning

Toy catalogues abound with claims about the ways their toys will stimulate creativity, imagination, discovery, and active learning. One toy called a "Skwish" consisted of a number of colored plastic tubes and balls connected by elastic strings. This "multisensory toy" will, the catalogue claims, "capture the imagination of all ages" (*Constructive Playthings*:6). Similarly a "Giant Animal Transport" (a truck that carried four animals) was advertised as a "truckload of imaginative play and creative learning" (*Constructive Playthings*:7). Toys and costumes involving fantasy role play also were marketed for their ability to stimulate imagination. A firetruck and uniform could "fire their young imaginations," and a medieval fortress, and knight in shining armor and Robin Hood costumes were "sure to set young imaginations ablaze" (*Childcraft*:12,17). The importance of imagination as a part of learning was also evident in catalogue subtitles and section headings. The *Troll Learn and Play* catalog carried the subtitle "A Child's World of Imagination, Fun and Creativity." Others had sections entitled "Just Imagine" (*Toys to Grow On*:16–17), "Fun: Imagine Amazing Adventures" (*Childcraft*:12–13), and "Watch as Their Imaginations Run Wild" (*Lilly's Kids*:22–23).

The celebration of creativity as a valued trait also features prominently in toy catalogs. Arts and crafts and musical toys almost invariably link the toy itself to the development of creativity in the child. *Childcraft's* arts and crafts sections, for example, are headed "Creating Masterpieces," "Toys That Teach: Creativity, Fun, Imagination," "Create: Crafts for Older Kids," and "Create: The Art of Expression" (pp. 6–7, 24–29). *Toys To Grow On* heads its array of coloring and art toys "Color Me Creative" (pp. 44–45). These catalogues stress the connection between creativity and self-expression. One advertisement for modeling clay warns: "Don't bottle up creativity" (*Troll Learn and Play*:20). A second advertisement, this time for a collage kit, claims that "young artists can express themselves in exciting new ways" (*Childcraft*:7). Here and elsewhere we find that toys are valued to the extent that they help develop expressive and independent individuals, capable of creative expression.

Discovery and activity often, though not always, are linked together in the claims merchants make about their toys. *Fisher-Price* markets a number of "Activity Centers" and other "infant-activated" toys designed to "excite a baby's curiosity" (*Fisher-Price*:2–9). These toys include a "Discovery Cottage," "Discovery Farm," and "Discovery Schoolhouse" each of which is "activity filled," requiring the child to open doors and windows to reveal additional play objects. Discovery is also used to suggest learning about other historical eras or about the natural world. *Childcraft* (p. 18) sells a series of toys including western wear for girls and boys, plastic logs for building log cabins and forts, and horses. Children are urged to "discover the American frontier." Farm animals, dinosaurs, and astronomy toys are also framed in terms of the ability of children to discover aspects of nature. As with claims about creativity and imagination, discovery and activity claims imply no specific knowledge to be gained but, instead, a general trait useful in learning all manner of information. Thus, although discovery of stars and planets may be important, toy merchants' claims suggest that the very process of discovery itself is a fundamental skill that their toys can cultivate in young children.

Claims regarding toys' value for moral education primarily focus on sharing and cooperation. These claims are generally limited to books and toys spun off from educational television programs for children. For example, three of the catalogs analyzed included a variety of toys, books, and videos drawn from the PBS television show *Shining Time Station* and its character Thomas the Tank Engine. *Troll Learn and Play* included a Thomas the Tank Engine Rescue Game in which children "help Thomas achieve his goal" and learn the "values of creative problem solving and working together" (p. 18). A set of Thomas the Tank Engine Videos advertised in *Constructive Playthings* offered, according to the catalogue, "subtle lessons on cooperation, safety, manners, friendship, etc." (p. 2). *Constructive Playthings* also includes a set of Barney videos based on the PBS series *Barney and Friends* about a group of children and their imaginary dinosaur friend. The videos feature "happy songs" that "stress positive values" (p. 23). Other books also offer lessons in sharing and cooperation. A set of Berenstain Bears books "teaches valuable lessons about sharing, manners, safety, and much more" (*Troll Learn and Play*:30)

Toy merchants also promote their products with claims about the toys' ability to develop hand-eye coordination, motor skills, and visual skills. Infant toys in particular stress the learning of visual skills. *Fisher-Price*, for example, sells a music box animal mobile for the crib that "lets you choose the visual stimulation for your baby." The black-and-white side of the animals is for the "first few months." Later the animals can be reversed to reveal "bright primary colors" (p. 2). *Constructive Playthings* also promotes their infant toys, including black-and-white "newborn flash cards," as meeting "the need for visual stimulation." A set of black-and-white crib animals with velcro tabs that attach to crib bumpers also gives "tactile experience" to the baby. Catalog text informs parents and others that the flash cards in particular are "endorsed by medical professionals," lending an air of authority to the toys (p. 7).

Toys designed for toddlers and older preschool children are frequently marketed with claims about their ability to stimulate hand-eye coordination and motor skill development. Tool sets (*Childcraft*:10; *Constructive Playthings*:22), sand-diggers (*Constructive Playthings*:30), shape-sorting puzzles (*Troll Learn and Play*:14; *Lilly's Kids*:53), and other toys "teach hand-eye coordination," provide children with "lots of hand-eye coordination while having fun," and "build . . . coordination and motor skills." *The Early Learning Centre*, which fashions itself as "the intelligent toy store," actually provides four icons in its catalog to help parents and others assess the educational value of the toys. These include a hand holding a block (hand-eye skills), profile of a face showing the mouth and ear (hearing and voice skills), two stick-figure children holding hands (social skills), and a stick-figure child running (motor skills). As a further aid to adults, the order form includes a chart labeled, "How to Select Age-Appropriate Toys for Children." This chart lists developmental skills and related toys for each of the four areas of development at five different age levels. Although not all of the catalogues were so systematic in their educational claims, they did use the same rhetorical appeals to link their toys to culturally valued educational goals.

Specific Learning

Each catalog analyzed for this study also claimed that some of its toys could teach basic concepts for literacy, numeracy, time, and science. *Troll Learn and Play*, for example, sells a "Shapes, Letters, and Numbers Learning Set" (p. 15) to teach the alphabet, numbers, shapes, colors, words, and simple math to 3- to 7-year-old children. The catalogues are filled with a host of similar products, as well as puzzles, books, and clocks that also focus on language, mathematics, and time. Nature toys dominate the market for science toys. Replicas of sea creatures, land animals, and birds are sold with claims about the need for children to learn about the wonders of nature. Collections of rocks and minerals, telescopes and astronomical charts, butterfly gardens, and other toys also are advertised in terms of their educational qualities.

Marketing claims regarding these toys build on the themes of discovery and activity used in promoting toys for general skills learning. One collection of 12 miniature whales and an accompanying book urges parents to help their children "discover the whales of the world" (*Toys to Grow On*:36), and an advertisement for a "geoscope," or water-resistant microscope, describes a "wide range of discovery activities" (*Constructive Playthings*:33). These advertisements also rhetorically link science play with "exploration" as a valued trait. For example, *Lilly's Kids* markets a light scope with which children can "explore the secrets of botany, geology, and zoology" (p. 44). Significantly, this advertisement links the toy to academic disciplines rather than, say, plants, rocks, and animals, reinforcing the notion that these toys are educational in specific rather than general ways.

Often, the claims made for these toys also suggest a parental obligation to provide early education to their children. A set of interlocking railroad cars bearing the letters of the alphabet and the numbers 1 through 10 carried the message that "Youngsters will get started on the right track" by learning with the toy (*Constructive Playthings*:28). Similarly, parents are urged "help your child master color and shape recognition and hand-eye coordination" by purchasing a shape-sorting puzzle (*Troll Learn and Play*:14). Such claims imply that parents who do not provide such toys are doing their children a disservice by failing to give them the added advantage of educational toys. As a result, the catalogues indirectly suggest, parents may not adequately prepare their children for future learning.

Parents' Definitions of Educational Toys

The image conveyed by mail-order toy catalogues is one in which toys can help children learn a wide array of intellectual, social, and physical skills. Parents interviewed for this study expressed a concern with the same kinds of learning and development. When asked what the term *educational toy* meant to them, parents responded primarily in terms of creativity, imagination, and learning basic concepts such as numbers, shapes and letters. Many parents had very broad understandings of educational toys. One defined them as "anything a child learns from," whereas another said they were "anything that fosters some kind of learning process." In part, these broad definitions reflected the parents' belief that educational toys need not be store bought. Several parents suggested that children could learn by playing with common household objects such as Tupperware, measuring spoons, and other kitchen tools. Others also expressed their belief that children learn the most when they take objects found around the house or in their yards and make imaginative use of them.

The parents' broad definitions of educational toys also reflected an emphasis on general rather than specific learning. Toys that fostered "experimentation and discovery" or that "stimulated thinking or motor skills or emotions" were singled out more frequently. Parents also spoke of toys that provided lessons about "real life" and developed "life skills" as being educational. The latter included toy telephones for one parent who viewed the telephone as an essential tool for modern living. Although most parents emphasized general learning in their definitions of educational toys, some focused on specific skills, including the recognition of numbers, shapes, and letters as well as the ability to tell time.

When asked what kinds of toys they preferred their children to play with, parents interviewed for this study overwhelmingly mentioned toys consistent with their definition of educational toys. Most parents initially responded with general categories rather than specific kinds of toys. For example, parents frequently expressed a preference for toys that fostered "creativity," developed "social skills," required "imagination," or had some "educational value." When asked to specify particular toys that served these ends they often mentioned Lego building blocks, puzzles, arts and crafts, and coloring books as creative toys that required children to use their imaginations. In discussing their preference for these toys, parents could have been reading from developmental psychology textbooks. Some praised their "constructive" nature, whereas others claimed these toys promote self-expression, help children to learn ideas and concepts, help children to organize their ideas, teach independence, and have learning objectives. Other parents who favored balls, bats, and other sports toys spoke of a need to develop their children's motor skills.

Parents also described the toys they do not like their children to play with. Three categories of toys dominated the interviews: violent toys, video games, and action figures. Guns, knives, swords, and other toys representing real-life weapons were highly criticized by many parents. Some believed that toy weapons teach that violence is an acceptable means of resolving disputes and that violent play produces violent children. Others claimed that young children have difficulty differentiating fantasy from reality and that a child who plays with toy guns may accidentally use a real gun as a toy.

Video games were criticized by some parents for their "addictive" or "mesmerizing" effects. These parents found that their children or children they knew became "obsessed" with Nintendo games in particular and wanted to spend all of their free time in front of the video screen. Other parents claimed Nintendo and other video games overstimulated their children and that it took a long time for children to "wind down" after playing with them. Video games were also identified as violent by some parents who objected to the use of weapons and depiction of death as common features in the games.

Action figures such as G.I. Joe, Masters of the Universe, and especially the Teenage Mutant Ninja Turtles also received criticism from these parents. In addition to promoting violence, overstimulation, and obsessiveness, some parents also claimed action figures served as "false heroes" and lacked positive moral values. Others commented on the "ugliness" of the turtles, or what parents perceived as the grotesque features of the figures. Still others complained about the faddishness of the toys and expressed an unwillingness to spend money on toys that would soon lose interest for their children.

If parents are clear in their preference for what they consider educational toys, they are less certain whether these toys or others have any discernible effect on their children. In part, parental ambivalence about the effects of toys on child development stemmed from what they viewed as their inability to keep "bad" toys away from their children. Several parents spoke of problems with other children in their neighborhood who had toy guns, Nintendo, or other toys of which the parents disapproved. Short of preventing their children from playing with their peers they saw no way to keep their children from playing with these toys. Gifts from friends and relatives posed another problem for parents. Several parents said they had made it clear to their friends and relatives what were acceptable and unacceptable gifts for their children. Others, however, had faced situations in which their children received guns or other disfavored toys as gifts. Parent responses to such situations ranged from thanking the giver but asking them to select a different toy to allowing the child to keep it. Some parents waited until after the giver had departed to exchange or hide the toy so as to avoid any possible offense or embarrassment. Others talked with their children about why the toy was unacceptable. Still others let the children play with the toy for a short time and then hid it. One parent said he would rewrap the toy and let the child give it as a gift to some other child.

Faced with the likelihood that their children would play with disfavored toys, the parents were reluctant to view this as causing irreparable harm to the children. In this context they offered a variety of disclaimers. For example, one parent claimed that the negative effects of toy guns could be counteracted by other, more positive toys. Others claimed that the use of the toy, not the toy itself, was the issue. Hence, even an ostensibly negative toy could be put to positive use under the parent's guidance. Another disclaimer focused on the age of the child. Preschool children, several parents claimed, are too young to be permanently affected. Brief exposure could do no real harm.

Ambivalence about the effects of toys also applied to those preferred by parent. When asked whether they believed educational toys would help their children learn more in school parents commonly responded with: "I hope so," or "I'd like to think so." Although some were definite in their belief that toys set the stage for learning in school, most said instead that the toys could at least do no harm and might show their children that learning can be fun. Indeed, encouraging children to enjoy learning was the most common positive educational effect of toys mentioned by parents.

SYMBOLIC ASPECTS OF TOY SELECTION

The strong preference of parents for "educational" toys over toy weapons, video games, action figures, and other disfavored toys is paradoxical given the ambivalence the same parents have regarding the actual effects of toys on child development. The paradox arises, however, only if we view toy selection as an instrumental act, whether designed to educate children or let them have fun. If we instead analyze the symbolic dimensions of toy selection, the paradox dissolves.

My thesis is straightforward. Parental beliefs about and selection of toys are best viewed in terms of ritual and magic. Specifically, parents face many anxieties and uncertainties as they raise their children. In an effort to cope with these anxieties, parents seek to reduce the uncertainty they face by using toys as ritual objects imbued with magical powers to shape their children's lives. I first discuss the sources of parental anxiety, then the ways in which toys are used in a ritual fashion to alleviate that anxiety.

Hazards of Child-Rearing

During the 1980s a host of social problems threatening the health and welfare of children gained the attention of the American public. In his study of these threats, Joel Best (1990) analyzes the ways in which problems such as missing children and sexual abuse are constructed through rhetorical claims.

In addition to these physical threats to children, parents increasingly were exposed to warnings about two sorts of educational threats to their children. On one hand, the media reported warnings by educational analysts about perceived failings in American education. Some stories focused on declining scores on various standardized tests of academic achievement, including the Scholastic Aptitude Test; others made unflattering comparisons between the performance of American students and students from other countries, especially Japan. These stories claimed that American schools were inadequately preparing children to compete with other nations.

The second kind of educational threat involved fears of the rising costs of a college education. News media, especially business publications, ran stories projecting that the costs of a college education would escalate beyond the means of even the upper middle class. These stories urged readers to begin savings plans for their newborn children's education based on projected average annual increases in college costs. Banks and other financial institutions began offering special investment programs aimed at parents concerned about future college costs.

The parents interviewed for this study expressed anxiety over some of these perceived hazards of childrearing. In general, parents expressed more concern over noneconomic than economic problems affecting their children. For example, 88 percent (23) either agreed or strongly agreed with the statement: "Children today face more dangers than when I was a child." Similarly 69 percent (18) believe that "the moral fabric of American society is deteriorating," and 96 percent (25) "worry about my child being exposed to illegal drugs as s/he grows older." Moreover, nearly one-half (11) of the parents expressed concern over their "child's prospects of attending the college of his or her choice."

The parents also expressed a general concern over economic problems, with 73 percent (19) agreeing or strongly agreeing that "the cost of living today makes it difficult to raise a family." Yet, when responding to statements about their personal economic situation, most of the parents interviewed expressed optimism. For example, 77 percent (20) of the parents were "confident about [their] ability to finance a college education for [their] children," 88 percent (23) believed their "family is better off now than in the past," and 65 percent (17) believed their children would have a "better standard of living . . . when they are adults."

These findings suggest that despite the relative economic security of these families, the parents find cause for concern about the future of their children. Parents fear factors seemingly outside their control. Exposure to drug use, a source of great concern for parents, is not something they can control. Public service announcements, newspaper stories, and grim statistics construct a serious national problem affecting all communities. Even such programs as Drug Abuse Resistance Education (D.A.R.E.), which are designed to reduce the use of illegal drugs, may serve to increase parental fears by bringing the subject to their attention.

The educational outcomes of children also lie, at least in part, outside the realm of parental control. The quality of schools, a child's diligence or laziness, the future costs of higher education, and competitive admissions all shape the educational opportunities and outcomes of children, yet are not easily controlled by parents. News stories about declining standardized test scores for U.S. students, unfavorable comparisons with foreign students, rising tuition costs at prestigious state and private universities, and other educational issues construct an educational future for children that is problematic if not downright ominous.

Ritual, Magic, and Toys

Faced with these perceived hazards of childrearing, parents may resort to the use of ritual and magic to ease their anxiety. Homans (1941) discusses two ways in which anxiety and ritual are related. First, magical rites may be employed to ease the anxiety resulting from the limits of practical knowledge. In this context, rituals are said to bring good luck and give people the "confidence which allows them to attack their work with energy and determination" (1941:164). Anxiety itself arises when people "feel certain desires and do not possess the techniques which make them sure of satisfying the desires" (1941:166). Here, anxiety results from an internal conflict between individual desires and limited resources for satisfying the desires.

The second means by which anxiety and ritual are related is the result of external pressures on the individual. According to Homans, there are certain occasions on which "society expects the individual to feel anxiety," for example, at childbirth (1941:168). Ritual allows individuals to persuade themselves and others that they do indeed feel anxious. In short, ritual may produce anxiety at socially appropriate times, or ritual may be designed to cope with anxieties generated in daily life.

In a related analysis of ritual and magic, Mary Douglas (1984/1966) cautions against the view that people perform rituals with an expectation of miracles. Instrumental efficacy, although hoped for, is not the primary motive behind ritual behavior. Rather, ritual serves the symbolic purpose of "making visible statements" about the kind of world we are trying to create and the moral rules we profess to live by. In this way, ritual is more an enactment of cultural values and beliefs than an effort to alter the course of natural events. Viewed in this light, Douglas suggests that the annual ritual of "spring cleaning" is less an effort to protect against disease than it is to make a symbolic statement about the type of home one wishes to establish.

Drawing on the ideas of Homans, Douglas, and others, one recent analysis of "modern magic" documents the many magical practices used by college students prior to taking examinations. Magic, the authors suggest, allows college students "to allay anxiety and so increase their chances for success" (Albas and Albas 1989:604). Similar studies have demonstrated the use of magic by baseball players and gamblers (Gmelch 1971; Henslin 1967).

Toy selection may be viewed as a ritual through which parents establish positive identities for themselves as parents. There are at least two ways in which this ritual process may work. On one hand, the ritual construction of identity through toy selection has the parents themselves as the audience. That is, the parents are seeking to create a positive self-image. This positive identity is built around a belief that children are threatened by powerful forces in society and that parents are responsible for protecting their own children from these perceived threats. By giving certain kinds of toys to their children (e.g., puzzles, crafts, and other "creative" toys) and preventing them from playing with other kinds of toys (e.g., guns, action figures, and other "violent" toys), parents can symbolically construct positive identities for themselves. In the face of multiple and elusive threats to their children, parents can in effect tell themselves they are doing something to ensure positive and deter negative outcomes for their children.

Identity construction through toy selection also has an external audience comprised of relatives, friends, teachers, and others who know the parents and their children. In this context parents may find themselves with a need to persuade others that they are indeed good parents, that is, that they seek to construct a positive public image. Even parents who themselves are skeptical about the putative threats to their children, may nonetheless engage in ritual toy selection if they have significant others who do believe in those threats.

Following Homans, I suggest that the ritual use of toys to construct a positive self-image "gives them the confidence to attack their work" as parents "with energy and determination." It allows them to escape the fatalism that might otherwise result from belief in the reality of the many putative threats facing their children. Likewise, there are certain times, such as toy-giving occasions at birthdays and Christmas, when society expects people to demonstrate commitment to their children's welfare. Parents may ignore these social expectations at their own peril, for to do so is to risk a negative evaluation of one's identity as a parent. In the celebrated Baby M surrogate-parenting custody trial, Mary Beth Whitehead had her fitness as a parent questioned in part because of her selection of toys for her 9-month old daughter. A child psychiatrist testified that during a court-ordered observation of Whitehead interacting with the infant, she offered inappropriate toys to, and did not play properly with, the child (Whitehead 1989:142–46).

As magic, therefore, toy selection by parents serves to ease the anxiety produced by the uncertainties involved in childrearing. Parents can symbolically reassure themselves and others that they are doing something to shield their children from the dangers of everyday life. Likewise, parents can symbolically use toys to demonstrate their commitment to educational values and the educational opportunities and success of their children. In the words of Mary Douglas, they are "making visible statements" about their identities as parents. Parents who make symbolic use of toys in these ways need not expect instrumental efficacy from the toys. As the interview data suggest, many parents are quite ambivalent about the effects of toys, good or bad, on children. Indeed, from the point of view of ritual and magic, the actual effects of toys on children are quite irrelevant to the parents. The point is that educational toys let parents establish their credentials as good parents.

CONCLUSIONS

In this essay I have shown that quite apart from whatever instrumental effects toys may have on the cognitive, moral, or social development of children, toys carry important symbolic meanings for the parents who purchase them. I have focused on the meaning of educational toys among middle-class parents and the ways in which these toys offer ritual opportunities to validate their status as parents.

A well-developed sociology of toys requires explorations into the varied ways class, race, and gender shape the cultural meanings of children's playthings and how these meanings influence patterns of toy selection. How, for example, do working-class parents differ from the middle-class parents analyzed here in terms of toy preferences; and how are these preferences related to their experiences and concerns as working-class parents? Similar questions about gender and race deserve analysis. Fashion dolls remain popular among young girls, but what do these toys represent to parents and how do dolls shape or reflect parenting experiences? In recent years, toy manufacturers have offered dolls with varying skin colors and facial features. Of what significance are these and other racially defined toys in the lives of parents of diverse racial and ethnic backgrounds?

The cultural analysis of toys also may shed light on the cultural meaning of childhood. As part of the material culture of childhood, toys reflect adult anxieties, fears, hopes, and general concerns about threats to children, as well as threats posed by children. Historical changes in the types of toys selected by parents may yield insights into changes in cultural perceptions of the role of childhood and children. In a similar vein, cross-cultural studies of parents' toy preferences can highlight divergent cultural understandings of childhood.

In short, a cultural approach to the sociology of toys has much to offer to the sociology of childhood.

ACKNOWLEDGMENTS

I would like to thank Gary D. Jaworski and David Rosen for their comments and suggestions.

APPENDIX A: TOY CATALOGS

Childcraft: Toys That Teach. Holiday 1991. Mission, KS: Childcraft, Inc.
Constructive Playthings. Summer 1992. Grandview, MO: Constructive Playthings.
Early Learning Centre: The Intelligent Toy Store. Summer 1992. Milford, CT: Early Learning Centres, Inc.
Fisher-Price 1991 Shopping Guide. East Aurora, NY: Fisher-Price, Inc.
Lilly's Kids. Vol. 140. Christmas 1992. Virginia Beach: Lillian Vernon Corporation.
Toys to Grow On. Holiday Preview 1992. Long Beach, CA: Toys to Grow On.
Troll Learn & Play: A Child's World of Imagination, Fun and Creativity. Halloween 1992. Mahwah, NJ: Troll Learn & Play.

REFERENCES

Albas, D., and Albas, C. 1989. "Modern Magic: The Case of Examinations." *Sociological Quarterly* 30:603–13.

Best, J. 1990. *Threatened Children*. Chicago: University of Chicago Press.

Brown, K. D. 1990. "Modelling for War?: Toy Soldiers in Late Victorian and Edwardian Britain." *Journal of Social History* 24:237–54.

Buettner, C. 1981. "War Toys or the Organization of Hostility." *International Journal of Early Childhood* 13:104–12.

Carlson-Paige, N., and D. E. Levin. 1987. *The War Play Dilemma: Balancing Needs and Values in the Early Childhood Classroom*. New York: Teachers College Press.

Cox, D. R. 1977. "Barbie and Her Playmates." *Journal of Popular Culture* 11(Fall):303–07.

Douglas, M. 1984/1966. *Purity and Danger: An Analysis of the Concepts of Pollution and Taboo*. London: Ark Paperbacks.

Gmelch, G. 1971. "Baseball Magic." *Trans-action* 8(June):39–41.

Henslin, J. 1967. "Craps and Magic." *American Journal of Sociology* 73:316–30.

Homans, G. C. 1941. "Anxiety and Ritual: The Theories of Malinowski and Radcliffe-Brown." *American Anthropologist* 43:164–72.

Kinder, M. 1991. *Playing with Power in Movies, Television, and Video Games*. Berkeley: University of California Press.

Kline, S. 1989. "Limits to the Imagination: Marketing and Children's Culture." Pp. 299–316 in *Cultural Politics in Contemporary America*, edited by I. Angus and S. Jhally. New York: Routledge.

Kunkel, D. 1988. "From a Raised Eyebrow to a Turned Back: The FCC and Children's Product-Related Programming." *Journal of Communication* 38(Autumn):90–108.

Masters, A. L. 1990. "Some Thoughts on Teenage Mutant Ninja Turtles: War Toys and Post-Reagan America." *Journal of Psychohistory* 17:319–26.

Motz, M. F. 1983. "'I Want to Be a Barbie Doll When I Grow Up': The Cultural Significance of the Barbie Doll." Pp. 123–36 in *The Popular Culture Reader*, edited by C. D. Geist and J. Nachbar. Bowling Green, OH: Bowling Green University Popular Press.

Provenzo, E. F., Jr. 1991. *Video Kids: Making Sense of Nintendo*. Cambridge: Harvard University Press.

Pursell, C. W., Jr. 1979. "Toys, Technology and Sex Roles in America, 1920–1940." Pp. 252–67 in *Dynamos and Virgins Revisited*, edited by M. M. Trescott. Metuchen, NJ: Scarecrow Press.

Sutton-Smith, B. 1988. "War Toys and Childhood Aggression," *Play and Culture* 1:57–69.

Whitehead, M. 1989. *A Mother's Story: The Truth about the Baby M Case*. New York: St. Martin's Press.

Wilkinson, D. Y. 1987. "The Doll Exhibit: A Psycho-Cultural Analysis of Black Female Role Stereotypes." *Journal of Popular Culture* 21 (Fall):19–29.

Winn, M. 1977. *The Plug-In Drug*. New York: Penguin.

Chapter 7

The Changing Meanings of Spanking

Phillip W. Davis

The general consensus is that adults in the past treated children in ways that seem especially harsh by today's standards (e.g., deMause 1974; but see also Pollock 1983). In fact, "whipping" children with buggy whips, cat-o'-nine-tails, riding crops, plough lines, sticks, switches and rods, as well as hair brushes and the "maternal slipper," did not generally lose favor in the United States until the 1830s, when "spanking" became more popular (Pleck 1987). Since then, the topic of spanking has arisen repeatedly in public and private arenas, with ministers, popular child-rearing experts, researchers, parents, media representatives, and even politicians debating whether spanking is too harsh.

Some critics argue for national legislation such as that found in Sweden and a few other European countries banning all physical punishment of children, but the issue has not led to much activity among policymakers. Even though many critics link spanking and physical punishment with child abuse, policymakers have generally resisted treating physical discipline as abuse (Nelson 1984:127). As a columnist wrote decades ago, "Despite years of debate on the matter, 'spanking' remains a fighting word" (D. Barclay 1962).

Why examine the debate over spanking? Like the other authors in this book, I am interested in the links between children and social problems. By looking at this particular debate, I think that we can better understand how seemingly simple matters of childrearing often involve complex, changing, and competing ideas about the essential nature of children and their appropriate place in society. I also think that we can see how the social meanings of a seemingly simple practice such as spanking can emerge, develop, and shift as one kind of social issue transforms into another.

There have always been controversies over how best to deal with children (Elkin and Handel 1989). As those controversies develop, the key themes, issues, and definitions associated with the problem frequently change. Take child care. The debate in the popular press over daycare shifted in its key concerns over time (Cahill and Loseke 1993), and issues of institutional sponsorship arose only after attention shifted from the desirability of daycare to its availability (Klein 1992). Or take child abuse. First "discovered" and publicized by medical experts, its meanings have changed since the 1960s in response to claims by a widespread child-protection movement (Best 1990; Johnson 1985; Nelson 1984).

Researchers usually ignore the spanking controversy, focusing instead on spanking behavior. Most define spanking as a kind of physical punishment, perhaps the "prototypical" punishment (Sears, MacCoby, and Levin 1957), although Straus (1991a:134) recently defined physical punishment as a "legally permissible physical attack." Sociologists have focused on spanking's developmental effects for the child's conscience and aggressive behavior (Steinmetz 1979), its uneven distribution by social class (Duvall and Booth 1979; Erlanger 1974), the widespread cultural approval for the practice (Straus, Gelles, and Steinmetz 1980), how often people spank (Wauchope and Straus 1990), the influence of religious fundamentalism on attitudes towards physical punishment (Ellison and Sherkat 1993; Wiehe 1990), and the role of physical punishment in shaping juvenile and adult deviance (Erlanger 1979; Straus 1991a).[1]

Spanking, however, is more than mild physical punishment to make children behave. It is also the focus of competing ideas, beliefs, and vocabularies put forth by critics and advocates in a debate over spanking's definition, appropriateness, and implications. There is a long history of religious and secular justifications for spanking (Grevens 1991). Beliefs that spanking is natural, normal, and necessary form a "spare the rod ideology" that may perpetuate the practice (Straus, Gelles, and Steinmetz 1980). Trivializing terms such as "smack," "spank," and "whack" are at the heart of a rhetoric of punishment that presupposes the legitimacy of parental authority and makes assumptions about the impersonality of adult motivation (Harding and Ireland 1989; Maurer 1974). Spanking is a socially constructed reality; it means what people say it means.

Controversial topics such as spanking cause people to trade competing images and moral vocabularies. They look selectively at certain parts of the "problem" and not at others. They also name and characterize the problem in the course of making claims and counterclaims about its essential nature, typical features, and social implications (Best 1990; Miller and Holstein 1993; Spector and Kitsuse 1987). Sometimes, they identify types of people with certain characteristics and moral qualities as part of the problem (Loseke 1993).

My purpose in this chapter is to compare the traditional defense of spanking with the emergent criticism of spanking, identifying the claims and counterclaims spanking's advocates and critics have made in the popular press since mid-century. I also want to link both formulations to wider cultural influences. I will limit my focus to the debate over spanking by parents, recognizing that there is a parallel debate about spanking in schools. In general I argue that the debate over spanking has become more complex in its themes and vocabularies. New definitions of spanking supplement older ones, and what was once primarily a childrearing issue has become a child-protection issue as well.

DATA AND MATERIALS

My research strategy involves an ethnographic content analysis (Altheide 1987) of newspaper and popular magazine articles that either focus on spanking or consider spanking in the course of discussing something else. This kind of analysis is appropriate when the research goal is to document and understand social meanings. First, I examined articles indexed in *The Reader's Guide to Periodical Literature* (RGPL) between 1945 and 1993. I chose articles spanning nearly half a century because I wanted to compare more recent statements about spanking with older arguments. The RGPL listed "spanking" as a subject category for those years and also referred readers to "corporal punishment" for specific articles. Most of the 142 articles listed under "corporal punishment" dealt with paddling in the schools; only 47 (33 percent) focused on spanking by parents. The RGPL excludes most religious periodicals, although it indexes a few (e.g., *Christianity Today* and *U.S. Catholic*). I also searched RGPL for the same years under "children—behavior and training," collecting more items on spanking and screening many pieces on discipline to see if they addressed spanking in any way.

To sample newspaper coverage of spanking, I searched the *New York Times Index* from 1945 to 1993, collecting articles and columns listed under "corporal punishment" or "children—care and training." I also searched a computerized index of seven major newspapers from 1985 to 1993 under the subject "spanking." I collected over 100 magazine articles and over 80 newspaper articles and columns about spanking.

Not all of these articles are by self-identified advocates or critics. Many summarize the debate, often presenting what are described as the "pros" and "cons" of spanking. Others are news reports about conference activities or research reports having to do with spanking. The reactions and opinions of pediatricians, sociologists, psychologists, childrearing "experts," and others are incorporated into many articles, usually couched in terms of their support or rejection of spanking. Occasionally, a magazine or newspaper article inspired letters to the editor criticizing or applauding the article, and I collected these as well.

Large-city newspapers and mainstream magazines are but one arena or claimsmaking setting in which contrasting ideas and images of spanking appear.[2] Of course, these materials do not reveal what is written in small-city newspapers, religious magazines and pamphlets, child-rearing manuals, parent-education texts, and abolitionist pamphlets. We also miss what is said on radio and television shows and in other popular cultural sources.[3] Debates over spanking also occur in semipublic arenas such as churches and parent-education classes and in private arenas where parents, children, and others formulate their own claims about spanking as an issue in their everyday lives.[4]

My materials represent a mix of primary and secondary claims (Best 1990:19). Most newspaper articles present the secondary claims of reporters, recasting the claims of the "experts" interviewed for the story. Editorial and letter writers, however, as well as family columnists, take sides and write as primary claimsmakers—champions or critics of spanking. Most magazine articles also present primary claimsmaking by advocates or critics exhorting readers to support or condemn spanking. They also tend to rely heavily on the opinions of experts and the findings of researchers in making their case. Written to sway an audience, these materials are an example of what Lofland (1976:113) calls "mediated exhortatory encounters." The readily available data are "frozen in print."

This paper begins by identifying themes associated with traditional defenses of spanking and noting how critics traditionally respond to those defenses. I take up the newer critiques of spanking that have appeared since the early 1970s, arguing that spanking is compulsive, violent, and abusive. Finally, I identify some of the likely influences on the development of these newer meanings and discuss the implications of these changes for understanding spanking and the social transformation of social issues.

TRADITIONAL DEFENSES OF SPANKING

Spanking's advocates traditionally use a rhetoric and vocabulary that paints spanking as the reasonable reaction of responsible parents to their wayward children. They claim that spanking is (1) the sign of nonpermissiveness; (2) anticipatory socialization; (3) God's will; (4) a morally neutral childrearing tool; and (5) a psychic release.

The Sign of Nonpermissiveness

Advocates often present spanking as an answer to the problem of permissive parents who are responsible for much of the "youth problem." The argument is that parents' lax attitudes result in the "undercontrol" of their children who go on to become delinquents, hippies, political activists, liars, cheaters, and thieves who lack respect for authority. In this view, failure to spank becomes the standard or benchmark of nonpermissiveness. The close association of nonspanking and the "permissive" label is clear in an interview with Dr. Benjamin Spock:

> He laughs when the subject of permissive child-raising is brought up, and how he is often blamed for the recent youth rebellions in this country: "In the first place, as anybody who has read my books knows, I was never permissive," he said. "I never said that parents shouldn't spank their children. To some parents, spanking is a natural way of making children behave. I would never tell them not to spank," he added. (Klemesrud 1970)[5]

Advocates also argue that character flaws lie behind the permissiveness of parents who do not spank; they lack the courage and responsibility that spanking is said to require. Parents who don't spank have neglected their responsibilities, taken the easy way out, or let themselves be duped by experts into taking a scientifically progressive but unwittingly troubled path. One father wrote how he and his wife started out permissive, despite his "itching palm." Finally they decided to try some real "action":

> More than once, the palm of my hand itched, but our textbook made it plain that the ultimate parental weapon, physical discipline, was arbitrary and old-fashioned. . . . Eight years of "permissiveness" had made my boy a liar, and an unrepentant and defiant one at that. "All right," I said heavily, realizing there was no alternative, "over my knee!" . . . George is 13 now and in the intervening five years, I don't think I have had to spank him more than three or four times. Once my wife and I steeled ourselves to substitute action for pleading words, we had no hesitations about spanking Linda, or Johnny as he grew older. (Conway 1955)

This statement suggests that spanking requires an admirable degree of decisiveness, in contrast to the inadequacy of permissive nonspankers who follow textbooks advising parents to use pleading words. Textbooks, experts, and scientists are part of the "new enlightenment" that appeals to permissive parents with disastrous effects:

> as the new enlightenment spreads its gentle glow in more and more of our modern American homes, the infant emperor is scientifically nurtured into a demanding little tyrant who relatives and neighbors detest ... free to develop into a youthful vandal, a car-thief, a thrill-sadist, or perhaps just into an arrogant boor, too selfish for an enduring marriage. (Kilbourne 1958)

Anticipatory Socialization

A second claim is that spanking effectively prepares children for the tribulations of life and the vagaries of adulthood. Some advocates argue that children will profit from spankings once they enter the real world, a world that is characteristically more difficult and demanding than family life. Although the idea that physically harsh treatment somehow hardens and toughens children, especially boys, is centuries old (deMause 1974; Grevens 1991), it is the hard realities of an industrialized world that these modern advocates care about. One father described spanking as a sign of caring:

> To have rules for behavior without the threat of physical punishment is like having laws without jails. ... Better to punish children than to be indifferent to them, since it is the neglected child who is more likely to grow up to be a problem. A father who spanks can at least be said to care. ... may I say that life spanks us all for mistakes which, had they been caught in time by a parent who cared enough to correct them, need never have happened? (Dempsey 1958)

Another advocate wrote that going "back to the hairbrush" prepares children for life's "booby-traps":

> The "permissive" parents have to suffer through the uncurbed tantrums and general hell-raising of their offspring. ... And the poor kids, when they eventually break out of the cocoon of an undisciplined childhood, are completely unprepared for the fenced-in and booby-trapped pattern of conventional adult life. (*Colliers* 1951)

This statement appeals to the idea that modernity and nonspanking are an unfortunate combination and that old-fashioned approaches better prepare children for the confinements of adult life.

God's Will

When religious themes appear in the materials I examined, it is usually when authors mention "biblical sanctions" as a traditional argument for spanking. Some ministers are quoted in support of spanking, but they are just as likely to emphasize effectiveness as divine sanction. James Dobson, author of *Dare to Discipline* and *James Dobson's New Dare to Discipline*, writes from the standpoint of Christian fundamentalism and is notorious among critics for his advocacy of spanking and switching: "I think we should not eliminate a biblically sanctioned approach to raising children because it is abused in some cases" (Neff 1993).

Although the definition of spanking as a "biblically sanctioned approach" figures prominently in the fundamentalist Christian press (Grevens 1991), it is relatively uncommon in the materials I examined. More often, articles make passing mention of religious themes or mention them in setting up a more secular discussion. Most people probably believe that the phrase, "spare the rod and spoil the child" comes from the Bible, but it first appeared in a poem by Samuel Butler published in 1664 (Gibson 1978:49).

A Morally Neutral Childrearing Tool

Advocates often refer to spanking as a tool, technique, or method, writing about it as if its "use" were but the impersonal and mechanical application of a morally neutral procedure. The virtues of this technique are said to include speed, efficiency, and efficacy. Spanking creates obedience and respect with minimum effort and without long, "dragged-out" discussions. These claims contend that the good child is an obedient child and that faster techniques are superior to slower ones. Defining spanking as a tool or method suggests that spankers are purposive rather than aimless and depicts spanking as a logical activity rather than an emotional outburst. The overall image of parents who spank is that their "applications" are part of a method that is reasonable, systematic, and even merciful:

> Why spank? Simply because there are times when spanking is the easiest, best method of correction—best for the children, easiest for me. I believe in spanking because it works! (Bramer 1948)

> A spanking is concrete enough to be effective, soon over, and more merciful than a prolonged bout or clash of wills. (English and Foster 1950)

The definition of spanking as a childrearing tool or technique is especially clear in the widespread claim by advocates in the popular press

that spanking should be used as a "last resort," only after other, presumably less harsh, efforts have failed. The rhetoric of "last resorts"
implies that spankers possess the knowledge and ability to mete out
penalties of varying severity in the proper sequence.

A Psychic Release

Another common contention is that spanking resolves particular conflicts by somehow allowing parents and their children to start over,
because it "clears the air." The popularity of this phrase no doubt
derives from its use in Spock's popular *Baby and Child Care*, first published in 1945. Some authors elaborate on the phrase, claiming that
spanking frees children from guilt by providing them with an opportunity for repentance or offers a cathartic release of the parent's tension
and anger. One parent wrote:

> One salubrious effect of spanking, which is often overlooked by those who
> hold out for other methods of punishment, is the resulting feeling of expi-
> ation. . . . A child likes to feel that "it's all over now," that he's paid the
> price for his bad behavior, the slate's clean, the air clear, and the fresh start
> made. (Bramer 1948)[6]

Advocates also contend that parents who don't spank will find other,
less healthy, ways of expressing their anger:

> This is frequently the best reason for doing it—tensions that might other-
> wise remain bottled up are given a therapeutic release. While it is true that
> the child is not happy about this, he might be far less happy with a father
> who restrains his temper at the cost of continued irritability. (Dempsey
> 1958)

If they don't become neurotically guilty, insecure, or repressed, parents
may erupt later and do greater harm to the child, for all their progressive efforts to conform to the new psychology.

The Critics Respond

Critics of spanking claim that these traditional defenses are flawed for
a variety of reasons. They argue that, rather than preventing youth
problems, spanking creates them. For one thing, spanking makes children untrustworthy:

> Few children feel as kindly toward a parent after a spanking as they did
> before. In time, bitter resentment, antagonism and strained child-parent
> relationships develop. To escape spankings, many a child develops into a
> sneak, a cheat or a liar. (Hurlock 1949)

Critics also claim that, although spanking may "work" in the immediate situation, its effects are highly limited: "It's true that a spanking can, very occasionally, work wonders with the child who has gotten a bit frisky, but it usually causes rebellion and resentment instead, especially in a preteen" (Kelly 1989). They also argue that, while it may be effective, it is effective for the wrong reason. Instead of complying voluntarily out of respect based on reason, children who are spanked comply out of fear. Critics claim that spankers are irresponsible, because they are avoiding the harder but superior alternatives. Spankers worry too much about teaching the values of respect and authority, oblivious to the fact that spanking really teaches the legitimacy of aggression, brute strength, and revenge. Critics also contend that spanking can easily escalate. A physician answered questions about spanking in his *McCall's* column:

Q: *Should I hit my child back when he hits me?*
A: No, you should not. If you strike him back, you are simply teaching him that the only way to respond in anger is by physical blows, and it may turn into a fist fight. (Senn 1957)

Critics argue that the true meaning of discipline involves teaching children the lesson of self-control, whereas "physical discipline" only teaches them "might makes right."

In sum, since mid-century advocates and critics in the popular press have been invoking several different meanings of spanking. Advocates claim that children are "underdisciplined," that they need to be spanked, that parents who do not spank are mollycoddling their children, that being spanked doesn't harm children, and that nonspanking parents are irresponsible. Critics respond that spanking is futile at best and counterproductive at worst. In this traditional debate, advocates emphasize the drawbacks of permissiveness as a cause of delinquency and rebellion, and critics argue that discipline should involve teaching and self-control.

EMERGENT MEANINGS

The traditional claims about spanking persist. Popular experts, columnists, researchers, professionals, and parents still argue for or against spanking by talking about effectiveness, lessons, psychic release, preparation, and permissiveness. Spanking is still said to work or not work, to counter permissiveness or encourage aggression, to reflect concern for the child's well-being or indicate a lack of self-control, to clear the air or breed resentment. Although claims about delinquency prevention and rhetoric about the woodshed have generally faded from view, along with worries about hippies and the youth rebellion, most of the other claims appear routinely in contemporary materials. One recent letter to a magazine, for example, echoes older claims: "Spanking is immediate, sharply focused, and lets everyone get on with their lives. It should be used sparingly and only as a last resort. But believe me, it can be effective." (*U.S. Catholic* 1993). But spanking's critics bring newer, supplementary meanings to the debate, meanings that coincide with changing concerns and arguments borrowed from debates over other issues.

Spanking Is Compulsive

The critics' first new claim is that spanking is compulsive, habit-forming, or addictive. This claim depicts parents as people who have lost their autonomy by becoming dependent on a highly satisfying behavior that they can abandon only with considerable difficulty. Critics compare spanking to smoking, because both practices are legal, harmful, and habitual. A mother described the day she decided to "kick the habit": "It was akin to the evening I found myself digging through a trash basket for a half-smoked cigarette butt and decided to quit smoking. And like the days that followed that decision, kicking the spanking habit proved to be tough" (Hyde 1980). A psychologist extended the analogy:

> People who smoke claim that it makes them feel better and helps them to relax; parents who spank their children also feel better by getting out their anger . . . there is liberal evidence that both are fraught with potential harm. Of course, most people who smoke never get cancer, and most children who are excessively spanked do not become delinquent. Yet for those who are affected, it is a serious matter indeed. (Welsh 1985)

Others associate spanking and smoking, because, given the widespread criticisms of each, they are increasingly secretive practices. Responding to a report that time out is more popular with parents than spanking, for example, one pediatrician was skeptical, saying that "spankers today are like closet smokers" (*Atlanta Journal/Constitution* 1993). A therapist and father asks spankers why they "reach for spanking, much as an alcoholic or drug addict reaches for their fix? . . . It takes great diligence to cultivate a new way of being and prevent the old addiction from taking hold again" (Dale 1993). Spanking in this rhetorical vein is an irrational attachment to a druglike experience. The attachment is so intense for some spankers that their "recovery" may require changes in their being.

Spanking is a Demeaning, Violent Act

Critics in the popular press routinely echo the view of most family violence researchers that spanking is a form of violence. Critics frequently quote researchers such as Murray Straus and Richard Gelles in their articles. They describe spanking as an act of violence that models violent behavior for the child and teaches children that violence is socially acceptable. Penelope Leach, an extremely popular British author, argues for no spankings and fewer time outs in the name of clear thinking and nonviolence: "a spanking humiliates and devalues the whole child, overwhelms thought with anger, and demonstrates that physical violence is a good way to solve problems" (Leach 1992). A newspaper columnist points to the lessons in violence that spanking teaches: "Spanking demeans parents as well as children by presenting violence as an acceptable way to solve problems" (Ashkinase 1985). Other critics define spanking as an assault. In a *Psychology Today* reader survey on spanking and physical punishment, "one woman said that hitting a child should be considered assault: 'It gives the message that size and power make abusive behavior acceptable'" (Stark 1985). For critics, spanking is a prime example of minor violence that later causes adult violence, especially by those who experience frequent, severe spankings as children.

Spanking Is Abusive

With increasing frequency, newspaper and magazine articles interweave references to spanking and abuse, although the nature of the claimed connection varies considerably. I found no flat statements that "spanking is child abuse," but one article noted: "Parents Anonymous, a group for parents who want to avoid abusing their children, recently declared that any physical punishment is emotionally abusive and should not be sanctioned" (Lehman 1989). Some critics argue that spanking is associated with future abuse by the spanked child:

> Clearing the air with a quick spank sometimes *seems* to halt the progress of a deteriorating situation. . . . Nevertheless, the short-term utility must be weighed against the real possibility, gleaned from clinical evidence, that corporal punishment is not associated, in the long run, with self-discipline; rather, it is associated with the abuse of the child of the next generation. (Katz 1980—emphasis in original)

Others emphasize that a "fine line" separates spanking and abuse, a line that is too easily crossed. The notion of fine lines appears frequently in professional writings, and its popularization has been successful:

> You should never hit your children, even when you've reached the end of your rope because that's exactly when you are the least in control of yourself. Lines can blur and a hitting can turn into real, if unintentional, child abuse. (Schlaerth 1993)

In discussing "The Three Cardinal Rules of Good Discipline" (don't insult or demean your child, don't forget that you are a role model, and "spare the rod, period"), a psychologist concludes: "Worst of all, for many grown-ups, the line between physical punishment and child abuse can become blurred with frightening ease" (Segal 1986).

The Advocates Respond

Advocates have had little say about the idea that spanking is a compulsion, but they take issue with critics who claim it is violent or abusive. They go about this in various ways. Some claim that critics are less concerned about raising children than they are about social appearances. One professor emeritus of English wrote in a *Wall Street Journal* commentary (with the headline, "The Bottom Line on Spanking"):

> My wife recalls that when she misbehaved as a child, her mother cut a switch from a tree in the backyard and whaled her with it then and there. Any mother so thwacking today would be condemned. . . . Joan Beck, a nationally syndicated columnist, equates corporal punishment in schools with child abuse. Thus has political correctness befogged one of civilization's most useful ways to raise the young. . . . I do not recommend beating children. . . . Spanking a child is but a single act—among many—that supports civilized behavior against the natural barbarism of the American brat." (Tibbetts 1992)

Not only does he imply that critics worry more about political correctness than raising children, but also he writes about thwacking and spanking as if they were the best hope of turning back the barbaric child. Lest his defense of thwacking is taken to mean he is insensitive, he issues a disclaimer about beatings. Several days later the paper printed 10 letters about the article. Only three favored "thwacking," echoing the refrain that "It didn't hurt me" and the idea that the only alternative is permissiveness. One writer said he started out a spanker, got trendy, and then resumed:

> Several years ago, however, I suffered a nasty bout of enlightened guilt. Trendy psychologists almost had me convinced I was a child abuser causing long term damage to my kids. I was almost ready to confess my sins and flog myself in front of the American Academy of Pediatrics. (Bell 1992)

Another put a twist on a contemporary theme by suggesting that the unspanked child may be an unguided child and that parents who don't spank may be guilty of "neglect."

In his syndicated column William Raspberry reacted to the publicity given a 1989 conference on physical punishment.[7] After a disclaimer, he ridiculed the idea that spanking and abuse are different points on the same continuum:

> Well, it's time to confess. My parents, for all their surface warmth and respectability, were into physical cruelty—child abuse, to put it plainly. You see, they spanked their children. I'm no advocate of child abuse, but it strikes me that the experts at Wingspread . . . are guilty of what might be called the fallacy of the false continuum . . . child abuse—the depressingly frequent incidents of child battering—is, for these experts, just another point on a continuum that begins with spanking. . . . Ordinary fanny dusting, to which some parents resort when more intelligent approaches fail, teaches children that violence is an acceptable way of settling disputes. . . . I think these experts are nuts. (Raspberry 1989)

The columnist notes that other approaches are more intelligent but also normalizes spankings by calling them "ordinary." His vocabulary pits "fanny dustings" against abuse, making light of what the critics take too seriously—spankings, after all, are only a light brushing of an unimportant part of the child's body. He also claims that people who confuse something inconsequential with something as important as violence are irrational and not to be taken seriously. A letter to the editor complained:

> I object to Columnist William Raspberry's characterization that we are "nuts" to link spanking to child abuse. . . . Without love, hitting children— no matter how euphemistically described—very easily becomes severe child abuse. (Hare 1989)

Some writers make increasingly sharp distinctions between spanking and abuse, between "an occasional swat" and spankings, or between rare swats and corporal punishment. They then discuss the differences these distinctions represent, emphasizing how rare swats are more defensible and less incriminating than the other things. One columnist reporting on a conference noted, for example: "Several specialists left the door open for that rare swat of a child who repeatedly endangers himself" (Lehman 1989). The occasional swat was also the topic of a syndicated column after Lady Di spanked Prince William, age 8, when he wouldn't stay at her side during his school's sports day in 1990. The writer wondered whether such a swat is the same as corporal punishment:

> The incident has revived debate over how parents should respond when their children misbehave and whether there is a difference between cor-

poral punishment and a rare swat from a loving parent. . . . "She sounds pretty human," said Dr. T. Berry Brazelton. . . . "What Princess Di did, and what I probably would have done too, is to react in a way that lets the boy know that you really mean it," he said. "All of my kids will tell you that I've swatted them on the bottom when I've been upset with them." He added that he sees this as different from unacceptable physical punishments like planned or protracted spankings. (Kutner 1990)

The headline for the story in a different paper was, "Crowning Blows," comically suggesting that Lady Di's action was relatively unimportant. Advocates who use phrases such as the "occasional swipe" rhetorically suggest that there are important differences between what critics argue is so damaging and what is an inconsequential if not valuable practice. Some advocates tell parents just what to do so that they will not be considered abusive:

Spank only for a few specific offenses, such as blatant disrespect and defiance. . . . John Rosemond, in his Knight News Service newspaper column "Parent and Child," gives these guidelines: "With no threats or warnings, spank with your hand, not a wooden spoon, paddle, belt or switch. A spanking is not more than three swats to the child's rear end. *A swat to any other part of the child's body is abuse.* (Oliver, 1987—emphasis added)

This statement tells readers what to spank with, how many times to spank, and where to spank. Not only does it promote a bottoms-only definition of spanking, but also it equates "a swat to any other part" with abuse.

DISCUSSION

I have examined spanking as a controversial topic rather than a behavior. Spanking remains a fighting word, and what people are fighting about is both complex and changing. I have identified arrays of older and newer meanings of spanking in a long-lived controversy filled with fluid, shifting claims by spanking's advocates and critics. In the course of formulating, defining, and characterizing spanking over time, a topic traditionally approached as a childrearing issue in a debate over "what works" is now also a child-protection issue in a debate over whether spanking is violent and abusive.

I have shown that advocates and critics employ rhetorical formulations that define and characterize spanking in ways meant to resonate deeply among readers, exhorting them to accept or reject "good old-fashioned" spankings. Advocates of spanking extol its virtues in the name of tradition, effectiveness, efficiency, and responsibility, defining it essentially as a tool, technique, or method for making children behave. Spanking is said to offer an antidote to the youth problem, release tension for both parent and child, and prepare children for life's hardships. Advocates generally ignore or trivialize children's suffering, portray nonspankers as irresponsible, and cite their own positive personal histories as spanked children. Critics counter that spanking ironically promotes, rather than deters, misbehavior. They contend that it is usually an expression of the parent's anger and frustration and teaches children that violence and aggression are acceptable. More recent critics also define spanking as a bad habit, an act of violence, and a form of abuse. All too often, they argue, spanking leads to abuse later in life or is closely linked to the abuse of the spanked child.

In the context of increasingly broad definitions of child abuse, some advocates argue for narrow definitions of spanking (e.g., bottom-only). Narrow definitions, as well as distinctions between planned spankings and the occasional smack, are ways of maintaining a "place" for spanking on the list of what parents can rightfully do to their children without lapsing into a new category of "putative person" (Loseke 1993). Otherwise, the moral character of spankers is vulnerable to allegations of being "old-fashioned" if not sadistic. To look at their rhetoric, advocates seem to embrace the notion of being old-fashioned, but they ridicule the idea that there is something incriminating about a normal form of discipline.

Activities in wider professional, scientific, religious, and political contexts have no doubt prompted and shaped these changing meanings for spanking. Psychological research and popular writings on aggression in the 1950s and 1960s challenged behaviorist assumptions about the role of punishment. Some well-publicized studies provided dramatic ironies such as the finding by Sears, Maccoby, and Levin (1957) that physical punishment for aggressive behavior is associated with more, not less, aggression by children. Many of these scholarly ideas and facts made their way into articles and stories in the popular press.

Moreover, in the 1960s and early 1970s, the development of a modern child-protection movement, the discovery of child abuse, and the continuing emergence of violence as a major policy issue led to a series of controversies associated with the idea that children are increasingly "at risk" (Wollons 1993). As these issues developed, spanking was mentioned, and sometimes its importance was highlighted. Working for the National Commission on the Causes and Prevention of Violence, for example, Stark and McEvoy (1970) wrote about spanking alongside fist fights, vigilantism, police violence, assassination, and military violence.

In his influential book on child abuse, David Gil (1970) stressed how approval of physical punishment creates a cultural climate in which abuse can flourish. Both studies received national media attention.

There has also been a convergence of interests and activities among anticorporal punishment and antiabuse organizations. Organizations such as the National Coalition to Abolish Corporal Punishment in Schools, the National Center for the Study of Corporal Punishment and Alternatives, and End Violence against the Next Generation, although they focus on educational settings, regularly point to spanking and physical punishment by parents as an analogous issue (Hyman 1990).[8] The National Committee for the Prevention of Child Abuse (NCPCA) has been actively seeking the primary prevention of child abuse through pamphlets, surveys, and press releases about physical punishment and spanking since the mid-1980s.[9]

We cannot make a flat statement that the newer meanings of spanking are now dominant. The themes in the newer debate suggest only a partial transformation of the traditional childrearing issue into a contemporary child-protection controversy. There is certainly the potential for definitions related to abuse to become dominant. Whether the transformation proceeds further depends in part on the discourse, resources, and activities of advocates and critics in organizational, political, media, and movement contexts.

Activities in medical settings will have an impact. The Centers for the Study of Disease Control instituted a division for the study of domestic violence in 1992. The June 1992 issue of the *Journal of the American Medical Association* was devoted to family violence and included an article on spanking as a form of corporal punishment. Some physicians now claim that "corporal punishment is child abuse" (Leung, Robson, and Lim 1993:42). These medical developments, if they are recognized by the press, policymakers, and agency officials, should encourage spanking's association with child abuse.

Other activities are likely to inhibit the ascendance of abuse meanings. Religious action groups are sensitive and alert to any move to broaden definitions of abuse to include spanking, or to remove existing legal protections of parents who use "reasonable physical discipline." We may see other spanking-related controversies develop as groups organize to resist further involvement by the state in family matters (Johnson 1986). In addition, some critics promote the idea that spanking is really a civil rights issue, and civil rights organizations may make spanking part of their agenda. Their constructions of the problem might easily bypass the issue of abuse or make it secondary to the issue of discrimination on the basis of age. Similarly, critics campaigning for state and national legislation comparable to that in Sweden may successfully promote the association of spanking with the violation of human or children's rights rather than child abuse. Finally, it is likely that child-protection officials will continue to warn that their limited resources should be reserved for "truly" abused children. Whether spanking ever fully becomes a child-protection issue, these emergent meanings challenge the assumptions that spanking is natural, normal, and necessary on a fundamental level.

ACKNOWLEDGMENTS

I would like to thank Sarah Buchanan-Gereau for her assistance in collecting data for this chapter. I would also like to thank Denise Donnelly and Cynthia Davis for their helpful comments on an earlier draft.

NOTES

1. Some critics argue that these studies overemphasize the importance of physical punishment and fail to appreciate the importance of context, inequality, authority, and control (Kurz 1991; Loseke 1991; see also Straus 1991b).

2. Ibarra and Kitsuse (1993) point to at least three settings where claims-making rhetoric occurs: media, academic, and legal-political. Advocates and critics of spanking have made their points in each arena, with considerable crossover. Researchers, for example, appear in the press when interviewed about their findings.

3. The highly rated television show "20/20" did a segment on spanking in October 1992 and reran it in July 1993. In addition to interviewing Murray Straus, noted family violence researcher at the University of New Hampshire, the show included videotape of children in four families being "spanked." The gist of the segment was that experts condemn the practice and recommend alternatives. Spanking is said to be "wrong" and interviewer John Stossel tells one set of parents, "It's almost as if you're abusive, that you're cruel" (*ABC News*, 1992).

4. Elsewhere I examined situations when strangers debate spanking and punishment in the context of one person trying to stop another from hitting a child (Davis 1991).

5. Spock later modified his position and, by 1988, he explicitly rejected the practice, stating that spanking and punishment were linked to the nuclear arms race and increasing rates of murder, wife abuse, and child abuse (Grevens 1991:95–97).

6. The assumption that spanking spares the guilty child is also found in the 1962 version of the Children's Bureau booklet, "Your Child from One to Six." The text refers to mild physical punishment as superior to prolonged disapproval and scolding with the advantage that, "a mild physical punishment can actually relieve the child who wants to shed his guilty feelings."

7. The Wingspread conference in Racine, Wisconsin, was sponsored by the University of Wisconsin and the American Academy of Pediatrics' Provisional

Committee on Child Abuse. Conference activities led to a call to stop parents from using physical punishment (Haueser 1990:68).

8. Two new organizations devoted to the abolition of all physical punishment of children are EPOCH (End Physical Punishment of Children) and EPOCH-USA. The former started in 1989 in the United Kingdom, soon after that country legislatively abolished corporal punishment in its public schools in 1986. EPOCH-USA started in 1990 (Haeuser 1990).

9. Daro and Gelles (1992) believe the surveys show that such public awareness and education campaigns are effective in reducing the overall amount of physical punishment and promoting the belief that physical punishment can be injurious.

APPENDIX A: SAMPLE ARTICLES

Ashkinaze, C. 1985. "A Tradition We Can Do Without." *Atlanta Journal/Constitution* June 21:22.

Atlanta Journal/Constitution. 1993. "Time Out's Most Popular Discipline" August 4:B.3D.

Barclay, D. 1962. "A Guide for Uncertain Spankers." *New York Times* July 8:VI.31.

Bell, J. 1992. "Thwack!" *Wall Street Journal* September 9:A.15.

Bramer, J. 1948. "I Believe Children Should be Spanked!" *American Home* 39 (April):118–121.

Colliers. 1951. "Back to the Hairbrush [editorial]." 128 (September 29):94.

Conway, T. 1955. "Children Need Spanking!" *Coronet* 38 (July):138–41.

Dale, S. 1993. "Spanking Is An Addiction." *Mothering* 69 (January):30–35.

Dempsey, D. 1958. "Whether, How and Why to Spank." *New York Times Magazine* July 6:11–12.

English, O. and C. Foster. 1950. "How Bad is it to Spank Your Kids?" *Better Homes and Gardens* 28 (June):197+.

Hare, I. 1989. "More on Spanking." *Chicago Tribune* April 29:1.10.

Hurlock, E. 1949. "Substitutes for Spanking." *Hygeia* 17 (January):70.

Hyde, C. 1980. "Confessions of a Nonspanker." *Parents* 55 (October):86–87.

Katz, L. 1980. "Spank or Speak?" *Parents* 55 (February):84.

Kelly, M. 1989. "Another Kind of Discipline." *Washington Post* March 23:D:5.

Kilbourne, W. 1958. ". . . and Why Not Spank Children?" *American Mercury* 86 (March):119–120.

Klemesrud, J. 1970. "Dr. Spock Tells Youth: 'Civilizations are Built on Restraint!'" *New York Times* November 3:C.30.

Kutner, L. 1990. "Swatting a Future King of England, or Any Child." *New York Times* June 21:C6.

Leach, P. 1992. "Instead of Spanking." *Parenting* (January):90.

Lehman, B. 1989. "Making a Case Against Spanking." *Washington Post* March 23:D.5.

Neff, D. 1993. "Dobson's New Dare" [interview with J. Dobson]. *Christianity Today* 37 (February 8):69–70.

Oliver, S. 1987. "How to Stop Spanking: Try a Lot of Tenderness." *Essence* 18 (April):98.

Raspberry, W. 1989. "Ultimate Child Abuse." *Washington Post* March 27:A.15.

Schlaerth, K. 1993. "Adults Should Never Hit Kids." *U.S. Catholic* 58 (January):25.

Segal, J. 1986. "The Three Cardinal Rules of Good Discipline." *Parents* 61 (April):82.

Senn, M. 1957. "What's Wrong With Spanking?" *McCall's* 84 (July):132+.

Stark, E. 1985. "Taking a Beating." *Psychology Today* 19 (April):16.

Tibbetts, A. 1992. "The Bottom Line on Spanking." *Wall Street Journal* August 24:A.8.

U.S. Catholic. 1993. "Feedback" 58 (January):26–29.

Welsh, R. 1985. "Spanking: A Grand Old American Tradition?" *Children Today* 14 (January):25–29

REFERENCES

ABC News. 1992. "20/20 Transcripts." *Journal Graphics, Inc.* October 30.

Altheide, D. L. 1987. "Ethnographic Content Analysis." *Qualitative Sociology* 10:65–77.

Best, J. 1990. *Threatened Children: Rhetoric and Concern about Child-Victims.* Chicago: University of Chicago Press.

Cahill, S., and D. Loseke. 1993. "Disciplining the Littlest Ones." *Studies in Symbolic Interaction* 14: forthcoming.

Daro, D., and R. J. Gelles. 1992. "Public Attitudes and Behaviors with Respect to Child Abuse Prevention." *Journal of Interpersonal Violence* 7:517–31.

Davis, P. W. 1991. "Stranger Intervention into Child Punishment in Public Places." *Social Problems* 38:227–46.

deMause, L. 1974. "Our Forebears Made Childhood a Nightmare." *Psychology Today* 8 (April):85–87.

Duvall, D., and A. Booth. 1979. "Social Class, Stress and Physical Punishment." *International Review of Modern Sociology* 9:103–17.

Elkin, F., and G. Handel. 1989. *The Child and Society: The Process of Socialization,* 5th ed. New York: Random House.

Ellison, C., and D. Sherkat. 1993. "Conservative Protestantism and Support for Corporal Punishment." *American Sociological Review* 58:131–44.

Erlanger, H. S. 1974. "Social Class and Corporal Punishment in Childrearing: A Reassessment." *American Sociological Review* 39:68–85.

_____. 1979. "Childhood Punishment Experience and Adult Violence." *Children and Youth Services Review* 1:75–86.

Gibson, I. 1978. *The English Vice: Beatings, Sex and Shame in Victorian England and After.* London: Duckworth.

Gil, D. 1970. *Violence Against Children: Physical Abuse in the United States.* Cambridge, MA: Harvard University Press.

Grevens, P. 1991. *Spare the Child*. New York: Knopf.

Harding, C., and R. Ireland. 1989. *Punishment: Rhetoric, Rule, and Practice*. New York: Routledge.

Haeuser, A. A. 1990. "Can We Stop Physical Punishment of Children?" *Education Digest* 56 (September):67–69.

Hyman, I. A. 1990. *Reading, Writing, and the Hickory Stick: The Appalling Story of Physical and Psychological Violence in American Schools*. Lexington, MA: Lexington Books.

Ibarra, P., and J. Kitsuse. 1993. "Vernacular Constituents of Moral Discourse: An Interactionst Proposal for the Study of Social Problems." Pp. 21–54 in *Constructionst Controversies: Issues in Social Problems Theory*, edited by G. Miller and J. Holstein. Hawthorne, NY: Aldine de Gruyter.

Johnson, J. 1985. "Symbolic Salvation: The Changing Meanings of the Child Maltreatment Movement." *Studies in Symbolic Interaction* 6:289–305.

_____. 1986. "The Changing Concept of Child Abuse and Its Impact on the Integrity of Family Life." Pp. 257–75 in *The American Family and the State*, edited by J. Peden and F. Glahe. San Francisco: Pacific Research Institute for Public Policy.

Klein, A. G. 1992. *The Debate over Child-Care: 1969–1990*. Albany: State University of New York Press.

Kurz, D. 1991. "Corporal Punishment and Adult Use of Violence: A Critique of 'Discipline and Deviance'," *Social Problems* 38:155–61.

Leung, A., W. Robson, and S. Lim. 1993. "Corporal Punishment." *American Family Physician* 47:42–43.

Lofland, J. 1976. *Doing Social Life*. New York: Wiley.

Loseke, D. R. 1991. "Reply to Murray A. Straus: Readings on 'Discipline and Deviance'," *Social Problems* 38:162–66.

_____. 1993. "Constructing Conditions, People, Morality, and Emotions: Expanding the Agenda of Constructionism." Pp. 207–16 in *Constructionist Controversies*, edited by G. Miller and J. Holstein. Hawthorne, NY: Aldine de Gruyter.

Maurer, A. 1974. "Corporal Punishment." *American Psychologist* 28:614–26.

Miller, G., and J. Holstein (eds.). 1993. *Constructionist Controversies: Issues in Social Problems Theory*. Hawthorne, NY: Aldine de Gruyter.

Nelson, B. 1984. *Making an Issue of Child Abuse*. Chicago: University of Chicago Press.

Pleck, E. 1987. *Domestic Tyranny: The Making of Social Policy against Family Violence from Colonial times to the Present*. New York: Oxford University Press.

Pollock, L. 1983. *Forgotten Children: Parent-Child Relations from 1500–1900*. New York: Cambridge University Press.

Sears, R., E. Maccoby, and H. Levin. 1957. *Patterns of Child Rearing*. White Plains, NY: Row, Peterson.

Spector, M. and J. I. Kitsuse. 1987. *Constructing Social Problems*. Hawthorne, NY: Aldine de Gruyter.

Stark, R., and J. McEvoy. 1970. "Middle-Class Violence." *Psychology Today* 4 (November):52–65.

Steinmetz, S. 1979. "Disciplinary Techniques and Their Relationship to Aggressiveness, Dependency, and Conscience." Pp. 405–38 in *Contemporary Theories about the Family*, edited by W. Burr, R. Hill, F. Nye, and I. Reiss New York: Free Press.

Straus, M. 1991a. "Discipline and Deviance: Physical Punishment of Children and Violence and Other Crime in Adulthood." *Social Problems* 38:133–52.

_____. 1991b. "New Theory and Old Canards about Family Violence Research." *Social Problems* 38:180–97.

Straus, M., R. Gelles, and S. Steinmetz. 1980. *Behind Closed Doors*. New York: Doubleday.

Wauchope, B., and M. Straus. 1990. "Physical Punishment and Physical Abuse of American Children." Pp. 133–48 in *Physical Violence in American Families*, edited by M. Straus and R. Gelles. New Brunswick, NJ: Transaction Books.

Wiehe, V. R. 1990. "Religious Influence on Parental Attitudes toward the Use of Corporal Punishment." *Journal of Family Violence* 5:173–86.

Wollons, R. 1993. "Introduction." Pp. ix–xxv in *Children at Risk in America: History, Concepts, and Public Policy*, edited by R. Wollons. Albany: State University of New York Press.

Chapter 8

The Positive Functions of Rock and Roll Music for Children and Their Parents

Joseph A. Kotarba

Lay and professional critics have long cast a wary eye toward children's pop culture. They have been especially critical of materials emanating from the electronic media, such as television violence, which allegedly leads to violent behavior among young viewers; music videos, some of which contain sexist messages; and rap music, which is criticized for many reasons (Wilson 1989). Rock and roll music has been criticized most often and most harshly, being designated as a "social problem" ever since its inception over 40 years ago. The purpose of this chapter is to qualify this argument by illustrating some positive functions of rock and roll music.

Rock and roll music has become an integral feature of American culture. I define rock and roll as popular music that: (1) is created for and marketed toward young people; (2) is primarily guitar driven and electrified or amplified; (3) has its musicological origins in African-American musical styles; (4) is usually danceable; and (5) sounds better when played or performed loud (Kotarba 1992). Rock and roll performers thus range from Elvis Presley and Dion and the Belmonts to the Beatles and Kiss to Metallica and the Butthole Surfers . . . and everybody in-between. In fact, it may be easier to list those forms of popular music that do not fit this definition. These include country and western (geared toward adults and young people seeking an adult viewpoint on life); serious jazz (also geared toward adults and not requiring amplification); classical music (geared toward adults and those who want to act even older than adults); and folk music (which is geared toward limited audiences). My admittedly broad definition of rock and roll is intended to envelope comprehensively all the particular styles, schools, and forms of rock music that come and go as Top 40 listings, fashions, and social conditions change.

For three generations, rock and roll has functioned as a primary source of meaning and leisure-time activity for young people. Since its inception in the 1950s, rock and roll has been associated with adolescents and has thus become a medium for both understanding and critiquing the adolescent generation. Some of the earliest sociological observers of rock and roll focused on its positive functions for adolescent development. Talcott Parsons (1949) argued that the adolescent culture, including rock and roll, that emerged after World War II was a functional mechanism for the societal control of the energy of this burgeoning generation.

James Coleman (1961) conducted a now classic survey of adolescent attitudes and behaviors in various northern Illinois communities in 1955. Coleman was interested in studying both the secondary school experience and adolescent status systems. He found that rock and roll was the most popular form of music among both boys and girls. Girls liked to listen to records or the radio more than boys, a phenomenon Coleman explains with the observation that boys had a wider variety of activities available to them. Nevertheless, both boys and girls used rock and roll to learn prevailing values for gender roles. Girls used romantic ballads and fan club memberships to learn about boys, dating, and so forth. Boys used "less conventional" stars such as Elvis Presley to learn about adventure and masculinity. Overall, Coleman (1961:236) viewed rock and roll positively, as "music and dancing provide a context within which (teenagers) may more easily meet and enjoy the company of the opposite sex." Many teenagers were "passionately devoted" to rock and roll (Coleman 1961:315).

These early sociological observations have been lost in a sea of criticism of the impact of rock and roll on adolescents (Martin and Seagrave 1992). This criticism began in the 1950s with dramatic efforts to eliminate rock and roll. Organized burnings of Elvis Presley records because of their alleged association with sinfulness and sexuality were common in fundamentalist communities. In the 1960s critics argued that rock and roll music was unpatriotic, communistic, and the cause of drug abuse. In the 1970s and 1980s the criticism became organized and sophisticated. Middle-class activist organizations, such as the Parents Music Resource Center (PMRC) led by Tipper Gore, opposed rock and roll for its alleged deleterious effects on the health of young people. In the 1990s we find several court cases in which the prosecution or the defense have attempted to legally link rock and roll with suicide and criminal behavior, respectively (Hill 1992).

Allan Bloom (1987) wrote one of the most elegant intellectual attacks on rock and roll. Bloom, a professor of social thought at the University of Chicago, argued that American universities are in a state of crisis because of their lack of commitment to traditional intellectual standards.

Bloom further argued that young people live in a state of intellectual poverty: "Those students do not have books, they most emphatically do have music" (Bloom 1987:68). Plato, Socrates, and Aristotle all viewed music as a natural mechanism for expressing the passions and preparing the soul for reason. University students' overwhelming choice in music today, rock music:

> has one appeal only, a barbaric appeal, to sexual desire—not love, not *eros*, but sexual desire undeveloped and untutored . . . young people know that rock has the beat of sexual intercourse. . . . Rock music provides premature ecstacy and, is like the drug with which it is allied. . . . But, as long as they have the Walkman on, they cannot hear what the great tradition has to say. And, after its prolonged use, when they take it off, they find they are deaf. (Bloom 1987:68–81)

In general, critics have viewed rock and roll as either a social problem or a major cause of other social problems. This chapter provides a contrasting argument. I am not arguing that rock and roll music does not have its shortcomings. My purpose is to show, however, that the effects of rock and roll music on its audiences vary. The specific positive function discussed in this paper is the many different ways rock and roll integrates families and serves as a bridge across generations. This generational bridge allows children, adolescents, and adults to share communication, affect, morality, ethics, and meanings.

One major reason critics focus on the dysfunctions of rock and roll is because they ignore the increasingly obvious fact that rock and roll is pervasive in American culture (Kotarba 1994). We now have three generations who have grown up with rock and roll music. For them, rock and roll is the preeminent form of popular music. It serves as the soundtrack for everyday life, providing the context for phenomena such as commercials, patriotic events, high school graduations, political conventions, and so forth. The functional or positive experiences of rock music simply do not attract the attention of observers, such as journalists and social scientists, whose work is structured around the concept of "the problem." In order to understand the pervasiveness of rock and roll and its positive as well as negative functions, I propose to reconceptualize it as a feature of children's culture.

ROCK AND ROLL AS A FEATURE OF CHILDREN'S CULTURE

Conventional social scientific thinking posits rock and roll as a key element of youth culture. The concept "youth culture," which can be traced at least as far back as the works of Talcott Parsons (1949), commonly denotes those everyday practices conducted by adolescents that serve: (1) to identify them as a specific generational cohort, separate from children and adults; (2) as common apparatus for the clarification and resolution of conflict with adults; and (3) to facilitate the process of socialization or transformation into adulthood. Conventional thinking isolates certain socioeconomic and cultural developments since World War II to construct an explanation for the historically integrated, coevolution of teenagers and rock and roll (Frith 1981). This theory argues that teenagers were a product of the postwar family. The general cultural portrait of this family is one of middle-class aspiration if not achievement, suburban orientation, affluence, and consumption. Teenagers in the 1950s comprised not only a demographic bulge in the American population but also an economic force. Teenagers are viewed as a product of the following formula: allowances + leisure time + energy + parental indulgence. Rock and roll music became an available and useful commodity to sell to teenagers. The music could be readily duplicated, the themes could directly address the angst and adventure of adolescence, and the 45 rpm record could be made disposable through the process of the Top 40.

As the postwar generation grew into adulthood in the 1960s, they took the previously fun-filled rock and roll and turned it into a medium for political dissent and moral/cultural opposition to their parents' generation. But, as the baby boomers reached full adulthood, they traded in their passion for rock and roll for country music and muzak, leaving succeeding generations of teenagers to consume the hegemonic cultural pablum of formulaic rock and roll and MTV (Grossberg 1987).

A powerful cultural experience such as growing up with rock and roll cannot be simply be left behind by moving through the life cycle. One would reasonably expect to find at least some residual effects of rock and roll on adult baby boomers. If rock and roll affected the way they dated, mated, and resisted, then one would reasonably expect rock and roll music to affect the way they work, parent, construct and service relationships, and in other ways accomplish adulthood. Paradoxically, the presence of rock and roll in the lives of adults as well as adolescents can be discovered by locating it in the lives and culture of children.

Postmodernism is a useful analytical framework for guiding the search for rock and roll music in the nooks and crannies of everyday life. Postmodernism reminds us that contemporary social life is mass mediated. Culture is less a reflection of some underlying, formal, firm, structural reality than it is an entity in its own right (Baudrillard 1983). Postmodernism allows the observer to see things not previously visible. For example, postmodernism recently has let us see gender as a critical factor in the process of writing history. Instead of gazing directly at the alleged facts of the past, postmodernism allows historians to focus on the process by which history itself is written. Similarly, postmodernism lets the sociologist analyze cultural forms such as rock and roll as free-floating texts with their own styles of production, disseminations, interpretations, and applications to everyday life situations. Therefore, at least hypothetically, rock and roll is no longer (if it ever was) simply a reflection of the structural positions of adolescents in western societies, no longer a possession of youth. Rather, cultural items in the postmodern world become available to anyone in society for their individual and subcultural interpretation, modification, and application. We now witness white, middle-class kids listening to and enjoying gangsta' rap music. We see Bill Clinton belting out a bluesy-groove on his tenor sax, first at his appearance on Arsenio Hall's television program during the presidential campaign and later at one of his inaugural parties. To see rock and roll as a feature of children's culture helps us see its presence in all generations. The concept "children's culture" denotes those everyday practices: (1) used by children to interpret and master everyday life; (2) created, acquired, disseminated, and used by adults to construct and define parental relationships with children; and (3) ordinarily associated with children and childhood, yet used by adolescents and adults to interpret, master, or enjoy certain everyday life situations. Children experience rock and roll as children. Adolescents experience rock and roll to extend childhood. Adults experience rock and roll to relive childhood.

In the remainder of this Chapter I offer an inventory of rock and roll experiences across generations to illustrate this argument. I emphasize those rock and roll experiences most taken for granted by professional and lay observers alike, because those experiences function positively as elements of children's culture. I conclude with a brief discussion of the contribution of this style of analysis to the social scientific literature on rock and roll.

METHODOLOGICAL APPROACH

My methodological strategy is *ethnographic tourism*. This study is ethnographic, because it attempts to describe rock and roll in terms of the natural situations in which it occurs and in terms of the language, feelings, and perceptions of the individuals who experience it. The metaphor "tourism" applies to this study the following way. Most social scientific research occurs in the researcher's native land. The researcher assumes that the phenomena (or features of the phenomena) in question are to be discovered, because they are hidden by a background of an otherwise familiar and plausible world. The researcher identifies cases for analysis through rational, systematic sampling. This logic fits best when the researcher assumes that the phenomena in question are relatively rare (e.g., deviant behavior or minority groups).

When the researcher assumes that the phenomenon in question is everywhere, then he or she should act like a stranger or tourist in a foreign land. No setting should be taken for granted. The goal is to *see* the phenomenon where it was previously ignored by both researchers and members. Rock and roll fits this scenario. My primary research strategy involved observation of ordinary, everyday life activities of ordinary people.

I enlisted two kinds of assistance from the students in my undergraduate course in the sociology of rock and roll. First, they each wrote a narrative description of a typical week in their families. They described all the ways rock and roll music became relevant to parents, siblings, and themselves. Second, they conducted conversational interviews with a sociological range of individuals (i.e., of differing gender, age, and ethnicity). They interviewed these respondents not as rock and roll fans but simply as people for whom rock and roll is in any way relevant.

Other sources of data or information were derived from my own observations of myself, my wife, and our three children—all rock and roll fans. Finally, I derived ideas from formal studies of rock and roll phenomena (Kotarba 1994).

ADOLESCENTS AS CHILDREN

As mentioned above, standard wisdom on rock and roll argues that it functions largely to establish adolescence as a distinct stage in the life cycle. Furthermore, rock and roll is seen a weapon in conflicts between adults and adolescents. The mass media contribute to this overstated, overromanticized view of rock and roll and adolescence. The film *Footloose*, for example, portrays the plausible scenario in which fundamentally conservative, small-town adults view rock and roll as an evil influence on their teenagers. Rock and roll is portrayed in the film as the gauntlet that forces teenagers to choose between good and evil by choosing their parents or dancing. The rebellious imagery of Elvis Presley portrays a prevailing cultural myth that allies rock and roll with youthful rebellion, unbridled sexuality, cross-ethnic intimacy, and a wide range of delinquent activities.

These cultural images support an ideological vision of youth culture that overemphasizes the independence, rebellion, and integration of teenagers. A revisionist or postmodernist reading of this history finds much more diversity within youth culture. For every Elvis Presley fan in the 1950s and 1960s, there was an "American Bandstand" fan. "American Bandstand," especially in its early days when it was broadcast live after school from Philadelphia, portrayed rock and roll in much milder and more acceptable (to adults as well as teenagers) ways. The kids on "American Bandstand" were all-American kids. They dressed modestly and neatly. They all chewed Beechnut gum, provided by the sponsor of the program. And, above all, they were extremely well-behaved. The boys and girls, especially the "regulars," tended to match up as boyfriends and girlfriends, not as potentially promiscuous dates and mates. "American Bandstand" probably represented most teenagers in American society at that time. And, teenagers could not participate in activities such as "American Bandstand" without the approval, if not support, of their parents. After all, someone had to drive the kids to the studio or at least give them permission and money to take the bus there, just as someone had to provide the television and permit watching "American Bandstand" at home.

Parents were and continue to be cautious supporters of their children's rock and roll activities. There is more tendency among parents to manage rock and roll as though their teenagers are children who need to be nurtured and protected, rather than adolescents who must be controlled, sanctioned, and feared. For example, my current research on heavy metal and rap music has found the continuance of three generations of ambiguous parental feelings of cautious support toward rock and roll. At a recent Metallica concert at the Astrodome in Houston, numerous teenagers indicated that their parents did not approve of heavy metal music for various reasons (e.g., volume, distortion, immorality, and potential affiliation with evil such as satanism). Yet, the same parents carpooled their teenagers and friends to the Astrodome on a school day and, in most cases, bought or provided the money for tickets. A similar situation exists among African-American and Hispanic parents facing the popularity of rap music among their teenagers (Kotarba 1994). Mass media–generated images of obstinate, if not rebellious, youths generally ignore the reflexive relationship between teenagers and their parents. As long as teenagers live at home as legal, financial, and moral dependents—that is, as children—their parents provide the resources for creating rock and roll identities (e.g., allowances, free time, and fashionable hip hop clothing). Parents then respond to the identities they helped create by controlling, criticizing, sanctioning, and punishing their teenagers for living out their rock and roll–inspired identities—responding to them as if they were autonomous, responsible adults.

From the teenagers' perspective, rock and roll is commonly an extension of childhood experiences. The Summer of Love in 1967 is a case in point. Mass media accounts treat the Monterey Music Festival and Haight-Asbury as benchmarks in the emergence of the youth counterculture. The Summer of Love marked the fulfillment of rock and roll as an instrument of adolescent rebellion, within a context of heavy drug use, free love, and political liberation—a clash between young people's values and those of their parents. The media argue that the political events of the late 1960s institutionalized and radicalized the unbridled, individualistic and existentially youthful rebellion of the 1950s and early 1960s.

A revisionist, postmodernist reexamination of these events suggests that the innocence of middle-class, postwar, baby boom childhood served as the primary metaphor for these young people. High status was attributed to the "flower child," whom the counterculture posited as the innocent who simply rejected the oppression of the adult establishment. Women in the movement with high status were known as "earth mothers," who nurtured themselves and their peers through natural foods, folk arts, and the ability to roll good joints for the group. Whereas the mass media stresses the centrality of Jimi Hendrix and Jim Morrison to the music of this period, more childlike songs such as Peter, Paul, and Mary's "Puff, the Magic Dragon" and Jefferson Airplane's "White Rabbit" (inspired by *Alice in Wonderland*) were at least as significant. The 1960s generation popularized the use of animation as a format for rock and roll (e.g., the Beatles' *Yellow Submarine*). Perhaps most interesting to my argument is the way the 1960s generation drifted away from the adult world of commercialized and confined concert halls to the parklike atmosphere of the open-air concert festival, where the audience could play with frisbees and other toys.

The baby boomer generation's attempts to maintain the feeling of childhood through rock and roll extends into their encounter with adulthood. Through the 1980s and 1990s, the baby boomer generation has been the strongest supporter of contemporary versions of the rock and roll festival. Every large- and most medium-size cities now have what are referred to as "shed venues." These outdoor concert sites, such as Ravinia in Chicago, Wolf Trap in Washington, D.C., and Miller Theater in Houston, serve as the setting for baby boomers to bring their blankets and their picnic baskets—and often their children—to hear concerts by New Age performers. New Age music, by the way, fits my broad definition of rock and roll. It is simply mellow, electronically amplified music appreciated by adults who want to extend their rock and roll experiences, but who for physical or status/cultural reasons choose to give up the volume and anxiety of pure rock and roll.

Adolescents today continue to experience rock and roll qua children at play. In 1984, Van Halen's "Jump" was a very popular, hard rock song. Many lay and professional critics of hard rock chose to interpret the song as an invitation to youthful suicide. It appeared that the kids did not. At the Van Halen concert held in the Summit in Houston that year, the fans—who appeared to range mostly from 14 to 17 years of age—let out a collective scream when Eddie Van Halen began the song with the now-famous keyboard riff. At the chorus, when David Lee Roth shouted "Jump," 18,000 teenagers did just that: they all jumped up together like a bunch of little kids in the playground during recess.

Even the darker moments of rock and roll have their childlike attributes. Teenage fans commonly experience heavy metal music as a mechanism for managing lingering childhood anxieties. Metallica's "Enter Sandman" was a popular video on MTV during 1991–92. As part of an ethnographic study of homeless teenagers, we asked these kids to talk about their music. This particular video was very popular with them. We asked them specifically to interpret a very old, scary-looking man in the video. The street kids tended to see the man as a reflection of their own real nightmares, such as physically abusive parents and drug-infested neighborhoods. In a contrasting set of interviews with middle-class kids, we commonly heard them say that the man represented nightmares, but only the inconsequential nightmares children have and ultimately outgrow (Kotarba 1994).

CHILDREN AS CHILDREN

The pervasive mass media increasingly expose young children to rock and roll. The Teenage Mutant Ninja Turtle rock concert tour, Saturday morning television (e.g., the "M.C. Hammer" cartoon program), and performers such as Michael Jackson all focus on preadolescent audiences. It does not stop there. Several school supply companies are now marketing math and reading enhancement programs based on the rock and roll idiom.

But beyond simple marketing, rock and roll informs our general cultural views of children. "Honey, I Blew Up the Kid" was a popular film comedy in 1992. The story line had a bumbling, scientist father mistakenly turning his infant into a colossus. As the child innocently marched down a boulevard in Las Vegas, he grabbed the large, neon-lit guitar from the roof of a bar and proceeded to pretend to play a rock and roll song. (A generic, rock-a-billy song was actually playing in the film's background). The guitar served as a toy for the baby. The imagery suggested the baby as adolescent, an absurdity that helped establish the overall absurdity of the story.

Young children can grasp rock and roll even when it is not intentionally produced for or marketed to them. When Los Lobos recently covered the 1950s hit "La Bamba," it became a hit among elementary school-age children. Like many rock and roll songs, young kids find its simple lyrics silly and its beat fun to dance around to. As country music broadens its appeal by "crossing over" to rock and pop music audiences, it also creates an audience of children. Billy Ray Cyrus's recent rockabilly hit "Achy Breaky Heart" has become a fun song for many children.

ADULTS AS CHILDREN

Adults who grew up on rock and roll may want to relive the fun, excitement, or meaningfulness of their earlier music experiences. This can happen two ways. First, adults may simply retrieve the past through nostalgia. In many cities, oldies rock music stations are the most popular radio stations, catering to an audience approximately 24 to 45 years of age. Rock and roll nostalgia also appears in the guise of circa 1950s and 1960s clubs. These clubs are often decorated in postwar diner motif, offering period food such as meatloaf sandwiches and malted milk shakes. Parents and their children dine to piped-in oldies, within an atmosphere resembling that of the "Happy Days" television program.

Rock and roll nostalgia is interesting because of the types of music chosen by programmers to attract and please their audiences. The music is typically 1950s style rockabilly or early 1960s pop rock (e.g., the Beach Boys and Motown groups). The primary audience for oldies programming, however, grew up with the somewhat harsher and harder music of the later 1960s (e.g., psychedelia and antiwar music). Most choose to forsake their own music for the easygoing, fun music of their older siblings. In the language of postmodernism, the oldies culture is a *simulacrum* (cf. Baudrillard 1983). It never existed in its original state as it is now presented to consumers. Again, adults commonly choose to relive the childlike side of their reconstructed adolescence, not the adult side.

Second, adults may engage in continuous rock and roll experiences that are constructed in the present. Many adults, especially males, maintain their original interest in rock and roll. They are visible at live concerts of 1960s performers who are still "on the road" (e.g., the Rolling Stones, the Who, and the Moody Blues). They continue to buy recorded music, although much less than teenagers do. An intriguing bonding and gift-giving ritual among middle-class and middle-age adult males is the exchange of tape dubs. One fan will purchase a new recording (preferably on compact disc) and proceed to dub high-quality cassette tape copies for distribution to neighbors, coworkers, business associates, and others with similar tastes. Van Morrison fans are a good example.

Adults may also use rock and roll as a medium for rebellion. Practical and proven strategies developed during adolescence to enrage parents and other adults are retrieved to use against current opponents, such as wives. I have heard of men who turn up their stereos at home simply to aggravate their wives. In contrast, I have also heard of wives who banish their husbands to the basement or the garage to play their loud music, similar to the shaming banishment of a cigarette-smoking spouse to the backyard.

ADULTS AS PARENTS

As we have seen, members of all generations use rock and roll music in everyday life. The major argument of this chapter, however, is that rock and roll also serves as a bridge across the generations. Rock and roll is shared by children, adolescents, and adults. As one would easily guess, much of this sharing takes place within the family. Yet, contrary to common wisdom, we will argue that much of this sharing is functional and positive: rock and roll helps integrate families.

From the early days of Elvis Presley to current issues surrounding rap music, our mass culture has portrayed rock and roll as a source of tension within families (Martin and Segrave 1988). Whether this conflict is over lyrics or volume or whatever, the fact is that children could not experience rock and roll without the implicit if not explicit support of their parents (as we have seen in the cases of "American Bandstand" and Metallica). The cultural pervasiveness of rock and roll lets rock and roll function in many different ways in the family, much like religion or television. In this section, I will present an inventory of these-largely-taken-for-granted positive features of rock and roll.

Mother and Daughter Bonding

Rock and roll has always served as a special commonality between mothers and daughters. They shared Elvis Presley in the 1950s, Frankie Avalon and the Beatles in the 1960s, and Neil Diamond in the 1970s. In the feminist era of the 1980s and 1990s, however, the object of sharing shifted to other women. Madonna is a case in point.

Madonna represents a rock and roll phenomenon that is attractive to both mothers and daughters. Madonna is a multifaceted star whose appeal rests upon life-style, clothing style, and attitude as well as musical performance. During the Houston stop on the "Like a Virgin" tour, I interviewed a number of mother-daughter pairs who attended. The pairs typically were dressed alike, in outfits such as black bustiers and short black skirts, with matching jewelry. During the interviews, they talked about Madonna in similar ways and appeared more like friends than family. In virtually all cases, they noted a distinct lack of true appreciation of Madonna by the men in their lives (e.g., fathers, husbands, brothers, and boyfriends who may look at Madonna and only see a sex object). In most cases, the mothers also indicated that Madonna served to bring them closer to their daughters. Other female rock and roll performers who fit this category include Cindy Lauper and Annie Lennox.

Father and Son Bonding

Fathers and sons also use rock and roll music to bond, but in different ways than one might expect. Fathers who learned to play guitar in the 1960s teach their sons how to play. Sharing music is difficult, because today's younger generation adopts the traditional ideological belief that their music is better than that of their parents. Fathers and sons are considerably more vehement than women in their allegiance to their generation's music. During our study of the rave phenomenon in Houston (Kotarba and Hurt 1993), we heard one 16-year-old boy exclaim: "I hate my dad's music. He listens to that old shit, like Led Zeppelin." On the other hand, recent trends such as rave (i.e., dance parties held in clandestine locations, to the beat of loud synthesized music) display a renaissance in the 1960s counterculture. Psychedelia is "in," for example, with LSD as the drug of choice and lighting provided by mood lamps. Teenagers see rave as a way of retrieving the romance and simplicity of the 1960s. In a way, these kids accept their parents' claim that growing up in the 1960s was special. Another example is Deadhead fathers and their sons sharing the Grateful Dead experience.

In my own family, I recall a very special rock and roll experience with my oldest son, when he was 5 years old. We were driving out to a fishing hole in my old pickup truck, when the local hard rock radio station began playing songs from the Van Halen album "1984." This is one of my all-time favorite albums and, in a sociological sense, definitive of the state of rock music in the mid-1980s. When the pounding, driving anthem "Panama" came on the radio, it began with the loud rumble of a motorcycle taking off. Chris proceeded to jump around in his seat to the excitement of what he knew as the "motorcycle song." Like any proud baby boomer father, a tear left my eye when I realized that my son was okay . . . he liked rock and roll.

Family Leisure Activities

Rock and roll fits well with the burgeoning family leisure and vacation industry. Family theme parks typically have some attraction related to rock and roll, such as the complete mockup of a 1950s small town main street in the Fiesta Texas park in San Antonio. The artists performing at the amphitheaters in the Six Flags parks included (in the summer of 1993) REO Speedwagon, an Eagles reunion band, and the latest version of the Jefferson Airplane/Starship.

Whereas the concept of family entertainment in the 1950s, 1960s, and 1970s referred to phenomena such as wholesome television programming, Walt Disney films, and home games, it increasingly refers to rock and roll today. The rock and roll presented usually addresses a common denominator acceptable to both parents and children, such as rockabilly or 1970s power pop (e.g., REO Speedwagon and Cheap Trick).

Religious Socialization

Rock and roll functions as a mechanism for teaching religious beliefs and values in families, whether or not rock and roll is compatible with the particular family's religious orientation. For mainstream Protestant denominations, rock and roll increasingly fits the liturgy. For example, when Amy Grant played the Summit in Houston several years back as part of her "Angels" album tour, her music was loud and fast (e.g., seven- piece band with double drummers and double lead guitars). Parents accompanying their children to the concert peppered the audience. One father, in his thirties, brought his wife and 10-year-old daughter to the concert (which he learned about at his Lutheran church). When I asked him about the compatibility of Christian rock music with Christianity, he stated: "We love Amy Grant. She is married and tours with her husband, which is not the case with regular rock stars. Her songs are full of Christian messages. Any way you can get the message of Christ to your kids is OK with us."

The variety of Christian rock styles is growing. A particularly intriguing version is Christian heavy metal (Kotarba 1991). One rock club in Houston routinely books Christian heavy metal bands on Sunday evenings. One evening, they booked a Christian speed metal band, which played extremely loud and fast music about Christ. I talked to several parents who accompanied their children to the concert. The parents were very polite, clean-cut, middle-class, Southern Baptists surrounded by a sea of punk rockers and headbangers. They struck me a being much like the parents of the "American Bandstand" generation discussed above. They created the opportunity for their teenagers to attend the concert by carpooling them and their friends in from the suburbs. They hoped that the message emanating from the long-haired rockers was indeed Christian, but they wanted to see for themselves to make sure that Satan was not infiltrating the event.

Certain Christian denominations, such as Assemblies of God Church, view rock and roll of any kind as evil, whether under the guise of Christian rock or not. Parents in this faith focus their attention on rock and roll as a way of establishing moral boundaries for their children. For example, a very popular video among Assemblies of God youth ministers is called "Rock and Roll: A Search for God." The producer, Eric Holmberg, displays numerous rock album covers to illustrate his argument that rockers, especially heavy metal rockers, advertently or inadvertently proclaim satanic messages. For fundamentalist parents, rock and roll functions as a convenient and accessible way of teaching their children clearly and directly that Satan and evil are present in today's world and can take various attractive forms.

Moral Socialization

Rock and roll functions as a mechanism for articulating general moral rules and values for particular groups. Although the PMRC has a broader political base, it supports the religious right's concern for the threat rock and roll poses to the moral, physical, and psychological health of children (Weinstein 1991). For middle-class and upwardly mobile African-American parents, rap music clarifies the issue of gender abuse within their community (cf. Light 1992). In a more institutionalized sense, rap music is becoming the medium of choice among inner-city teachers for transmitting emerging moral messages. For example, rap music is now allowed in the Houston public schools' student talent shows. The local news regularly highlights school programs in which students use the rap idiom to convey antismoking and antidrug messages.

Historical Socialization

Families use rock and roll to relay a sense of history to their children. For example, every year on Memorial Day in Houston, various veterans' organizations sponsor a concert and rally at the Miller Outdoor Theater. Most of the veterans present fought in Vietnam, the first war for which rock and roll served as the musical soundtrack. Most of the veterans bring their children to the event. Among the messages and information available to the kids is the type of music popular during the war. A popular band regularly invited to perform is the Guess Who, whose "American Woman" was a major anthem among soldiers. I have observed fathers explaining the song to their teenage and preteen children, who would otherwise view it as just another of Dad's old songs. The fathers explain that the song had different meanings for different men. For some, it reminded them of girlfriends back home who broke up with them during the war. For others, the title was enough to remind them of their faithful girlfriends back home. For still others, the song reminded them of the occasions when they were sitting around camp, smoking pot and listening to any American rock and roll songs available as a way of bridging the many miles between them and home. In Houston, Juneteenth and Cinco de Mayo activities function much the same way for African-American and Hispanic families, respectively.

CONCLUSION

I have only touched on the many ways rock and roll music functions positively for people, especially in terms of family integration. There are obvious limitations to this study. The illustrations certainly do not represent all rock and roll experiences in a systematically sampled way. My generalizations are clearly based on the experiences of white, middle-class rock and roll fans and their families. Nevertheless, I would argue that the principles of culture use discussed here apply across subpopulations in our society.

The intellectual field of social problems is predicated on the assumption that social phenomena can be denoted as "problems," because they somehow differ from the norm, the reasonably expected, or simply other phenomena. When a phenomenon is pervasive throughout or endemic to a group, it is difficult to call it a problem. Rock and roll is a social problem only if one assumes that it is limited to a portion of the population (teenagers) who use it to harm themselves or others. However, rock and roll "belongs" to all portions of the population.

These findings are evidence for the argument that the true "cause" of social problems associated with children and adolescents lies beyond the music they choose to listen to. On the one hand, rock and roll simply serves too many positive, integrative functions for its audiences to be considered a "problem" in its own right. On the other hand, these findings strongly suggest that we look deeper for the roots of children's and adolescents' problems, for example, in the structure of the family itself. Rock and roll is all too often merely a convenient scapegoat for other problems.

REFERENCES

Baudrillard, J. 1983. *Simulations*. New York: Simeotext.
Bloom, A. 1987. *The Closing of the American Mind*. New York: Simon & Schuster.
Coleman, J. S. 1961. *The Adolescent Society*. Glencoe, IL: Free Press.
Frith, S. 1981. *Sound Effects*. New York: Pantheon.
Grossberg, L. 1992. "Rock and Roll in Search of an Audience." Pp. 152–75 in *Popular Music and Communication*, edited by J. Lull. Newbury Park, CA: Sage.
Hill, T. 1992. "The Enemy Within: Censorship in Rock Music in the 1950s." Pp. 39–71, in *Present Tense: Rock & Roll and Culture*, edited by A. deCurtis. Durham, NC: Duke University Press.
Kotarba, J. A. 1991. "Postmodernism, Ethnography and Culture." *Studies in Symbolic Interaction* 12:45–52.
_____. 1992. "Conceptualizing Rock Music as a Feature of Children's Culture." Presented at the annual meeting of the Society for the Study of Symbolic Interaction.
_____. 1994. "The Postmodernization of Rock Music: The Case of Metallica." Forthcoming in *Adolescents and Their Music*, edited by J. Epstein. New York: Garland.
Kotarba, J. A., and D. C. Hurt. 1993. "The Rave Scene in Houston, Texas: An Ethnographic Analysis." Paper presented at the annual meeting of the American Sociological Association, Miami, FL.
Light, A. 1992. "About a Salary or Reality: Rap's Recurrent Conflict." Pp. 219–34 in *Present Tense: Rock and Roll and Culture*, edited by A. DeCurtis. Durham, NC: Duke University Press.
Martin, L., and K. Segrave. 1988. *Anti-Rock: The Opposition to Rock 'n' Roll*. Hamden, CT: Archon.
Parsons, T. 1949. *Essays in Sociological Theory, Pure and Applied*. Glencoe, IL: Free Press.
Weinstein, D. 1991. *Heavy Metal: A Cultural Sociology*. New York: Lexington.
Wilson, S. Le R. 1989. *Mass Media/Mass Culture*. New York: Random House.

Part V

SCHOOLS AND CHILDREN

Chapter 9

Normalizing Daycare—Normalizing the Child: Daycare Discourse in Popular Magazines, 1900–1990

Donileen R. Loseke and Spencer E. Cahill

While I personally believe that children benefit much more from having a full-time parent, I realize it is wishful thinking to expect a return to "Ozzie and Harriet" style families.

—Senator Orrin Hatch, *Nation's Business* 1988

Who cares for America's children? Increasingly, the answer is "paid daycare providers." True, some Americans still object to the extrafamilial care of young children, and some children do not react to such care as positively as expected or hoped. Yet, from all indications, parental reliance on daycare is growing and will continue to do so in the immediate future (Hofferth and Phillips 1987). "Whatever the effect on the children . . . high quality, reliable day care is a blessing for parents" (*Newsweek* 1984). Daycare has been transformed from a "luxury" into a "right" (*McCalls* 1968). It now is described as a "basic family need" (*Newsweek* 1984) and a "permanent necessity for modern mothers" (*Parents'* 1982). In the words of the celebrity pediatrician T. Berry Brazelton, "daycare is here to stay. It's not whether we do it, but whether we do it right" (*U.S. News and World Report* 1987, emphasis in original).

But how did daycare become such an unquestioned part of modern American life? In an earlier article (Cahill and Loseke 1993), we examined discourse about daycare in popular magazines published between the end of World War II and 1985. There, we drew inspiration from Foucault (1977), who suggests that social formations, such as commoditized extrafamilial care of young children, are neither sudden inventions nor the inevitable products of historical development. Rather, they are gradually and often haphazardly constructed out of multiple, overlapping, and sometimes contradictory forms of social discourse and practices with long histories. Our examination of popular daycare discourse indicated that the construction of extrafamilial child care as an unquestionable necessity of modern American life involved the discursive linkage of daycare to the special needs of modern children, the childrearing deficiencies of modern families, irresistible economic forces that necessitated mothers' employment, and the plight and rights of modern women. Throughout this discourse, the authoritative voice of "scientific experts" on child development repeatedly advised that the correct training of children required an expertise that few modern parents possessed. With this scientific seal of approval, daycare was normalized, and its opponents could be dismissed as a "vociferous minority" who are "out of touch with parents' feelings, behaviors, and the realities of modern life" (Kamerman and Kahn 1979:81).

Although the normalization of daycare is the central plot in popular American discourse, it is not the whole story. The normalization of daycare both depended on and contributed to the discursive normalizing of child care and the child. In this work, we focus on the discursive construction of "normal child care" and the "normal child" as crucial subplots to the normalization of daycare in popular American discourse.

THE DISCURSIVE FIELD

In our earlier analysis of popular daycare discourse, we examined 62 articles published from 1946 through 1985 in popular American magazines. Here we reach deeper into the past and closer to the present. From its first edition in 1900 though the 1990 edition, the *Readers Guide to Periodical Literature* lists 989 articles under such headings as "Day Care," "Nursery School," and "Play Schools." The following examination of popular daycare discourse draws from 122 of those articles (see Appendix A for a list).

Because our interest is in popular daycare discourse, we excluded from consideration articles published in magazines with limited and specialized audiences. These included articles published in periodicals with limited regional markets (e.g., *The New York Times Magazine*), in those appealing to an occupationally specific audience (e.g., *Architectural Record*), and in those published by or on behalf of voluntary, religious, or professional associations (e.g., *Rotarian, American Catholic, Elementary School Journal*). Excluding these left us with 386 articles.

Based on two further considerations, we selected 122 of these articles for examination. First, we wanted an adequate basis for historical comparison. Because only 30 of the 386 articles were published from 1900 through 1945, we selected all of these. Second, we wanted to sample a broad sweep of daycare discourse, so we classified the 356 articles published from 1946 through 1990 into three broad types: family/home (e.g., *Parents'*, *Good Housekeeping*), women's (*Redbook*, *Ms.*) and news/business (e.g., *Time*, *Business Week*). We then randomly selected about 26 percent of each type in each decade.[1] Our sample of 122 articles therefore is a historically diverse collection published in different types of magazines and written by a variety of authors with seemingly different interests and purposes. The following analysis of these articles focuses on the scientific normalization of childcare, children, and the means of their correct training.

THE SCIENTIFIC NORMALIZATION OF CHILD CARE

For it is a great new principle—the discovery, coming in along a dozen lines of science, that every single part of the raising of little children is as important for their future as every other part; that right daily habits of digestion, sleep, exercise, are as important for health as feeding; that these same daily habits, and right emotional control, are the very center of moral training and mental health; that moral training and mental health are necessary to enable the child to learn.

—*Woman's Home Companion*, 1933

Our earlier article (Cahill and Loseke 1993) concluded that the authoritative voice of scientific experts was critical to the discursive normalization of daycare as an unquestioned necessity of modern American life. Because that powerful scientific voice also formed the crucial discursive building blocks of normal child care and the normal child within these mass media articles, we will begin with this scientific normalization of child care and the child.

The twisted history of organized daycare in the United States reaches back into the nineteenth century when "child saver" reformers provided custodial care for the "day orphans" of poor working women. These philanthropic and reformist efforts are one thread of daycare's history. Another thread was spun by the early twentieth-century nursery schools that appealed to upper-middle class, primarily academic parents (Joffe 1977). Although these two forms of extrafamilial child care were initially quite distinct and their respective proponents often at odds, they soon became entangled. For example, by the early 1900s, many philanthropic reformers were convinced that it would take more than mere custodial care to save disadvantaged children from their certain and unfortunate fates. Reformers then hoped that day nurseries would use educational principles to transform the "puny, nerveless, half-fed offspring" of the poor (*Charities* 1904) into "good men and women and good citizens, instead of [the] invalids, insufficients, or mendicants" (*Charities* 1902) that they would otherwise become. By 1919, the "enlightened nursery" was posed as a model for the "community of the future" where all children were "owed" the experience of extrafamilial care. Although distinctions continued to be drawn between "day nurseries" and "nursery schools," those two threads of extrafamilial child care were gradually woven into a single discursive cloth. During World War II, *Parents' Magazine* (1944a) declared that "the child-care center" was the "wartime name for all day-nursery school." In 1963, *Ladies Home Journal* informed its readers that "early-childhood educators are generally agreed that, no matter what the preschool groups call themselves, all are essentially the same in that they provide care, protection and education for children." Two decades later, *Better Homes and Gardens* (1984) announced that the "distinction between preschool and daycare has blurred as more centers offer educational programs and more preschools offer full-day care." Reflecting this discursive conflation, the *Readers' Guide to Periodical Literature* dropped the heading "Nursery School" in the mid-1980s in favor of the single heading, "Day Care."

Although the history of daycare practice is one of custodial care and educational training, the history of daycare discourse in these popular magazines is that of constructing daycare as a single discursive form of scientific, and therefore, educational child care. The foundation for that construction was the definition of early childhood as the most developmentally crucial stage of life. The folk wisdom, "as the twig is bent, the tree is inclined" (*Parents'* 1937), received scientific confirmation on the pages of these magazines. As early as 1919, Olivia Howard Dunbar reported that "psychologists, physiologists, and educators" were in agreement that early childhood was critical for education and that "education can not begin too early" (*Good Housekeeping* 1919). Nearly 50 years later, the venerable Dr. Benjamin Spock informed the readers of *Redbook* (1967) that from the "point of view of psychological principles, the first three years of a child's life are the most formative." And, as the Educational Policies Commission sponsored by the National Education Association and the American Association of School Administrators concluded, this suggests that "starting a child to school at six is out of date" (*Good Housekeeping* 1967). Indeed, parental education might even help ensure that "babies" and "infants yet unborn" get the best start in life

(*Ladies Home Journal* 1971). According to popular daycare discourse, the human twig is bent quite early and it should be bent with scientific precision through early childhood education.

Clearly, "education" is about far more than intellectual development, for a "wealth of research on early childhood development [attests] to the now widely held conviction that the preschool years are crucial in setting the pace and tone for a child's future intellectual and emotional development" (*Parents' Magazine and Better Family Living* 1972). Daycare could set the proper pace and tone through its "para-academic program ... [focusing] on the child's whole development—social, creative, aesthetic, emotional, physical and intellectual" (*Ladies Home Journal* 1971). Just as clearly, the stakes reportedly were high. Because "unhappy childhoods lead to unhappy adults" (*Ladies Home Journal* 1956*)*, there is, according to Sarah Comstock, a "terrible truth: childhood maladjustments, if not corrected, may yield, in later years, unhappiness in home, social, and business life; in extreme cases, bodily or mental breakdown, delinquency, failure in lifework, divorce, crime, or death" (*Good Housekeeping* 1937). Given such a terrible truth, Doctor-Father Benjamin F. Miller drew the obvious conclusion: Because "emotional illness and instability are now the major problems of childhood and adult life ... Good nursery schools should be made available to all our young children" (*Parents'* 1952). Neglecting such education causes far more than intellectual problems—it "can often lead to delinquency and mental and health problems" (*U.S. News and World Report* 1976). The mothers of children enrolled in nursery schools reportedly learned this terrible truth and how to prevent their own children's lives from confirming it. For example, Billy's nursery school teacher convinced his mother that "the trouble must be cured. If it goes on, Billy will be an aggressive, selfish man, socially unfit" (*Good Housekeeping* 1937). Similarly, Skipper's mother learned that certain tendencies in children must be handled, because "if not curbed, [they] may warp the pattern of his living with other children" (*Parents'* 1944b).

The discursive formulation of daycare as the means of correct training for the young rested on its identification with the latest scientific principles of child development. Initially, those were scientific principles of physical growth. In the first article on daycare to appear in a truly mass media magazine, Mary Bronson Hartt informed the readers of *Good Housekeeping* (1911) that the ideal was for "scientific baby experts" to plan children's diets at daycare centers. In 1923, a little over a decade later, Ethel Puffer Howes praised nursery schools for their ability to "apply all our new knowledge about little children" (*Woman's Home Companion*). According to Edna Brand Mann (*Parents'* 1929), this "new knowledge" was about more than children's physical development, for in nursery schools "every activity, every toy, every move by the teachers is based on a scientific study of the needs and nature and educability of young children." Andrea Fooner (*Working Woman* 1982) was no less impressed over 50 years later by a daycare center that was "based on the most up-to-date knowledge of young children's intellectual, social and emotional development." The discursive construction of daycare as the correct means of training the young built on the authority of scientific discourse. The science of child development established the correct means of training, and daycare put those principles into practice.

This discursive formulation of childrearing as a scientific enterprise implied that care providers should be scientifically trained professionals: "Well run centers are designed to stimulate intellectual, social, cultural, and emotional development of children by employing experts in early education" (*Business Week* 1970). Because "child psychologists consider training especially critical for alerting providers to children's needs" (*U.S. News and World Report* 1987), it follows that untrained care providers are clearly inferior to certified child care professionals (*Good Housekeeping* 1988); a good daycare provider is necessarily "trained and certified in early childhood education" (*Good Housekeeping* 1967).

Although wrapped in the discursive cloak of science, this formulation of childrearing as a scientific enterprise did not necessarily involve a radical break with the more traditional emphasis on the importance of the home and mother to a child's training. Rather, nursery schools and daycare centers were compared to a disappearing traditional home. Popular discourse in the early part of the century likened the atmosphere at daycare centers and nursery schools to that of a "well-regulated home" (*Woman's Home Companion* 1920, 1931). In 1933 (*Woman's Home Companion*), Dorothy Canfield asked readers "Which corresponds more closely to that old-time home? The solitary young mother with one child or two in an apartment or small house . . . or the nursery school with a sizable group of children?" Her obvious answer was the nursery school. Daycare—not the modern family—provided "the preschooler the sort of education he got naturally in the homes of yesterday" (*Parents' Magazine and Better Homemaking* 1961). That is in large part because good daycare providers are women with a "true motherly instinct" (*Woman's Home Companion* 1931). They are "warm and sympathetic" (*Parents' Magazine and Better Homemaking* 1961), "warm and caring" (*Better Homes and Gardens* 1984), and just plain "motherly" (*Parents'* 1952).

Although popular discourse described the daycare center as "home for these children, and teacher is the daytime mother" (*Parents'* 1944a), traditional familial childrearing did not escape criticism. The training of children in the home was called "haphazard" and contrasted to "the needed skilled training" (*Good Housekeeping* 1937). The childrearing methods of older relatives were particularly suspect. In 1931 (*Woman's Home Companion*), a working mother complained that her child was becoming very unpleasant, because her mother was "raising him in the good old-fashioned way, based on mother love, in which child psychology played no part." Over 30 years later, a child development expert warned parents of just such a possibility if they relied on relatives for child care because there cannot be "complete confidence that the grandmother's methods are up to date" (*Redbook* 1967). Moreover, popular daycare discourse left little doubt that the "most up to date methods" of childrearing were those based on the scientific principles of child development and psychology—the methods employed in nursery schools and at well-run daycare centers.

Although experts complained that the majority of "American families don't necessarily believe that child care is much more than baby sitting" (*Business Week* 1989), on the pages of these magazines child care was discursively cast as a scientific enterprise and daycare as the most reliable method of this correct training. Daycare "extended scientific upbringing below the knee-pants level to youngsters aged 2 to 5" (*Newsweek* 1939), and parents were advised that they "should study [scientific] methods and conform to the same means of management at home to get the best results" (*Parents'* 1937). But, what are "the best results?" If the purpose of daycare is to "bend the twig in the right direction from the start" (*Parents'* 1937) we might well ask what kind of child and adult scientific daycare is designed to produce. How should the tree incline as a result of the scientifically precise bending of the twig?

THE SCIENTIFIC NORMALIZATION OF THE CHILD

> Whether a young child develops an active desire to learn, a belief that learning is attractive and that he can do it, or whether he becomes a passive endurer of schooling ... largely depends on what he gets to know about the world and his place in it during his preschool years.
>
> —*Parents' Magazine and Better Family Living* 1972

Although correct training seems necessarily guided by an image of its intended results, the discursive relation between daycare and guiding images of the normal and normative child and adult were complex. According to popular discourse during the first half of the twentieth century, daycare was as much a scientific means of establishing standards of normality as it was a scientific practice of producing children who conformed to those norms. For example, in 1919 (*Good Housekeeping*), Olivia Howard Dunbar praised the work of the Iowa Child Welfare Research Station for its "scientific conservation and development of the normal child" but she was chagrined when one of the professors there told her that "nobody knows what constitutes a normal child." As Nell B. Nichols reported to readers of *Woman's Home Companion* in 1930, "until a decade ago . . . little was known of the pre-school child," but that was changing thanks in no small part to daycare. In 1923 (like today) nursery schools provided a "wonderful opportunity for training student assistants" whose "absorbing interest in the psychological problems each of the children presented was a pleasure to see" (*Woman's Home Companion* 1923). At those managed by universities, "children are watched more particularly for scientific results of diet, habit and development" (*Woman's Home Companion* 1931), and daycare centers served as "laboratories to gather statistics on what makes Tommy tick and when and how" (*Parents'* 1944a).

This careful observation and study led to the establishment of scientific standards of normality. By the 1930s children's physical development could be precisely assessed in terms of a "government standard height, weight and age chart" (*Parents'* 1937). An even more impressive diagnostic tool was the method of "picturing and charting the child's personality" developed at the Merrill-Palmer School. As readers of *Woman's Home Companion* learned in 1930, "personality as it is rated at this school does not consist merely of pleasing smiles and neat bows." Rather, personality was divided into five parts: "pep," "mental effectiveness," "emotional control," "ease of social adjustment," and "skill in work and play." Each of these parts was further subdivided into 20 characteristics allowing precise comparison and ranking of children's personalities on a 100-point scale.

In addition to the development of scientific standards of normality and diagnostic methods, daycare provided an opportunity to identify and correct problems and characteristics that might adversely affect a child's "normal" development. During play at nursery schools, the "child airs certain disturbing problems which results from something in his home situation: difficulties with a new brother or sister, reactions toward an over rigid mother, competition with an older child" (*Parents'* 1952). These are easily observed and recognized by professional child care providers who "attempt to identify the strengths and weakness of each child and give him special opportunities to eliminate his deficiencies" (*Ladies Home Journal* 1971).

Thanks to daycare, then, it was possible to identify "children with unfortunate personalities" (*Woman's Home Companion* 1930), it was possible to "dream of a day when maladjustments may take their place with smallpox—among the almost-wiped-out diseases!" (*Good Housekeeping* 1937). The reported diagnostic and therapeutic benefits of daycare were indeed impressive. For example, it helped little Alvin recover from the frightening experience of confinement to a "preventorium" after his mother was diagnosed with tuberculosis (*Ladies Home Journal* 1956). Such schools were especially good for "youngsters who are physically and mentally handicapped" (*Parents' Magazine and Better Homemaking* 1967). The nursery school experience of a blind child, for example, was so "successful" that she "sailed through three grades in her local school" according to her mother (*Ladies Home Journal* 1956). Also as a result of his daycare experience, one "four year old considered retarded graduated to kindergarten a normal 5-year-old" (*Newsweek* 1967). Daycare even helped boys from female-headed households learn lessons about fathering and masculinity that they could not learn at home (*Newsweek* 1967). Such daycare success stories discursively demonstrate its normalizing influence and they also discursively imply some of the defining characteristics of the normal and normative child. The normal child has a "merry face," a "pleasing personality," no physical or mental disabilities, a healthy gender identity, and the intelligence to sail through school.

Popular daycare discourse also implied that the normal child came from a middle-class home. Throughout the twentieth century, readers of popular American magazines were informed that poor children especially needed and benefited from the normalizing influence of daycare. In 1923, a *Woman's Home Companion* story reported the success of a nursery school for poor children in "making over those little creatures, stunted in body and soul, into tall, beautiful, intelligent, normal children" Over four decades later, a nursery school in Detroit was reportedly introducing "slum children" who were used to hearing "one-syllable words" at home to "a brave new world" (*Newsweek* 1967). The normalizing influence of daycare was especially important for children of "welfare mothers" who lacked "a series of values and initiatives which would work against the poverty-welfare cycle." It could "provide the children with a program of education designed to make them healthier, happier, and better equipped for life than their parents" (*Redbook* 1971). The "necessity of early intervention to educate disadvantaged children" (*Ms.* 1988) was no less pressing at the close of the 1980s when Massachusetts Governor Dukakis told *Time Magazine* readers (1987) that "child care is an absolute precondition if one is serious about trying to help people lift themselves out of poverty." According to such popular daycare discourse, the normal child was articulate, respectable, and equipped for life. Daycare could produce children who were more successful—more normal—adults than their parents.

Although popular daycare discourse implied that certain characteristics were not normal and not normative, it was somewhat less clear and consistent about what characteristics are. As one author lamented, "we still lack a thoughtful discussion of what kind of person we want to develop through our present planning for children" (Ms. 1974). Vague assertions that daycare provides "education for citizenship" (Parents' 1934) or that "preschool education of the right sort helps lay the groundwork for a happy life as a useful member of the community" (Parents' 1944a, emphasis in original) had not encouraged such a discussion. Over time, popular discourse credited daycare with fostering quite different desirable characteristics. During the first half of the century, characteristics such as "obedience to authority" (Parents' 1929), "control of body, control of emotions" (Parents' 1931), and "good manners" (Parents' 1944a) were commonly mentioned as desirable characteristics promoted by daycare, whereas later in the century articles praise daycare for making children more "self-assured and outgoing" (McCalls 1985) and for fostering their "self-esteem and curiosity" (Working Mother 1989).

However, throughout these years, three normal and normative characteristics encouraged by daycare were consistently mentioned: independence, sociability, and academic readiness. For example, in 1937, the readers of Parents' were rhetorically asked why a preschool child should not learn "how to be self-reliant . . . through contact with his peers in nursery school." Thirty-four years later, parents were reportedly paying for costly daycare, because they "feel their children grow in independence" (Better Homes and Gardens 1972). The normal child also is sociable and therefore relishes the contact with peers that daycare provides. For decades, popular American magazines have been telling readers that children are "always anxious to play with other children" (Parents' 1943) and are "social creatures who enjoy the company of other children" (Parents' 1983). Finally—and not surprisingly—the normal child is the academically prepared child. Such children "always stand well in the competition of the public schools" (Charities 1904), they know how to "fit better into school routines" (Ladies Home Journal 1951), how to "adapt to regular school routines" (Better Homes and Gardens 1972). Simply stated, the normal child knows the "rules of the game before [getting] to elementary school" (Newsweek 1984).

Although often implicit, vague, historically variable, and multidimensional, the normal child of popular daycare discourse is self-reliant, socially adjusted, and schooled in schooling. Such a child is a product of the normal and normalizing training of daycare. What, then, are the specific scientific means of producing such an independent, sociable, and school-ready child? Popular daycare discourse provides some answers.

SCIENTIFIC MEANS OF CORRECT CHILD TRAINING

Mendel's 900 Kinder-Care Learning centers are clean, well lit places. . . .
Currently, the chain handles about 100,000 "units" in 42 states. In Kinder-
Care parlance, a "unit" is a child.

—*Newsweek* 1984

Popular daycare discourse is admittedly complex, inconsistent, and
often contradictory. Nursery schools and daycare centers reportedly
resemble both the idyllic home of the past and the formally organized
school of today; daycare providers are described as both caring surro-
gate mothers and serious professionals. Articles in popular magazines
also tell of vast differences among the varied forms of daycare provided by employers, proprietary chains, religious and community organizations, school districts, and so-called family care providers (e.g.,
McCalls 1977; *Parents'* 1989). These articles even inform readers that
there are sharp disagreements among child development experts concerning how, specifically, to organize "the best early childhood education" (e.g., *Better Homes and Gardens* 1972, *Parents' Magazine and Better
Family Living* 1972).

Despite such diverse and often conflicting images and opinions, popular daycare discourse does paint a consistent picture of certain defining characteristics of "good" daycare. Such magazines assure readers
that "fortunately, there *are* objective criteria you can use to assess the
quality of care in the facilities you visit" (*Parents'* 1986, emphasis in original), and they offer readers checklists for evaluating daycare facilities
(e.g., *Better Homes and Gardens* 1990; *Parents'* 1977). The picture of quality daycare that these advisory articles paint is similar to the one that
informs the many calls for increased regulation of daycare (e.g., *Good
Housekeeping* 1988; *Nation's Business* 1988; *Parents'* 1987), for federal
involvement in that regulatory effort (e.g., *Business Week* 1990; *Ms.* 1988;
Nation's Business 1988) and for campaigns to "recruit, license, train, and
monitor" the now-unregulated, untrained, and unprofessionalized family daycare providers (*Good Housekeeping* 1988). It is a discursive picture
of professionalized and governmentally regulated daycare that employs
scientific means of correct training. There are many details such as recommended ratios of number of providers to children of different ages
and specific health and safety measures. We are not concerned with
these details but with the principal means of correct training that define
high-quality daycare in the pages of popular American magazines. Normalized environments, activities, discipline, and parenting provide

insight into the modern technology of manufacturing normal and normative persons.

Normalized Environments

According to popular daycare discourse, high-quality daycare facilities are equipped with "child-sized furniture" and other fixtures (*Ladies Home Journal* 1963); these places are designed and built "for the comfort and convenience of the small child" (*Woman's Home Companion* 1931). Such a miniaturization of the physical features of the environment is not only for children's comfort and convenience, for "[e]verything is for small people [because] the first law of a well-managed school of this sort is self-service" (*Woman's Home Companion* 1931). As one author wrote about her visit to a nursery school, "these children care for themselves. You see them remove their own wraps, hang them in a special locker . . . you see them sit down at small tables. . . . You see them wash at tiny lavatories" (*Better Homes and Gardens* 1934). Unlike the adult-size environment of the home, the daycare environment facilitates correct training, because it is a physical environment allowing independence and self-sufficiency. In such places "small boys and girls learn to use every bit of power they had to take care of themselves" (*Parents'* 1936).

The daycare environment is also equipped in a particular way. At the nursery school of the 1930s, there were "tools and crayons, paints and modeling clay, small indoor blocks, trains and dolls and housekeeping toys" (*Parents'* 1935). Similarly, the daycare center of the 1980s contained "easy-to-use art materials like nontoxic crayons, paints, and playdough . . . building toys, such as different types of blocks . . . toy people, cars . . . soft toys and dolls, toy dishes, and dress up clothes" (*Parents'* 1986). Like its child-size furnishings, these materials are provided not merely for children's comfort and convenience. Rather, they are the "special equipment" (*Redbook* 1961, 1971) that, as readers of *Woman's Home Companion* learned in 1931, " has been subjected to scientific studies." What young children need for normal growth and development are toys that "develop the smaller muscles, to train the senses and encourage imaginative play" (*Parents'* 1935), "puzzles and manipulative toys to allow [them] to discover concepts of shape and size" (*Working Woman* 1982), and "toys and games to build eye-hand coordination" (*Parents'* 1986). The presence of such special equipment is a defining characteristic of the high-quality daycare environment as the state of California confirmed in 1960 (*Time*) when it revoked the license of a previously well-regarded preschool for lacking "loose dirt for mud pies" and "tubs for water play."

The daycare environment is expansive as well. "Preschoolers have always needed space to run and climb" (*Parents' Magazine and Better Homemaking* 1961), and the daycare environment "provides more play space" than the modern home or apartment (*Good Housekeeping* 1967). It offers children "opportunities to run and climb both indoors and out-doors" (*Parents'* 1982). According to the National Association for the Education of Young Children, the daycare facilities should have "at least 25 square feet of indoor space and 75 square feet of outside play space" for each child (*Nation's Business* 1988). This extensive space provides children opportunities not only to run and climb but also for privacy. Articles in popular magazines advise that cots for nap times should be "set two feet apart for privacy" (*Ladies Home Journal* 1951) and that space should be "provided for children to play alone . . . protected from the pressure and competition of the other children" (*Parents'* 1986). Even the sociable child of daycare, it seems, needs some solitude.

Thus, the high-quality daycare environment is not one large disorga-nized space. Indeed, it is divided into different work and play areas (*Parents' Magazine and Better Family Living* 1972). There is space for pri-vate play and different "interest areas" (*Good Housekeeping* 1967). The young inhabitants of the expansive and well-equipped daycare environ-ment "paint at an easel or play house in the Creative Expression Room, assemble puzzles in the Small-Muscle Room, listen to music in the Sense-Perception Room, and let off steam by shouting and tumbling in the Large-Muscle Room" (*Ladies Home Journal* 1971). In the daycare envi-ronment, each activity has its proper place in the correct training of the normal child.

Children of different ages also have their proper and separate place in the high-quality daycare environment. Normal development reportedly requires that a child be "in a group keyed to his own age level" (*Par-ents'* 1941), and that toys and activities be "graded to a child's physical and mental development" (*Parents'* 1952). Thus, in the interest of correct training, the high-quality daycare environment has "special areas for each age group" (*Working Woman* 1982).

The discourse of popular American magazines leaves little doubt that the high-quality daycare environment is an important means of correct-ly training the young. Its child-size furnishings foster self-reliance; its sheer size and scientifically selected equipment promote the acquisition of physical and cognitive capacities and skills; its special segregation of different-age children and activities encourages orderly development. Yet, although important in and of itself, such a normalized environment also is the site for particular types of activities promoting the correct training of the daycare child.

Normalized Activity

The furnishings, equipment, and compartmentalization of the high-quality daycare environment provide only the infrastructure for correctly training young children through scientifically structured activity. Just as the physical environment of daycare compartmentalizes by function and age, high-quality daycare is temporally regulated. The professional provider of high-quality daycare knows that a scheduled routine is the correct means of training the young. As *Parents'* reported in 1931, "habits of neatness, of independence, of regularity are also developed by the routine of the school." More recent articles in popular magazines apparently agree that temporal routines are important, because they advise parents to choose a daycare center with a "schedule covering basic care routines and play periods" (*Parents'* 1986) and to "look for a caregiver who structures the day into regular playtimes, mealtimes and nap times" (*Working Woman* 1982). Readers also are assured that such routines are in the best interest of the child, because children "crave routine" (*Working Mother* 1989).

Although a routinized day is discursively produced as good for the child, it seems that not just any set of activities will do. As *Ladies Home Journal* warned its readers in 1971, it is clearly "a disaster to waste a child's early years—when he is best amenable to environmental influences—by placing him in the average poor preschool with no organized program." A routine fostering normal development apparently should not include the activity of "watching television," because a horrified mother reported finding children at one daycare center "all lined up in front of the TV like a bunch of zombies" (*Time* 1987) and U.S. Representative Dale Kildee told a writer for *Ms.* (1988) of the daycare "horror stories" of "kids sitting around vegetating in front of a television all day." High-quality daycare is not a place where children are found "wandering aimlessly" or "just sitting and staring blankly"; it is a place where children are "busy and involved" (*Parents'* 1982).

As readers of *Good Housekeeping* learned in 1970, "a day-care center, says the U.S. Children's Bureau, should offer a program designed to promote a child's growth and development" High-quality daycare requires a "thoroughly planned program" (*Woman's Home Companion* 1953), a "planned program for the day, every day" (*Woman's Home Companion* 1933); it includes "planned activities that encourage child development" (*Nation's Business* 1988). Those planned activities may sometime include formal instruction. Some propriety chains of daycare centers, for example, provide teachers with curricular manuals such as "a social studies Theme of the week and cognitive activities in readiness and language arts" (*Ms.* 1975), and some preschool teachers are praised for making "lesson plans for infants" (*Time* 1987). Yet, even if there are no formal lessons, parents are instructed to look for daycare providers who "are observed to *teach* children" (Parents' 1982, emphasis in original). At the minimum, high-quality daycare provides "guided play" (*Working Woman* 1982). The professional provider of such daycare has "the training to be the kind of creative companion the child should have" (*Newsweek* 1967). She knows that "peek-a-boo" teaches an infant about "object permanence," that infants are engaging in "prehensile activities" when they are "shaking a toy," that a game of "finding the ball" is an exercise in "verbal decoding." Such a knowledgeable teacher, therefore, guides children's play along a course of normal growth and development (*Ladies Home Journal* 1971).

Popular daycare discourse has long maintained that children enjoy the planned and scheduled activities of high-quality daycare. As an author for *Woman's Home Companion* told an anonymous, fictional child in 1929 who had just arrived at a nursery school, "now you are ready for the day's work. You are not only ready but eager because all your work, though serious and important, is really play." At nursery school, "play is the *business* of the runabout child, for through it he learns about himself, his limitations, his powers and creative ability" (*Parents'* 1931, emphasis added). And, "then, as now, nursery-school life was a lark," for children "with plenty of room, air, and light, and constant opportunity for making friends, . . . have fun and at the same time absorb the complicated rules of social living" (*Newsweek* 1939). Such discursive formations of normalized activity within a normalized environment produce children as willing, happy, and active participants in their training. Daycare, though, is discursively produced as being about more than correct training disguised as fun.

Normal Discipline

The planned program of activities and temporal routine of high-quality daycare are means of correct training that introduce discipline into young children's often unruly lives. Popular daycare discourse leaves little doubt that young children require such discipline to "absorb the complicated rules of social living" (*Newsweek* 1939). Children are reportedly prone to "uncontrolled aggressiveness, natural curiosity about sex, the craving and competition for the teachers' affection, tantrums, excessive shyness" (*Parents'* 1952); the important principle of "social sharing" might be "quite incomprehensible to most three and four-year-olds" (*Woman's Home Companion* 1953). Given such a discursive production of the normal child, it is not surprising that "all nursery school experts believe that three and four year olds need control" (*Redbook* 1961).

High-quality daycare includes control, yet it certainly does not depend on harsh discipline. On the contrary, the professional providers of high-quality daycare seem keenly aware of the importance, power, and methods of gentle discipline. Unlike mothers who still rely on traditional methods of toilet training, "the women in charge of nursery schools have studied enough to understand the importance of bringing those bodily functions under control without leaving ragged scar tissue in the child's nervous system." Trained providers are far more professional than the mother whose "rotten day with her toddler ended with a spanking" (*Woman's Home Companion* 1933). Because trained teachers seek "an attitude of cooperation" rather than "blind obedience to authority" (*Parents'* 1941), "punishment is not practiced" (*Parents'* 1982). Because providers of high-quality daycare are far too knowledgeable and professional to resort to such harsh and psychologically ill-advised discipline, it follows that "no spanking or corporal punishment is *ever* used, nor is harsh discipline such as shouting, shaming, or withholding of food" (*Time* 1986, emphasis in original).

Rather than harsh discipline, high-quality day care relies on "gentle compulsion in the matter of manners and morals" (*Good Housekeeping* 1911). Apparently, the key to this gentle compulsion is young children's normal sociability. According to popular daycare discourse, the unruly child is powerfully influenced by the contrasting example of other children's compliance. "The force of good example" (*Woman's Home Companion,* 1931) is powerful, because a child is "readily controlled by desirable group example" (*Parents'* 1944). Mrs. Edna Brand Mann illustrates the power of the group's example by writing from the perspective of a child who is enrolled in a nursery school where all the children must first stand behind their chairs before being seated for lunch. He continues to play, so that none of the other children can begin to eat. "You look around and you are the only one out of place and you feel very foolish. Morton and Alice are looking at you as if to say, 'hurry up, will you? You're keeping us all waiting with your silliness.' You stand behind your chair and then everyone sits down" (*Parents'* 1929). Likewise, when little Tommy does not like the food he is served at nursery school he eats it anyway, because "all the other children eat" (*Parents'* 1944a). Or, when a 5-year-old refused to feed himself, the trained teacher "pointed out to him that other children smaller than he were feeding themselves." In a few days, "he was eating normally and feeding himself altogether" (*Women's Home Companion* 1920).

In addition to the gentle compulsion of a desirable group example, high-quality daycare reportedly relies on another effective method of gentle discipline that exploits young children's normal sociability. Because children "prefer the companionship of teacher and playmates to solitary play" (*Parents'* 1952), "isolation of the offending child from the group" (*Parents'* 1929) is effective discipline. By 1946, child development experts were reportedly agreed that "if discipline is necessary, isolation has proved to be the most practical and effective method" (*Parents'* 1946). Over the years, the pages of popular magazines reported numerous examples demonstrating the effectiveness of this method of discipline. One teacher, for example, reported that this method proved effective in changing one young girl's eating habits: "Her reward for eating a good meal is to take her nap in the nursery with other children. If she does not eat well she must sleep alone" (*Woman's Home Companion* 1931). Or, after Mrs. Rice's shouting and scolding proved ineffective in silencing her son Buster's "bellows of wrath," a nursery school leader and "trained mother" reportedly took charge and led the other children indoors, leaving Buster outside howling.

> All at once an astonished Buster finds himself alone. He doesn't know that child guidance prescribes, "For tantrums, isolate." But he does know that he wants to go with the crowd, and it is a much subdued youth who comes running after, forgetting his howls and kicking. And the happy ending is: Everybody else forgets them. There is no retribution, . . . Simply he finds the social machine running smoothly for him as soon as he makes himself an agreeable cog." (*Good Housekeeping* 1937)

By the 1980s, popular daycare discourse had abandoned the term *isolation* and replaced it with *time out*, yet modern writers are no less enthusiastic about its effectiveness. According to one advisory article, reasonable discipline is easily maintained when there is "careful supervision, clear limits, age-appropriate explanations and use of time out" (*Parents'* 1986).

Unlike the mother or other care provider who attempts to train one or a few children in the privacy of her own home, the professional provider of high-quality daycare has the apparent advantage of training children in groups. He or she has no need for spanking, corporal punishment, or other harsh discipline that leaves "ragged scar tissue in the child's nervous system." Rather, such a provider can rely on the gentle, safe, and effective methods of social comparison and isolation. As popular daycare discourse suggests, these methods of gentle discipline within the normalized environment with its normalized activities are essential to the correct training of the young. At the same time, such methods depend on another characteristic of daycare: examination.

Normalized Examination

Effective employment of gentle discipline and the means of correct training depend on the inextricably tied formulations of close observation, careful record keeping, and comparison—the examination. As *Woman's Home Companion* informed readers in 1921, nursery schools "offer both discipline and oversight." Since then, readers of popular American magazines have been repeatedly reminded that high-quality daycare is characterized by close and continuous observation of children: "Nothing escapes the teacher's eye" (*Parents' Magazine and Better Homemaking* 1961); "at least one adult is always with children" (*Parents'* 1982); "a caregiver closely supervises the children, staying near them all the time" (*Parents'* 1986). This careful and continuous oversight and supervision is about more than protecting children from physical harm. It is a means of maintaining "reasonable discipline" (*Parents'* 1986) and of identifying, diagnosing, and correcting problems that might interfere with the children's normal development. Indeed, a benefit of daycare is that the child in such care "can be more accurately measured than in any home" (*Parents'* 1934) and this "individual study of each child" is essential for the identification—and correction—of deviations from the normal and normative. With this goal, the "discerning" provider of high-quality daycare "can help a child with problems that are brought to her attention by observing his play" (*Parents'* 1952). Such a provider identifies problems through careful observation of each child and then "must quickly go on to help the child find the tools to solve his problem" (*Working Mother* 1989). Time out, in other words, is not enough for correct training. For example, after observing that Jamie was jealous of another child's possession of a favored toy, a nursery school teacher in the 1920s isolated him, yet she concluded on the basis of her observation that more elaborate measures would be required to ensure his normal development: "Jamie's fit of jealous temper was a problem needing serious study on the part of his teachers. He will be watched from now on, to be helped, and kept, to the right attitude" (*Woman's Home Companion* 1923).

According to popular daycare discourse, these diagnoses and prescriptions are based on scientific observation that involves "writing down the child's doings and sayings with scientific accuracy" (*Good Housekeeping* 1937). Furthermore, "results of these studies are [also] used for comparison" (*Woman's Home Companion* 1923). For example, the method of picturing or charting the child's personality developed at the Merrill Palmer school in the 1920s enabled precise comparison of a child's personality to those of "other children in the same group," and this allowed teachers to send parents "personality report cards" on their children (*Woman's Home Companion* 1930). Another nursery school teacher noted that they "grade the children according to cooperation; application; self-reliance; ability to carry out instruction; conduct [attitudes toward teacher and other children]; and health habits, rating them—poor, fair, good, excellent" (*Parents'* 1937).

Although such invidious comparisons and classifications of young children may seem antiquated, popular daycare discourse continues to imply that providers of high-quality daycare record their careful observations and evaluate each child's developmental progress and potential problems on the basis of those records. For example, in 1951, *Ladies Home Journal* informed its readers that "conscientious teachers note bowel movements" and conduct "monthly studies . . . of height, weight, and general physical development of each child" keeping "careful records" of the results. Twenty years later that same magazine informed readers that providers of high-quality daycare "attempt to identify the strengths and weakness of each child" and meet with parents "to discuss their child's progress" (*Ladies Home Journal* 1971). And, in the late 1980s, providers of such care still reportedly kept "parents closely informed about the child's development." The apparent implication is that providers of high-quality daycare closely observe each child, record their observations, and continually evaluate the child's progress and development in terms of scientifically established standards of normal development.

High-quality daycare becomes the means for the correct training of the young through the densely interrelated discursive formations of the normalized environment, activities, discipline, and examination. One further characteristic remains: extending such scientific methods of correct training into the home.

Normalized Parenting

By the 1990s the half-day, two-day-a-week nursery schools of the past have been all but replaced by all-day, everyday daycare centers. Although such a temporal extension of the daycare day is now discursively assumed a simple necessity for working parents, popular daycare discourse in the 1930s argued that the means of correct training required such extensive daycare. As *Better Homes and Gardens* informed readers in 1934, many nursery schools were now keeping "the small pupils from 8:30 or 9 in the morning until 3 or 4 in the afternoon . . . so that all the important habits—eating, sleeping, toilet training—can come under expert supervision, as well as attitudes toward their fellows and toward life itself." Another article lamented that a particular nursery school was only open from 9 to noon, because "the added benefits to the children of trained supervision of their eating and napping would make the longer day thoroughly desirable" (*Parents'* 1935).

Although the scientific means of correct training might be best for the child's development, it remains that children still spend time with their parents. And this time outside the daycare environment is discursively produced as a problem for normal development. Indeed, the majority of children "would be happy, reasonably well-behaved young citizens if the home in which they are acquiring their life pattern were not faultily adjusted" (*Good Housekeeping* 1937). Given this, it is important to extend scientific methods of correct training into the home. This "business of parent education is to get at the root disease" (*Good Housekeeping* 1937). "Teaching mothers is important work" (*Charities* 1904), for "it is important for mothers to know enough of what experts know about the mental and physical hygiene of little children" (*Woman's Home Companion* 1923). By educating parents, high-quality daycare can thereby extend its characteristic methods of correctly training the young beyond the nursery school and daycare center into the home.

The pages of these popular magazines report considerable success in training parents in the skills of scientific child training; they report how mothers are simply transformed for the better by what they learn in working with a trained director. Mothers, for example can learn the skill of scientific observation. So, mothers of children in one nursery school learned to observe their children more carefully and to make records while observing:

> the mothers sit informally around the edge of the group and each spends her time recording what her child does and says. ... [The teachers] encouraged the parent to write down exactly what she saw her child doing, how long he did a certain thing and what he said. The records are used by the mother to help her learn how to study her child. (*Parents'* 1944)

Mothers, then, can be taught to record "not the 'cute words' and 'sweet Dolly Dimple ways' of saucy young Jim and fluffy little Edna. But a scrupulously honest statement of facts to show you the child's and your own mistakes" (*Good Housekeeping* 1937).[2]

Mothers also can learn the scientific means of correct training by observing trained teachers, so "an untaught mother learns ... as much as she can absorb of the educational principles behind the nursery's mothering of her own and other children" (*Good Housekeeping* 1919). Through observing expert teachers, "she learns what you can and can't expect of small children. In watching a teacher handle specific problems, she learns new methods of dealing with these problems at home. Parent-orientation programs ... make her aware of specific teaching techniques and the needs of each age group" (*Good Housekeeping* 1960).

Mothers also can be taught to observe themselves. As Mrs. Jeanne Van Note (*Parents'* 1944b) confessed, "frankly, it had never occurred to me that I needed special training in my career as mother." Yet, she visited her son Skipper's nursery school and happily reported that what she learned there "is helping me to observe myself as well as my child. As a result I am becoming a more understanding and relaxed person."

Mothers also can learn the scientific method of comparison. For example, Josephine Poynter (*American Home* 1947) confessed that her son Dickie was "opposite of what I thought a little boy should be." However, after observing him with other children at nursery school and after talking to his knowledgeable teacher, Mrs. Poynter realized that she had been expecting too much of Dickie and that he was "actually a normal three-year-old." Betty's mother reportedly learned a more disturbing lesson. "Betty had . . . all sorts of fears and anxieties . . . that her mother didn't know how to cope with. It was at nursery school that the teacher and mother together discovered that she wasn't really ready for life in a group but we needed first the special help of a child guidance clinic" (*Woman's Home Companion* 1953).

According to popular daycare discourse, high-quality day care is as much about the correct training of parents as of children. Given the discursive construction of scientifically designed daycare as normal and normative, it is not surprising that in 1936, *Parents'* reported to their readers that the "meaning and value of nursery school procedures were interpreted to the parents, thereby helping to put child training on a twenty-four-hour-a-day basis." And popular daycare discourse left little doubt that home training should resemble the training provided by high-quality daycare. The prominent daycare advocate Edward Zigler's vision of the "21st Century School" is a case in point: "His idea was that the public school buildings already in existence could be used for more than formal schooling; they could also provide . . . on-site day care for three- to four-year-olds . . . assistance and home visitation to new parents, [and] information and referral services for parents from pregnancy on" (*Parents'* 1989). Within such a twenty-first-century school, the scientific methods of correct training are all-pervasive.

CONCLUSION

Adjustments to school, athletics, job, marriage and parenthood are all important ones. They are part of the tough, competitive world in which we must live. If a youngster is prepared for such experiences early in childhood . . . he has a better chance of adapting to new experiences smoothly. If not, nervous upset may be the result of stressful situations.

—*Parents'* 1952

An ideal form of scientific childrearing was discursively constructed in the pages of popular American magazines during the twentieth century. Articles published in those magazines defined that discursive ideal as the skilled practice of scientific means of correct training so as to bring young children into conformance with scientifically established standards of normal and normative human development. Popular daycare discourse provided numerous rhetorical justifications for this ideal during the first half of the twentieth century but eventually took the desirability of such scientific training for granted. Now it is simply dubbed "high-quality daycare" and implicitly assumed that this scientific child training is what both young children and their parents want and need. In these closing years of the twentieth century those who advise, train, and regulate child care providers are left with the responsibility of realizing this ideal of high-quality daycare (e.g., Goetz, Turnbull, and O'Brien 1984; Gotts 1988; Nurss and Hough 1983; National Association for the Education of Young Children and the National Association of Early Childhood Specialists in State Departments of Education 1991).

Twentieth-century Americans' increased and increasing reliance on extrafamilial child care may be a response to contemporary social and economic circumstances, but the discursive ideal that is now popularly called "high-quality daycare" has a more impressive genealogy. As we concluded elsewhere (Cahill and Loseke 1993), this discursive ideal—"institutionalized, professionalized and governmentally regulated group care of children"—is "a recognizable progeny of discourse and social arrangements which have proliferated since the beginning of modern times." Foucault's (1977) analysis of eighteenth-century discourse strongly suggests that the discursive and practical roots of such extrafamilial care reach at least that far into the past.

The defining characteristics of the popular discursive ideal of high-quality daycare in twentieth-century America are the means and methods of correct training and discipline that were developed and perfected in the prisons, armies, schools, hospitals, and asylums of eighteenth-century Europe. Like the factory, the school, the asylum, or the hospital, high-quality daycare, as described in the pages of popular American magazines, involves the "enclosure" of young children in a protected place (Foucault 1977:141). That enclosed place of daycare is further partitioned, creating functional sites for specific activities (p. 143) and a serial space of compartments for children of different ages or developmental rank (p. 145). Within such scientific daycare, the children's activities follow an expertly designed "time-table" (p. 149). Like the school, factory, hospital, or prison, children in daycare are under constant surveillance by trained daycare providers. Indeed, through hierarchical observation in a relay of gazes between daycare providers and parents, the surveillance of children is total (pp. 177–76). Daycare providers are among the latest "judges of normality" (p. 304) who identify gaps between each child's own development and scientific standards of normal and normative development. Once identified, they correct such deviations from the normal and normative through the application of gentle punishments that have proven effective in the school, the factory, the asylum (pp. 177–84). The providers of high-quality daycare repeatedly examine each child, document their findings and construct a textual "case" (pp. 184–92). They are even judges of parental normality who identify and correct parental deviations from scientific methods of normal and normative childrearing.

As Foucault (1977:211) argues, these means and methods of correct training and discipline constitute the modern technology of "making useful individuals." The discourse of popular American magazines during the twentieth century leaves little doubt that high-quality daycare is precisely such a technology. This discursively ideal form of child care reportedly trains young children to "substitute speech or reasoning for the more emotional forms of response" (*Parents'* 1941), to "accept and understand the rules and regulations, the prohibitions and rewards of our society" (*Parents'* 1952), to "accept a friendly adult as an authority figure" (*Ladies Home Journal* 1971), and to "become productive members of society" (*Nation's Business* 1988). Readers are warned that without such correct training of the young the workforce of the future will lack needed skilled labor (*Ms.* 1988).

High-quality daycare is apparently a necessary technology for making the useful individuals that American society will need in the future, because its defining methods and means of training and discipline resemble those of the modern barracks, factory, school, hospital, and prison (Foucault 1977:228). In an important sense, it is merely another application of a tried-and-true technology for making useful individuals. It merely starts that process earlier in life, producing a normal child who is prepared to be fashioned into a serious student, dedicated soldier, conscientious worker, cooperative patient, and contrite prisoner—a "useful individual." It is hardly surprising, then, that such scientific means of correct training would become an unquestioned fact of modern American life—a life lived within a great carceral network of disciplinary mechanisms (Foucault 1977:304). That is the fate of the normal child and useful individual of the twentieth and, perhaps, the twenty-first century. As the popular daycare discourse examined here seems to conclude, it only makes sense that the young should learn to accept this fate at the earliest possible age.

NOTES

1. For the period from 1946 to 1990 there were a total of 356 articles in popular magazines. We selected 31 (26.5%) of the 117 articles in news and business magazines, 34 (25.8%) of the 132 articles in family or home magazines, and 27 (27.6%) of the 98 articles in women's magazines. These proportions are close to the 25.8% of the 356 articles from 1945–90 that our sample of 92 represents.

2. Such observation reportedly is absolutely discreet from the point of view of the child. As a 1937 issue of *Good Housekeeping* reported, mothers learned during their visit to a nursery school that children "are as unconscious of grownups as if in some world of childhood all their own. Meanwhile, mothers sit apart with the Director, studying them in their revealing play." Or, as a more contemporary mother happily reports as a benefit of a particular daycare site: "I can go into an observation room with a one-way mirror and audio and see what kind of day she's having" (*Good Housekeeping* 1990).

APPENDIX A: SAMPLE ARTICLES

American Home. 1947. "I Went to Nursery School" (Josephine Poynter). 37(March):102–5.

Better Homes and Gardens. 1934. "Shall I Send My Child to Nursery School??" (Gladys Denny Shultz). 13(October):48+.

_____. 1972. "How to Pick a Nursery School" (Gerald M. Knox). 50 (April):44+.

_____. 1984. "Finding the Best Day Care for Your Child" (Dan Kaecher). 62 (June):25+.

_____. 1990. "Finding Quality Infant Day Care: Care That's Good for Baby and You" (John Rosemond). 68 (April):53.

Business Week. 1970. "Day Care: It's a Lot More Than Child's Play." (March 21):110+.

_____. 1989 "Ring around the Rosie at Kinder-Care" (Chuck Hawkins). December 18:45–46.

_____. 1990. "This Man May Have Mike Milken's Number" (Chuck Hawkins and Bruce Hager). November 5:56.

Charities. 1902. "Problems of the Day Nursery" (Helen Thornton Higbie). 8 (June 13):541–42.

_____. 1904. "For What Does the Day Nursery Stand?" (Marjory Hall). 12 (June 23):764–67.

Good Housekeeeping. 1911. "The Day Nursery Problem" (Mary Bronson Hartt). 52 (January):21–27.

_____. 1919. "Community Mothering" (Olivia Howard Dunbar). 68 (January):17–18.

_____. 1937. "The Happiest School in the World" (Sarah Comstock). 105 (October):34+.

_____. 1953. "Nursery Schools" (Robert L. Faucett, M.D.). 137 (November):172+.

_____. 1960. "Just What *Is* a Co-operative Nursery School?" 151 (October):200.

_____. 1967. "Should a Child Go to Nursery School?" 185 (September):182–83.

_____. 1970. "The Facts about Starting a Day Care Center." 171 (September):156.

_____. 1987. "Daycare for Sick Children" (Denise M. Topolnicki). 205 (November):245.

_____. 1988. "Good News for Working Moms" (Mary Finch Hoyt). 206 (January):64+.

_____. 1990. "How Employers Are Helping Working Moms" (James A. Levine). 211 (September):150+.

Ladies Home Journal. 1951. "Working Mothers: San Diego's Problem." 68 (September):25+.

_____. 1956. "Children Get Loving Care" (Margaret Hickey). 73 (August): 21–22+.

_____. 1963. "Before Selecting a Nursery School: Stop, Look & Listen" (Stanley Schuler). 80 (October):60+.

_____. 1971. "Nursery Schools: A Primer for Parents" (Elliott H. McCleary). 88 (November):74+.

McCalls. 1968. "The Day Has Come for Day Care" (Elisabeth Stevens). 95 (April) 6–7.

_____. 1977. "A Dozen Ways to Solve Your Day-Care Problem" (Holly Hyans). 105 (October):112–13.

_____. 1985. "Reassuring Answers to 10 Myths about Day Care" (Carolyn Jabs). 112 (January):22.

Ms. 1974. "What about the Children?" (Ruth Sidel). 2 (March):38–39.

_____. 1975. "From the Folks Who Brought You Fast Food, Nursing Homes, and Minigolf . . . Vacuum-Packed DayCare" (Joyce F. Goldman). 3 (March):80–82.

_____. 1988. "At last! A Major Push for Child Care" (Mary McNamara). 16 (February):17–19.

Nation's Business. 1988. "Caring for the Children" (Roger Thompson). 76 (May):18–20.

Newsweek. 1939. "Romper Classes: Teachers' Plea for More Nursery Schools Menaced by Economy Drive." 13 (April 24):34+.

_____. 1967. "When Mothers Work." 70 (August 28):73.

_____. 1984. "What Price Day Care?" 104 (September 10):14–21.

Parents'. 1929. "School before Five" (Edna Brand Mann). 4 (December):17+.

_____. 1931. "How to Organize a Nursery School" (Mona Ames Marsh). 6 (June):26–28+.

_____. 1934 "When Is a Child Too Young to Learn?" (John N. Washburne). 9 (April):17+.

_____. 1935. "When Babies Go to School" (Jean McPherson Kitchen). 10 (March):6–17+.

_____. 1936. "Uncle Sam's Nursery Schools" (Edna Ewing Kelley). 11 (March):24–25+.

_____. 1937. "Play School for the Very Young" (Ruby Mack Bush). 12 (November):28–29+.

_____. 1941. "The Young Child Needs Companionship" (LaBerta A. Hattwick). 16 (September):24–25+.

_____. 1943. "Wanted, a Playmate" (Helen T. Aschmann). 18 (August):31+.

_____. 1944a. "What Are Child Care Centers?" (Juliet Danziger). 19 (August): 20–21+

_____. 1944b. "Laboratories for Parents" (Jeanne Van Note as told to May F. McElravy). 19 (October):26+.

_____. 1946. "Time Off for Mother" (Mary Wright Moscrip). 21 (March):42+.

_____. 1952. "What a Doctor-Father Thinks of Nursery Schools" (Benjamin F. Miller, M.D.). 21 (August):30+.

_____. 1977. "All about Day Care" (Stevanne Auerbach, Ph.D.). 52 (April):41+.

_____. 1982. "The Day-Care Child" (Alison Clarke-Stewart). 57 (September): 72–74+.

_____. 1983. "Ready for Nursery School?" (Lillian G. Katz). 58 (August):86.

_____. 1986. "Finding Good Child Care" (T. Haims). 61 (August):105–6.

_____. 1987. "Finding Quality Child Care." 62 (August):15.

_____. 1989. "21st Century School" (Rita E. Watson and Karen FitzGerald). 64 (October):112–18.

Parents Magazine and Better Family Living. 1972. "The New Look in Nursery Schools" (Julie Hoss). 47 (September):53+.

Parents Magazine and Better Homemaking. 1961. "Programs for Preschoolers" (Reynolds Sherwin, Ph.D.). 36 (June) 45+.

_____. 1967. "Urgently needed: More Day Care Centers" (Katherine Brownell Oettinger). 42 (November):58.

Redbook. 1961. "How to Choose a *Good* Nursery School" (Ellen Prince). 118 (November):36.

_____. 1967. "When a Mother Goes to Work" (Benjamin Spock, M.D.). 129 (June):20–22+.

_____. 1971. "The Town That Closed Its Doors" (Jean Evans). 136 (March): 88–89+.

Time. 1960. "Mud Pies and Water Play." 76 (August 29):47.

_____. 1986. "Tender Loving Care Inc." 127 (February 17):57.

_____. 1987. "The Child-Care Dilemma" (Claudia Wallis). 129 (June 22)54–60.

U.S. News and World Report. 1987. "Second Thoughts about Infant Day Care" (Art Levine, Kathryn Johnson, Marilyn Noore, and Henry Fersko-Weiss). 102 (May 4)73–74.

Woman's Home Companion. 1920. "The House of Happy Children" (Christine Terhune Herrick). 47 (October):44.

_____. 1923. "The Nursery School" (Ethel Puffer Howes). 50 (December):34+.

_____. 1930. "—In the Way He Should Go" (Nell B. Nichols). 57 (April):58+.

_____. 1931. "What about the Children: The Other Side of the Mother-in-Business Situation" (Anna Steese Richardson). 58 (January):21–2.

_____. 1933. "The Babies' Utopia" (Dorothy Canfield). 60 (March):12–13.

_____. 1953. "Is Nursery School the Answer?" (Dr. Millie Almy). 80 (September):18+.

Working Mother. 1989. "Get Good Child Care: 30 Revealing Questions to Ask" (Susan H. Kuefener). (May):90+.

_____. 1982. "Who's Minding the Kids?" (Andrea Fooner). 7 (May):99–102.

REFERENCES

Cahill, S. E., and D. R. Loseke 1993. "Disciplining the Littlest Ones: Popular Day Care Discourse in Post-War America. Forthcoming in *Studies in Symbolic Interaction*, Vol. 14, edited by Norman K. Denzin. Greenwich, CT: JAI Press.

Foucault, M. 1977. *Discipline and Punish: The Birth of the Prison*, Translated by A. Sheridan. New York: Random House.

Goetz, E., A. P. Turnbull, and M. O'Brien. 1984. "Helping Parents Work and Raise Children." *Daycare and Early Education* 11 (Summer):31–36.

Gotts, E. E. 1988. "The Right to Quality Child Care." *Journal of the Association for Childhood Education International* 64 (June):268–75.

Hofferth, S. and D. Phillips. 1987. "Child Care in the United States, 1970–1995." *Journal of Marriage and the Family* 49:559–71.

Joffe, C. 1977. *Friendly Intruders*. Berkeley: University of California Press.

Kamerman, S. and Kahn, A. 1979. "The Day-Care Debate: A Wider View." *The Public Interest* 54 (Winter):76–93.

National Association for the Education of Young Children and the National Association of Early Childhood Specialists in State Departments of Education. 1991. "Position Statement." *Young Children*, 46 (March)21–42.

Nurss, J. R., and R. A. Hough. 1983. "Providing High Quality Child Care." *Daycare and Early Education* 11 (Fall):33–35.

Chapter 10

The Medicalization and Demedicalization
of School Refusal:
Constructing an Educational Problem in Japan

Atsushi Yamazaki

The modern era in Japanese education began with an 1887 decree that provided for founding elementary schools, middle schools, and universities throughout the nation (Stevenson 1991:110). In the Meiji era (1868–1912), leaders established the school system as an instrument to select and train the able among the largest possible segment of the population (Sumiya 1971:148). Rates of primary school attendance rose from 40 percent for men and 20 percent for women in the early Meiji period, to 60 percent for men and 25 percent for women in the 1880s (Frost 1991:297). In 1909, compulsory education was extended to six years of elementary school education. Since 1925, over 99 percent of Japanese children have been enrolled in elementary school (Stevenson 1991:110). Following World War II, the Japanese educational system underwent many profound changes. Japan's 1947 Fundamental Law of Education requires nine years of education: elementary school (6 years, age 7–12) and junior high school (3 years, age 13–15). Even though high school (3 years, age 16–18) is optional, the number of youths attending high school has increased dramatically. In 1950, only 42 percent of Japanese youths attended high school; attendance exceeded 96 percent in 1986 (Inagaki 1986).

Throughout modern Japanese history, young people were always encouraged to "be somebody." Stories about lower-class children who had risen to positions of eminence in the bureaucracy or military service were common. Education has been one way people from the lower classes can climb the social ladder. At the same time, as status is not ascriptive, even the upper classes must re-create their social and economic status by having their children acquire the prominent academic background needed to maintain their family ranking in society. As the Japanese middle class grew in numbers and wealth after the 1960s, more parents wanted their children to enter higher education. The proportion of senior high school students sitting for university exams rose from 44 percent in the late 1970s to 50.2 percent in 1991 (Rosario 1992:22). *Ronin*—literally "masterless samurai"—students sitting for examinations for the second or third time, increased from 195,000 in 1980 to 294,000 in 1991 (Rosario 1992:22). Vertical social mobility through education has created "educational fever" (*kyoiku netsu*).

Generally, Japanese parents set high standards for their children's academic achievement. Japanese parents seem less concerned with the child's ability or desires than with the child's future social status (Ishida 1971). Children who receive good grades at school tend to be viewed favorably by their teachers and parents regardless of their other accomplishments, such as volunteer work and extracurricular activities. Parents are eager to send their children to a good high school so that they have the best possible chance of getting into the more prestigious universities, which in turn ensure better jobs and higher status. The Japanese "educational mom" (*kyoiku mama*) is concerned with her children's education and gives personal instruction at home. Even elementary school children are sent to cram schools (*juku*) that offer after-school classes in subjects such as mathematics, science, English, calligraphy, abacus (*soroban*), and music. According to the Yano Research Institute, the proportion of elementary students attending *juku* rose from 16.5 percent in 1985 to 44.5 percent in 1990, and the proportion of junior high school students rose from 18.6 percent to 52.2 percent (Rosario 1992:21). For many students, childhood has become a time of stress, and learning is reduced to the process of mastering exam skills. Most exams feature multiple-choice questions requiring an encyclopedic knowledge of information that most Americans would consider trivial (Frost 1991:291). The need to do well on college entrance exams shapes education in Japan.

Teachers are well respected in Japanese society and enjoy considerable social and economic status. Especially in rural areas, teachers are part of the local social elite. For centuries, the term used for teachers—*sensei*—has denoted a position honored by all Japanese (Stevenson 1991:113). As churches have little influence as agents of socialization, many parents expect their children's teachers to strengthen moral training. Compared to American teachers, Japanese teachers have more power socially and politically. It is not rare for children facing contradictory opinions from teachers and parents to believe their teacher is right.

Although Japanese high school students' scores are near the top in cross-national studies of achievement in science and mathematics

(Stevenson 1991:116), the darker side of Japanese education, such as physical abuse by teachers, students' attacks on teachers, vandalism, overemphasis on academic achievement, severe bullying by other students, diplomatism (*gakurekishugi*), "entrance exams hell" (*juken jigoku*), and school refusal (*toko kyohi*), is little understood in other countries.[1] School refusal (SR) involves students who refuse to or say they are unable to go to school for various reasons. It began to be recognized in the 1960s but became a visible social problem during the 1980s. First, SR students were regarded as truants, then as sick, and later as normal. The history of SR as a Japanese educational problem demonstrates how a nation's social structure and culture provide the context for social problems construction.[2]

In this Chapter I examine how SR was medicalized and subsequently demedicalized and how the processes of medicalization and demedicalization of SR were shaped by Japanese culture and social structure.

THE MEDICALIZATION OF SCHOOL REFUSAL

From Truancy to School Phobia

According to the Minister of Education (MOE 1984), until the mid-1950s, students who refused to or could not go to school were regarded as truants, not only by the general public but also by medical professionals. During the mid-1950s, Japanese educational research organizations and journals of child psychiatry and clinical psychology began describing cases of such students, but they did not offer a general interpretation (MOE 1984). Although some students persistently complained of fever, headaches, or stomachaches, those symptoms were not taken seriously, because they disappeared when the students were allowed to stay home from school. Because most of these students were regarded as truants and there was a norm that students should go to school unless they were sick, these students were sometimes forced to attend school by their teachers and parents. Because these students showed no serious symptoms, physicians, mostly pediatricians, began to suspect mental illness and sent their patients to psychiatrists. When they referred to American and British studies, psychiatrists were confused, because they could not find appropriate diagnostic categories. Some cases were diagnosed as autism, autonomic imbalance, or schizophrenia. By 1960, child psychiatrists and clinical psychologists were using the term *school phobia* (*toko kyofusho*) to describe the personality and behavior pattern of students who refused to or could not go to school (MOE

1984). Those medical experts began to study treatments and educational policies (MOE 1984).

From School Phobia to School Refusal

School phobia was described first by an American psychiatrist, A. M.
Johnson. According to Johnson, school phobia is caused by the child's
separation anxiety from the mother. Studies of school phobia by Japanese psychiatrists stressed the separation anxiety from the mother (Satou
1968), immature personality (Arioka and Katsuyama 1974), and
matrism—families lacking a father's authority (Hisatoku 1985). Typically, school phobia involves children under the age of 10 (Johnson et al.
1941). Although Johnson's discussion of school phobia only included
students afraid of attending school, Japanese psychiatrists used the term
to describe other types of students as well. In the late 1960s, some psychiatrists began to favor a diagnosis of school refusal (SR) (Hirai 1968,
1975, 1991) rather than school phobia, because SR, which is also of U.S.
origin (Warren 1948), can include various types of students, including
children over the age of 10. School phobia was now considered one kind
of SR (MOE 1984).

Although SR includes school phobia as well as other students who do
not or cannot go to school for other reasons, there was no unified definition of SR. Nobuyoshi Hirai is an influential psychiatrist and one of
the medical professionals who introduced the concept of SR in Japan.
He insists that SR is caused by an underdevelopment of independence,
which in turn is caused by an overprotective family (Hirai 1968, 1975,
1991). Another influential diagnosis was presented by Hiroshi Inamura,
a psychiatrist at Tsukuba University, who was often quoted by the
media, and who helped prepare the MOE's 1984 student guidance materials. According to Inamura, SR can be seen as one aspect of the "adolescent break-down syndrome" (1989): "school refusal is a kind of social
inadaptability. Unless school refusal students are cured appropriately,
they will be spiritless in their 20s and 30s" (Inamura 1989:ii). Although
there are many definitions of SR, according to Inamura, they can be
summarized into three types. The first involves neurosis and excludes
truants, psychosomatic SR, temporal SR, and ideological SR students
who oppose the present educational system. The second type of definition is broader and includes all of the patterns above except psychosomatic SR. The third type includes all students who do not go to school
(Inamura 1991).

The first official definition of SR appeared in *Student Guidance Materials* published by the MOE in 1984. According to the MOE, SR is a condition in which students do not or cannot go to school for some psy-

chological or emotional causes, although no concrete reasons are found and some SR students think that they want to go to school. Such students tend to be very anxious, irresolute, unadaptable, inflexible, immature socially and emotionally, and nervous (MOE 1984). The MOE also characterized the families of SR students as overprotective, at their children's beck and call, and overcontrolling. Fathers of SR students tend to lack social skills, confidence, masculinity, and positiveness and to be taciturn and introverted. Mothers of SR students tend to be dependent, shy, emotionally immature, uneasy, and lacking confidence (MOE 1984). The MOE did not discuss the characters of SR students' teachers.

Teachers' Reaction to School Refusal

In the late 1960s, a few psychiatrists and pediatricians began to write medical certificates stating that their patients showed SR symptoms (Hirai 1991:13). However, teachers rejected these medical certificates, because they had never heard of this disorder (Hirai 1991:14). Some psychiatrists and pediatricians reluctantly rewrote their medical certificates for SR students, because teachers and school officials tended to think that a record attributing long-term absence to illness would be better than one mentioning SR (which had negative connotations about the school) when SR students went on to a higher school (Hirai 1991).

Media Attention to School Refusal

School refusal began to be recognized as a social problem during the 1980s and early 1990s, mainly because of two incidents involving SR students: the Totsuka Yacht School incident in 1983 and the Kazenoko School incident in 1991.[3] Totsuka Yacht School used yachts to train SR students, mainly teenagers, to be tough and independent. The idea for this school reflected the general public's view that SR students were not tough and independent. During the training, some students drowned (*Asahi Shimbun* 1983). As the media reported that the parents sent their children to the Totsuka Yacht School because they could not bear their children's disobedience, the general public began to pay attention to the SR problem, in particular to families damaged by the violence and disobedience of SR students at home. Like the Totsuka Yacht School, the Kazenoko School trained SR students to be tough and independent. In 1991, two students were confined in a container car as a punishment and died from the summer heat. Articles about SR in the *Asahi Shimbun* increased: During the 1970s, the paper averaged 0.4 articles per year; coverage rose to an average of 4.6 articles per year during the 1980s and 13.3 articles per year during 1990–92.

Medical Professionals and School Refusal

As SR received more attention during the 1980s, various medical professionals began paying attention to it. Some professions were relatively unknown to the Japanese. Treating SR seemed to offer them a way to establish their status. First, pediatricians began to recognize that they had an occupational advantage: They usually saw SR students first. Because SR students persistently complain of symptoms such as fever, headaches, or stomachaches, their parents brought them to pediatricians. Pediatricians who had sent their SR patients to psychiatrists now insisted on establishing a subspecialty—a psychiatric pediatrician who could cure SR students before they became serious cases (Wakabayashi 1990). School refusal was one of the principal concerns when the Child Psychosomatic Study Association was founded by pediatricians in 1983. Second, family therapists, a new occupation in Japan, began to pay attention to SR and insisted that "SR should be understood within family dynamics because the SR problem is not only the student's problem, but also the problem of the family" (Suzuki 1988:12). Some parents of SR students who were dissatisfied with the care of psychiatrists or educational counselors began to accept family therapy. Accordingly, as SR became more common, family therapy attracted more clients. Third, psychological therapists were not well established in Japan. There was no unified standard for psychological therapy. The Japanese Clinical Psychological Association was not founded until 1988. They began to claim the need for school psychotherapists to prevent SR problems (Uchiyama and Ibaraki 1992). Fourth, school nurses, who possessed lower status than teachers, could gain prestige. Interestingly, many students who refuse to or cannot enter classrooms will visit school nurses (MOE 1984). Those students often study in "the kingdom of the school nurse's room" (hokenshitsu okoku). School nurses are expected to act as school counselors (MOE 1984).

Although many medical professionals began treating SR, a few psychiatrists criticized the disease concept of SR and became recognized by the general public, especially the parents of SR students, because demedicalizing SR shifts blame away from the families. Logically speaking, if SR students are not sick but normal, their families, especially their mothers, can escape criticism for poor upbringing, overprotection, immature parenting, and also be seen as normal. Thus, parents of SR students strongly supported demedicalization, even though most medical professionals defined SR as a medical problem.

Although various kinds of medical professionals have tried to cure SR students and find the cause of SR, there is no evidence of organic impairment or abnormality in the brain or elsewhere in most SR students. Accordingly, like the learning disability problem that reflects the cultural significance of reading-based academic achievement in the United States (Erchak and Rosenfeld 1989), it can be said that SR clearly reflects the cultural significance of diplomatism (*gakurekishugi*) in Japan. It is important to note that most medical professionals are simply trying to get SR students back to school, even though they advise parents and teachers not to force SR students to go to school. Moreover, medical professionals tend to think that the successful return of SR students to school is proof of a cure.

The Nature of Medical Professionals

Professionals tend to think in terms of their specialties; many of them cannot see beyond their paradigm. For instance, psychiatrists tend to think of SR as a psychiatric disorder. Thus, most medical professionals originally viewed SR as caused by an immature personality and family dynamics; they ignored the educational system, the cultural significance of diplomatism, physical abuse by teachers, overemphasis on academic achievement, and severe bullying by other students. Takuma and Inamura (1991) (both prominent psychological authorities, who, as Tokyo University graduates, are products of the educational system) argued, "there must be some reasons why some students do not want to go to school *when most students go willingly*" (emphasis by the authors). As winners in the Japanese educational competition, medical professionals rarely criticize the school system and its teachers. Where SR is concerned, most medical professionals are politically conservative, because they cannot see beyond the micro level of individual and family. In other words, they unconsciously protect the status quo.

However, a few psychiatrists and pediatricians, such as Watanabe (1984) and Wakabayashi (1990), opposed the disease concept of SR. Ironically, these medical professionals gave the parents of SR students the opportunity to question other medical professionals. Even the demedicalization of SR relied heavily on the authority of some medical professionals.

THE DEMEDICALIZATION OF SCHOOL REFUSAL

The Function of Demedicalization

In the cases of Alcoholic Anonymous and learning disabilities (LD), taking on the "sick role" can neutralize blame from others. However, SR students could not take the sick role fully, because most medical professionals and others attributed SR to the character of those students and their upbringing. Although medical professionals believed that SR students were sick, they held the students and their families responsible for SR (Hirai 1991; Takuma and Inamura 1991). Thus, one function of the "sick role"—avoiding blame from others—did not work well. However, like LD, medicalizing SR benefitted teachers. Unlike in the United States, there are almost no free schools or home schoolers in Japan. Thus, SR is easily considered deviant, a target of severe social sanctions. Students were frustrated and sometimes desperate, because they believed they lacked a future without formal education. Thus, these students were violent or disobedient toward their family members and were often diagnosed as mentally ill by psychiatrists. Under such conditions, it was not rare for students or their parents to commit suicide or for parents to kill their children. Other SR students were institutionalized in mental hospitals; as a result, they were stigmatized and their self-esteem was low (*Asahi Shimbun* 1985). Accordingly, demedicalizing SR appealed to SR students and their parents, because it freed them from criticism by others, most important, from self-criticism. In addition, the demedicalization of SR redefines SR as a problem of the Japanese culture, educational system, and society (meso or macro level), rather than a problem of individuals and families (micro level).

The Demedicalization Process

Claimsmaking. Takashi Watanabe was an influential psychiatrist who opposed the disease concept of SR. According to him (1984), SR students are not sick; rather, the educational system is wrong. Mrs. Keiko Okuchi, a former teacher whose son was a patient of Watanabe, borrowed Watanabe's idea and founded the School Refusal Association (SRA) in 1984. She insisted that SR students are normal, that they are victims of Japanese society and its educational system's diplomatism, strict discipline, severe exams, and so on. Under such pressures, children's sensibilities are distorted. Thus, SR is a form of self-protection in order to protect students' essential humanity. She also claimed that students who are not aware of society's ills will reproduce such a society (Okuchi 1990, 1992). Okuchi's claims appealed to other parents of SR students, because the parents could avoid not only criticism from others but also self-criticism. Okuchi led the movement to demedicalize SR, establishing the School Refusal Association and Tokyo Shuray (a free space for SR students).

The Foundation of the School Refusal Association. Okuchi founded the SRA in 1984. The basic concept behind the SRA was that SR students are not sick at all but that the school system is wrong. SRA's members are parents of SR students. SRA's purposes are threefold: to fight the disease concept of SR; to offer support for the SR students' parents who are isolated and criticized; and to organize the parents of SR students (Okuchi 1990, 1992). The SRA taught members Okuchi's ideology about SR as well as practical methods for dealing with SR. For example, the SRA members learned that it is possible to graduate from elementary and junior high school without attending class if schoolmasters and principals approve. Okuchi also taught that one can graduate from junior high school by attending junior high school evening sessions (which are intended to educate adults over 15 years old). In 1988 SR students constituted one-fourth of the students in the evening sessions of eight Tokyo junior high schools (*Asahi Shimbun* 1988b). Students can also graduate from junior high school by taking comprehensive exams, which supposedly are not too difficult.

In November 1985 the SRA established a telephone hotline for SR students and announced that SR was mostly caused by violent teachers (*Asahi Shimbun* 1985). In 1988 the SRA denounced Inamura's study of SR. According to Inamura, SR students should be cured by psychiatrists or psychologists, otherwise they will become apathetic (*Asahi Shimbun* 1988b). Inamura's findings were reported by *Asahi Shimbun*, one of the largest Japanese newspapers (8 million subscriptions). The SRA responded that SR students were normal, that the school system was wrong. After the SRA's comments about the SR problem appeared in the media, both the SRA itself and Okuchi became well-known. The general public began to regard Okuchi as an expert on the SR problem. She was often invited to lecture about SR. Wherever Okuchi traveled to lecture, she tried to establish a new branch of the SRA. In fact, SRA branches in Hiroshima (1987), Kyoto (1987), Gifu (1988), and other cities were founded on Okuchi's advice (SRA 1992). The number of SRA members increased rapidly. In 1990, SRA had organized a nationwide network of 40 branches; there were 60 SRAs in 1992. Accordingly, the demedicalization of SR was growing more popular. The first SRA branch was founded in Tokyo in 1984, with eight members, including Okuchi. Today, the Tokyo SRA has 1,200 members.

The Foundation of Tokyo Shuray. Tokyo Shuray was founded in 1985 by Okuchi. Tokyo Shuray offered a free space for SR students who were isolated and had nothing to do at home except play Nintendo. Okuchi sought to offer an alternative to school for SR students who had no place to go. More important, Okuchi wanted to prove that SR students were not ill by showing lively SR students in Tokyo Shuray. Because Tokyo Shuray, unlike Totsuka Yacht School or Kazenoko School, was the first institution where kids were able to enjoy freedom, the media paid attention and reported stories about "lively SR students." Those articles criticized teachers and the school system. It seemed that the demedicalization of SR was gradually becoming accepted.

However, in 1988 the MOE announced that teachers regarded 54 percent of junior high SR students and 39 percent of elementary SR students as truants, and another 24 percent of junior high SR students and 35 percent of elementary SR students as neurotics (*Ashahi Shimbun* 1988a). This announcement made SRA members and Tokyo Shuray students angry because they attributed most SR to teachers and the school system. Tokyo Shuray students, led by Okuchi, energetically criticized that announcement and conducted their own survey of other SR students. Although heavily biased, this survey, if not its results, attracted media attention because it was unusual for SR students to ask other SR students about their motives. According to *Asahi Shimbun* (1989a), the survey identified the school environment, teachers, and schoolwork as the three main reasons why students began SR. This survey, with additional self-reports by Tokyo Shuray students, was published in 1991 (Tokyo Shuray 1991).

The success of Tokyo Shuray and of the activities of SRA comforted SR students and their parents. One student at Tokyo Shuray said that "contemporary SR students recover sooner" (because they now had a place to go and be with other SR students) (Okuchi 1991). This suggests that social pressures on SR students have weakened or that the pressures are offset by an alternative support system.

Changing the Rhetoric

"The school system is wrong, teachers are bad and kids are victims of the Japanese society and educational system." These remarks have often been repeated publicly by Okuchi since SRA was founded in 1984. However, Okuchi gradually changed her tone. For example, the SRA does not reject all school education but argues that the MOE should recognize private institutions as an alternative to school for SR students (*Asahi Shimbun* 1990d). Okuchi said this when the media asked her for a comment about the MOE's new acknowledgment that SR is not merely a problem of individuals and families but also a problem of schools and society. In addition, the MOE announced that SR could happen to anyone and that there was no common character of SR students (*Asahi Shimbun* 1990c). Okuchi changed or softened her claims as the SRA grew into a big organization; the SRA needed to soften its policies to keep various kinds of members, including new members such as teachers, college students, and others. Most important, there was a dilemma. If Okuchi kept saying that the school system is wrong and teachers are bad, what could she say about SR students who decided to go back to school? In fact, many SR students return to school, including Okuchi's son (who entered college) and her daughter (who was sent to Summerhill School in England—one of the most famous free schools). In addition, success stories of ex-SR students who became college students, lawyers, teachers, and artists were often told at SRA meetings. It seemed that many SRA members temporarily rejected the means (formal education) but not the goal (higher education). Thus, although they criticized teachers and the school system, many of them could not reject the whole educational system, and most returned to school. Thus, the SRA movement could change neither the cultural significance of diplomatism in Japan nor the "educational fever" (*kyoiku netsu*).

HIDDEN PROBLEMS WITH DEMEDICALIZATION

As mentioned before, the MOE expanded its list of official causes of SR in 1990 from problems of individuals and families to include problems of families, schools, and the whole society. The MOE also redefined SR students to include those absent 30 days in a year (instead of 50), if those absences are attributed to disliking school. These changes show that the MOE began to take the SR problem more seriously as the number of SR students increased and the SRA's claims began attracting attention. By 1990, there were 8,000 elementary school SR students, as well as 40,000 junior high school SR students (*Asahi Shimbun* 1990a, 1991c).

Although claimsmakers pointed to the increasing number of SR students, that increase reflected, in part, the success of the SRA and of Tokyo Shuray. Three factors contributed to the increase. First, since the SRA demedicalized SR and some medical professionals agreed that SR was not an ordinary disease, long-term absences by students, previously classified as due to illness, were more likely to be categorized as SR. Second, since the SRA discouraged forcing SR students to go to school and warned that force may make the students' condition worse, parents and even teachers became more tolerant of long-term absences by SR students. Finally, following the success of Tokyo Shuray, many other private institutions for SR students were founded; more choices were available. In short, before the SRA and Tokyo Shuray were founded, parents and teachers believed that school was the only place students could go. But the SRA gradually changed this belief. Because it supported the parents of SR ideologically and Tokyo Shuray offered SR students a place to stay during the regular school hours, being SR became less stigmatized than before, and the number of SR students increased.

On the other hand, the MOE statistics probably underestimate the extent of SR. First, they do not include students who skip some classes, although "those students have a high probability of being SR" (Morita 1991:15). Second, because the norm requires students to go to school unless they are sick, it is quite common for the parents of SR students to report short-term absences as illness. Finally, the concept of disliking school is ambiguous. Each school or district interprets it differently, and as "disliking school" and "school refusal" imply criticism of teachers and school administrators, some districts hesitate to classify SR students as such (*Asahi Shimbun* 1991a). In addition, because the concept of SR is not well-known in rural (e.g., Ehime) and semiurban prefectures (e.g., Nara), these areas still tend to define SR students as sick or truants. However, in most urban prefectures, long-term absences are attributed to students disliking school (SR). (See Table 1.)

In addition, there is a more important problem. Because of the successful claimsmaking of the SRA and of Tokyo Shuray, the demedicalization of SR is becoming more popular. At the same time, criticism about teachers and the school system is stronger. The SR problem as constructed by the SRA seems to suggest that all SR is caused by teachers and the school system; if there were no bad schools, there could be no SR. However, 30 percent of elementary and 26 percent of junior high school SR students in Tokyo blamed SR on aspects of their family environment, such as divorce, fights between parents, father's long-term absence for business (*tanshin funin*), and so on (*Asahi Shimbun* 1990b). The criticism of teachers and the school system is probably overemphasized by the SRA because those parents and SR students whose families have problems are reluctant to speak up.

CONCLUDING REMARKS

In this paper I examined how the SR problem was medicalized and subsequently demedicalized and how the processes of the medicalization and demedicalization were shaped by Japanese culture and social structure. Even though the SRA tried to destigmatize SR, it is fair to say that the SRA movement is conservative. As mentioned before, the SRA simply ends up advocating ways to bypass the schools while accepting the goal of higher education. At least since the 1920s, there have been

Table 1. Reasons for Long-Term Absences in Junior High Schools by Prefectures, 1989 (%)

| | Urban areas | | | | Semi-urban | | Rural |
Reason for absence	Tokyo	Osaka	Chiba	Aichi	Fukuoka	Hokkaido	Nara	Ehime
Dislike school	83	47	60	72	54	59	22	37
Sick	12	21	26	19	27	28	31	53
Financial reason	1	3	5	1	1	1	2	1
Other	4	29	9	8	18	12	45	9
Total	100	100	100	100	100	100	100	100

Source: Asahi Shinbun 1991a.

repeated complaints in the Japanese press that examination hell has prevented Japanese students from having a healthy childhood (Frost 1991), but no one has succeeded in offering an alternative. The SRA is no exception. As we have seen, the SR problem cannot be explained unless one considers SR in the larger context of Japanese society and social structure; the claimsmaking by the SRA and the MOE's countermeasures offer temporary, incomplete solutions to the SR problem.

Medical professionals were very important not only in the medicalization of SR but also in the process of demedicalization. If no medical professionals supported the demedicalization of SR, could demedicalization have succeeded? In addition, could the SRA have become popular without support from some medical professionals? Probably, the answers are no. Without medical professionals' support for demedicalization, the SRA could not have been established; certainly it could not have attracted so many members.

Regardless of the definition of SR, many SR students continue to have family problems. As mentioned before, a father's long-term absence for business (*tanshin funin*) is one common family problem; a father may be transferred by his company, while his family chooses to stay behind because of children's education or housing. The current construction of the SR problem clearly ignores such family problems.

What is the future of the SR problem? Since 1988, the MOE has started town classrooms (*machi no kyoshitsu*) that offer SR students counseling and basic education (*Asahi Shimbun* 1989c). Those classrooms are called "adjustment guidance classrooms" (*Asahi Shimbun* 1991b). Even though the MOE stressed the need for community cooperation to prevent SR (*Asahi Shimbun* 1989b), the name "adjustment guidance classrooms" suggests that the MOE still sees SR in terms of social inadaptability. The MOE does not present measures for reforming the educational system or schools, although many parents have started to question the trivial rules that so many schools impose on their students. For example, there are rules about how students should raise their hands in classes, the angle at which they should bow to their teachers, and even the order in which they should eat their school lunches (Kurita 1990). Many schools regulate dress and hair styles. Students who cannot tolerate those rules may become SR students.

In conclusion, SR is a very real problem in Japan; it warrants public attention, concern, and appropriate policy development. However, current perceptions of the SR problem do not foster the type of attention that is needed if the SR problem is to be addressed effectively, because current constructions of SR do not threaten the status quo. Until SR is redefined so as to focus critical attention on the larger social context, it will remain a problem in Japanese education.

NOTES

1. One exception is Kitsuse, Murase, and Yamamura's analysis of *Kikokushi-jo mondai* ("the returning student problem"). They examined how characterizations, analyses, policy proposals, and institutional responses were interrelated in the production of "the *Kikokushijo* problem" (Kitsuse, Murase, and Yamamura 1984).

2. This study adopts a contextual constructionist approach (Best 1989; Spector and Kitsuse 1977).

3. I examined coverage of school refusal in one of the largest newspapers in Japan, *Asahi Shimbun* (8 million subscriptions in the morning edition and 4 million subscriptions in the evening edition) between 1970 and September 18, 1992. I checked all entries under "School Refusal" (*Toko Kyohi*) in the paper's monthly indexes. I limited my examination of coverage to *Asahi Shimbun*'s Tokyo edition. My figures do not include articles about the Totsuka Yacht School incident (1983) or the Kazenoko School incident (1991).

REFERENCES

Arioka, I., and N. Katsuyama. 1974. *Toko Kyohi Sho* [*School Refusal Symptoms*]. Tokyo: Kanehara.

Asahi Shimbun. 1983. ["Totsuka Yacht School Incident"]. June 4.

_____. 1985. "Toko Kyohi no Kodomo o Ani ni Seishinbyoin Okuri" ["School Refusal Kids Are Sent to Psychiatrists Carelessly"]. November 22.

_____. 1988a. "Gakkou Gawa Taigaku to Ninshiki" ["Schools See School Refusal as Truancy"]. December 1.

_____. 1988b. "Moto Toko Kyohi no Kora Yakan Chugaku de Kyuzo" ["The Number of Ex-school Refusals Increases in the Evening Session of Junior High Schools"]. December 3.

_____. 1989a. "Toko Kyohi no Kikkake Wa" ["What Is the Motive for School Refusal?"] June 25.

_____. 1989b. "Toko kyohi, Koko Chutai" ["School Refusal and High School Dropouts"]. July 19.

_____. 1989c. "Toko Kyohi ni Machi no Kyoshitsu" ["Town Classrooms for School Refusal Students"]. September 2.

_____. 1990a. "Futoko Kyuzo Tsuzuku" ["Nonattendance at School Increases Rapidly"]. August 4.

_____. 1990b. "Kouritsu Shou Chu Sei no Toko Kyohi, 5,000 Nin Kosu" ["School Refusal Students at Public Elementary and Junior High Schools Number Over 5,000"]. December 4.

_____. 1990c. "Toko Kyohi, Dono ko mo Kanousei" ["School Refusal Could Happen to Anyone"]. December 7.

_____. 1990d. "Toko Kyohi Chukan Hokoku" ["The School Refusal Interim Report"]. December 8.

_____. 1991a. "Baratsuku Toko Kyohi" ["Ambiguous Interpretation of School Refusal"]. March 7.

_____. 1991b. "Gakko yo Sayonara" ["Good-bye School"]. November 9.

_____. 1991c. "Toko Kyohi ga Shogakusei ni Kyuzo" ["Elementary School Refusal Students Increase Rapidly"]. December 26.

Best, J. (ed.). 1989. *Images of Issues: Typifying Contemporary Social Problems.* Hawthorne, NY: Aldine de Gruyter.

Erchak, G. M., and R. Rosenfeld. 1989. "Learning Disability, Dyslexia, and the Medicalization of the Classroom." Pp. 79–97 in *Images of Issues,* edited by J. Best. Hawthorne, NY: Aldine de Gruyter.

Frost, P. 1991. "Examination Hell." Pp. 291–305 in *Windows on Japanese Education,* edited by E. R. Beauchamp. Westport, CT: Greenwood.

Hirai, N. 1968. "Shisyunki ni Okeru Toko Kyohi" ["Adolescent School Refusal"]. *Shouni no Seishin to Shinkei* [*The Mind and Nerve of a Child*] 8(2):51.

_____. 1975. *Gakko Girai* [*Disliking School*]. Tokyo: Nissin Hodosha.

_____. 1991. *Toko Kyohiji* [*School Refusal Children*], 15th ed. Tokyo: Sinyosha.

Hisatoku, S. 1985. *Bogenbyo wa Naoseru* [*Disease Caused by Mother Can Be Cured*]. Tokyo: Daisanbunmeisha.

Inagaki, T. 1986. "School Education: Its History and Contemporary Status." Pp. 75–92 in *Child Development and Education in Japan,* edited by H. Stevenson, H. Azuma, and K. Kakuta. New York: Freeman.

Inamura, H. 1989. *Toko Kyohi no Kokufuku* [*Overcoming School Refusal*], 4th ed. Tokyo: Shinyosha.

_____. 1991. "Toko Kyohi no Teigi to Bunrui" ["Definition and Classification of School Refusal"]. Pp. 12–22 in *Toko kyohi* [*School Refusal*], edited by T. Takuma and H. Inamura, 17th ed. Tokyo: Yuhikaku.

Ishida, T. 1971. *Japanese Society.* New York: Random House.

Johnson, A. M., E. I. Falstein, S. A. Szurek, and M. Svenson. 1941. "School Phobia." *American Journal of Orthopsychiatry* 11:702–11.

Kawai, H. 1992. *Gakko ni se o Mukeru Kodomo* [*Children Who Turn Their Backs on Schools*], 17th ed. Tokyo: Nihon Hoso Kyokai.

Kitsuse, J. I., A. E. Murase, and Y. Yamamura. 1984. "Kikokushijo: The Emergence and Institutionalization of an Educational Problem in Japan." Pp. 162–79 in *Studies in the Sociology of Social Problems,* edited by J. W. Schneider and J. I. Kitsuse. Norwood, NJ: Ablex.

Kurita, W. 1990. "School Phobia." *Japan Quarterly* 37:298–303.

Minister of Education. 1984. *Student Guidance Materials,* 2nd ed. Tokyo: Publishing Bureau of Minister of Finance.

Morita, Y. 1991. *Futoko Gensho no Sakaigaku* [*Sociology of Nonattendance at School*]. Tokyo: Gakubunsha.

Okuchi, K. 1990. *Toko Kyohi wa Byoki ja Nai* [*School Refusal Is Not Sickness*], 4th ed. Tokyo: Kyoiku shiryo shuppankai.

_____. 1992. *Tokyo Shoere Monogatari* [*Tokyo Shoere Story*], 3rd ed. Tokyo: Kyoiku shiryo shuppankai.

Rosario, L. D. 1992. "All Work and No Play: Cram Schools Keep Alive Education Nightmare." *Far Eastern Economic Review* 155 (March 12):21–23.

Satou, S. 1968. *Toko Kyohniji* [*School Refusal Child*]. Tokyo: Kokudosha.

School Refusal Association. 1992. *Futoko o Ikiru* [*Nonattendance at Schools*]. Tokyo: Kyoiku shiryo shuppankai.

Spector, M., and J. I. Kitsuse. 1977. *Constructing Social Problems*. Menlo Park, CA: Cummings.

Stevenson, H. W. 1991. "Japanese Elementary School Education." *Elementary School Journal* 92:109–20.

Sumiya, M. 1971. "The Function and Social Structure of Education: Schools and Japanese Society." Pp. 146–66 in *Selected Readings on Modern Japanese Society*, edited by G. K. Yamamoto and T. Ishida. Berkeley, CA: McCutchan.

Suzuki, K. (ed.). 1988. *Toko Kyohi [School Refusal]*. Tokyo: Kongo Shuppan.

Takuma, T., and H. Inamura. (eds.). 1991. *Toko Kyohi [School Refusal]*, 17th ed. Tokyo: Yuhikaku.

Tokyo Shuray. 1991. *Gakko ni Ikanai Boku Kara Gakko ni Ikanai Kimie [(Messages) from Tokyo Shuray Students to School Refusal Students]*. Tokyo: Kyoiku shiryo shuppankai.

Uchiyama, K., and T. Ibaraki. 1992. "Psychology." *Imidas '92*.

Wakabayashi, M. 1990. *Ejison mo Toko Kyohi Datta [Edison Was also a School Refusal Student]*. Tokyo: Chikuma Shobo.

Warren, W. 1948. "Acute Neurotic Breakdown in Children with Refusal to go to School." *Archives of Disease in Childhood* 23:266.

Watanabe, T. 1984. *Jidou Seishinka: Oya mo Kyoshi mo Kangaetai Tokokyohi no Kokoro [Child Psychiatry: School Refusal Should Concern Not Only Parents but also Teachers]*. Tokyo: President sha.

Part VI

CHILDREN'S PERSPECTIVES
ON SOCIAL PROBLEMS

Chapter 11

If We Don't Do Anything Now, There Won't Be Anything Left: Categories of Concern in Children's Drawings of Environmental Crisis

Donna Lee King

First save the planet, then you can watch cartoons.
—Slogan found on an infant t-shirt

THE ENVIRONMENTALIZATION OF CHILDREN

Messages to children about environmental crisis are evident in every realm of child life. Department stores display all manner of childrens' clothing—down to diapers—sporting brightly colored planets, rainforests, wildlife, and slogans, with colorful hanging tags that read "Kids Talk—Save Our Earth," "Enviro Team," and "Keep Our World Clean." The environmental targeting of children includes cereal boxes decorated with endangered animal species, fishsticks with "Clean Ocean Kids" activity books inside, and animal crackers admonishing children to "Help Save the Animals." Burger King bags depict a burger in the shape of the planet, and brag about their "New Earth Happy Packaging" in the handwriting of a child:

> You will probably notice that our sandwiches now come in paper wrapping instead of a box. That's because we figured the world could probably use *15,000* less tons of trash a year. And less trash means less trucks to carry it. Which means less gas, and a lot less air pollution. Not to mention the reduction in packaging the packaging has to be shipped in! All in

all, its just one of the ways we are trying to make the world a nicer place to eat.

Not only are children targets of "green" advertising campaigns but also there are a plethora of books, magazines, television shows, and school curricula specifically designed to educate children about environmental concerns. Barney and Sesame Street, Mister Rogers and Nickelodeon, MTV and VH-1 all devote a significant portion of their children's programming to environmental issues. There is an "Earth-based" environmental magazine for kids, an environmental cartoon called *Captain Planet and the Planeteers*, and a seemingly limitless supply of books telling children "how to save the earth." From breakfast in the morning until they climb into their "save the rainforest" pajamas at night, children eat, sleep, read, and watch TV about environmental crisis.

Elsewhere I have examined the conflicting cultural messages children are getting about "saving the planet" (King 1994). It is sometimes difficult to decipher what adults want from children regarding environmental crisis. Are children supposed to curtail their consumption and conserve? Or buy the latest Toxic Crusader or Captain Planet doll? Are they innocent victims of imminent global disaster? Or tyrannical "eco-terrorists" cowing their parents into recycling the trash? And when they are taught about the ecological hazards of strip mining, forest clear-cutting, driftnet fishing, toxic waste dumping, oil spills, nuclear waste storage, overcrowded landfills, ozone depletion, greenhouse effect, the effects of pesticides, ad infinitum—what exactly are kids supposed to *do*? In this chapter I explore different ways children are receiving and appropriating pervasive social messages directed at them about "saving the planet."

DISCOURSES OF CHILDREN AND THEIR CONCERNS

How are children responding to the bombardment of cultural messages about environmental crisis? I would like to address this question by first examining adult notions of children's concerns. For children do not "signify alone" as purely existential creatures. Children are also objects of representation. Visual, literal, and symbolic images and notions of children circulate throughout the culture. These representations, or what Roland Barthes calls "myths," congeal into various discourses or systems of knowledge about children. To understand children, therefore, we must place them within the discourses through which children are mediated and within which their meanings are articulated. Different representations of children will convey different meanings and, "lay down the terms and myths by which we [adults and children alike] come to recognize" children (McRobbie 1991:28). That is, much of our understanding about children comes from the ways they are represented in the culture.

From the adult perspective, children are perceived as social incompetents (Cahill 1990; Denzin 1979), as vulnerable victims (Best 1990), as precious commodities (Rothman 1989; Zelizer 1985), as an endangered species (Postman 1982; Winn 1983), as a marketing "goldmine" (McNeal 1992), or as little tyrants (W. C. Fields). This, of course, is not an exhaustive list. These social constructions, or in discursive terms myths, reveal much about adult notions of children's environmental concerns.

Many adults imagine that messages about "saving the planet" go right over the heads of little children, that such issues as environmental crisis are too abstract for children to comprehend. Others worry that children are being unfairly burdened by such "grown-up" concerns as global warming and nuclear disaster.

Research on children's responses to the threat of nuclear disaster often refers to "nuclear nightmares" and the "psychic numbing" of the nuclear concerned (Mesnikoff 1989). Although children could (reasonably) be expected to view global degradation or nuclear disaster as overwhelming problems beyond a child's ability to influence or control, this attitude leads, some adults argue, to cynicism, apathy, or even nihilism in children in relation to the larger society. In her study of the impact of nuclear threat on young people, La Farge (1987) worries that children are becoming "survival artists" in an effort to cope with intense vulnerability and "learned helplessness" (p. 89). In the face of nuclear proliferation, she states, many children are "restricting their emotions," retreating into private or even religiously fundamentalist worlds, and withdrawing from the political process (pp. 74–75).

Other critics writing about nuclear and other crisis socialization portray children in quite a different light: as overzealous, intolerant, and self-righteous proselytizers (Coles 1986; Quindlen 1990). Regarding environmental crisis, this construction is evident in the popular press, where images of environmentally tyrannical children are promoted with headlines such as, "The Enforcers: Teach Your Parents Well" (Garelik 1991), and "Newest Parental Nightmare: The Eco-Smart Child" (Slesin 1990).

Some adults wonder at the consumerist content of environmental crisis messages for children. Are children being educated as fully actualized, self-managing citizens in a cooperative, ecological, democracy? Or are they learning to be compliant "caring" consumers in a vast, global, "green" marketplace (Bolotin 1990; Bookchin 1990; Coward 1990)?

THEORETICAL FRAMEWORKS

The relationship between how children are perceived and how they perceive themselves is dialectical. Children simultaneously shape and are shaped by the prevailing culture (Alanen 1990; Power 1986). But this process has been interpreted in many different ways.

The notion that children are targets for social messages is, of course, nothing new. According to Ariès (1962:329), the modern concept of childhood as a distinct social status did not arise until after the invention of systematic "moral edification" or compulsory schooling. This implies a concerted effort on the part of society to shape, if not mold, new members to prevailing social norms and values. Consensual structural-functional approaches emphasize children's internalization of society, citing institutional arrangements of family, school, and popular media as primarily responsible for transmitting the culture to young initiates.

Marxist structuralists, critical of existing social arrangements, point to the same institutions as functioning (wittingly or unwittingly) to reproduce unequal and oppressive social relations based on class, through a practice of symbolic violence "wherein the consent of children is gained, or at least sought" (Bourdieu and Passeron 1977; Katz 1990:6). Marxist feminists advance the theory of social reproduction by examining the ways in which unequal gender arrangements are essential to the maintenance of capitalist social relations (Dalla Costa 1972; Laslett and Brenner 1989).

Structural approaches often view children as passive objects, empty vessels to be filled for the smooth maintenance of social structure. From this perspective, social messages to children are useful indicators of norms, values, and social relations of power and privilege in a society. Their importance lies more in the information they provide about adult society than in their relationship to the social experiences of children.

For interactionists, the process whereby a child becomes an emergent member of a particular social order implies a dialectical relationship between social constraint and the reflexive construction of self (Elkin and Handel 1989; Power 1986:260). That is, children receive social messages and proceed to interpret them; fashioning meaning from the objects, circumstances, and gestures of their everyday lives. They actively construct their social worlds, although always within the confines of existing social, cultural, historical, and biological boundaries (p. 261). Children are a largely untapped source of insight into various aspects of their society and their own conditions (Ambert 1986:7). Insights into the social experiential world of children also provide unique reflections of adult society. "A child, then, is a complex social object. The meanings brought to the child will be reflected in his [or her] actions" (Denzin 1979:112).

Thus, children reflect society; children interpret society; children cocreate society. When studying children's interpretations of social issues, we learn not only what children's concerns are, but also what *adults'* concerns are, and importantly, how the two intertwine and perhaps compete. This last point is noted by Ambert (1986) in her critique of the virtual absence of children in sociological research: "We know very little about how children manage or negotiate the points of divergence and of convergence between the realities presented to them by their parents, siblings, peers, teachers, and mass media" (p. 7).

Convergences and divergences in young people's experience of social life have been explored in different ways by Fiske (1989), Hebdige (1988), Katz (1990), McRobbie (1991), Willis (1977, 1990), and others in cultural studies. In their work on youth, these cultural analysts draw on three interlocking concepts: hegemony—whereby dominant values in a society become so taken for granted as to be invisible to members, despite their often pervasive oppressiveness—consumerism—simultaneously a means of social control and a medium of self-creation or "symbolic work" (Willis 1990)—and resistance—the subversive response by youths (in subcultures and other social settings) to push back against the structural constraints of late capitalist society, often through popular cultural expressions of personal style (McRobbie 1988).

There is, then, a dual argument for studying children's interpretations of social issues: Children are intimately bound up with the creation of society. Thus, their lived experiences are inherently valuable as social facts; and, children's perspectives and concerns reflect aspects of adult society that might otherwise remain occluded or merely implicit except as revealed "through the eyes of a child." Always there lurks a danger of sentimentalizing children—as pure and innocent surveyors of emperors (or empires) without clothes—but the fact remains that children provide unique—and grossly unexamined—perspectives on the social world (Ambert 1986; Waksler 1986).

Therefore, we might expect children's responses to social issues to reveal: (1) implicit adult agendas and concerns; (2) hegemonic or dominant social values that might otherwise remain obscured; and (3) vital strategies or tactics used by children to negotiate meaning within existing social structural constraints.

ON THE USE OF CHILDREN'S DRAWINGS
IN SOCIOLOGICAL RESEARCH

Before moving on to the present study, let me briefly discuss my decision to use children's drawings as a research method in sociology (cf. King, in progress). The idea came to me in the fall of 1990 while watching children recite essays and present pictures about environmental crisis on our local public television station (WMHT 1990). The use of children's drawings has turned out to be a rather novel method in sociological research.

Robert Coles, a child psychiatrist, uses drawings and paintings extensively in his prolific work on children (cf. Coles 1992). But despite an abiding interest in children's experiences of social issues, he typically looks at pictures as the product of a particular person, as an indication of what a particular mind is like. Taking the opposite tack, Dennis (1966), a social psychologist, utilizes children's drawings to trace group values. He sees children's drawings as a kind of social mirror reflecting those values most esteemed in a given society. Elsewhere, drawings by children have been employed in market research (McNeal 1992); as a curricular tool in the elementary schools (Warren 1991); and for a study on gender differences (Reeves and Boyette 1983). Only the last was conducted by sociologists.

Because my project is exploratory, I wanted to use drawings as a kind of qualitative survey tool; as a reasonably efficient means of casting a rather wide net to see the variety of concerns children have about environmental crisis. Drawings are a relatively quick and easy way to gather social information from and about children. I got interested and cooperative responses from teachers and camp directors and from all of the children who participated in the study. Another obvious advantage is that drawings are nonverbal, thus providing an alternative means of communication for children.

In lieu of direct observation of children's environmentally concerned behavior, drawings can provide ethnographic clues about children's social strategies, meaning construction, symbol making, role taking, differing levels of reflexivity, differing orientations to the environment, and differing orientations to adult messages. Like language and behavior, drawings can reveal "attempts by the child to act on his [or her] environment, to make that environment sensible and orderly" (Denzin 1979:141).

In a more "quantitative" mode of content analysis, children's drawings can also reveal "salient interaction objects" that can be studied by "recording the repeatability ratio of all [symbols] in the [drawings]" (Denzin 1979:123). Those symbols with the highest repeatability ratios are indicators of salient or problematic objects. "Such a mode of analysis permits the observer to focus centrally on the question, How do children take account of one another?" (Denzin 1979:123–24). From this I have extrapolated the question: "How do children take account of themselves and social issues in their drawings of environmental crisis?"

RESEARCH METHODS

A convenience sample of 325 children between the ages of 5 and 15 was drawn from 3 elementary schools, 3 summer camps, and 1 neighborhood center in upstate New York, and from 4 elementary schools in South Carolina throughout the summer and fall of 1991. The majority of children in the study were white, lower-middle to upper-middle class, and under 12 years old. Black children within the same age and class range are also represented. Because specific class status was not always available, a subsample of poor (low-income) black children from a small blue-collar city in upstate New York was selected for comparison according to race/class. Also included in the sample are: children attending special education classes (these account for most of the children over 11 years); two Chinese-speaking children; two wheel-chair using children; and a child with Down's syndrome.

Children were asked to "draw a picture about what it means *to you* when someone says, 'You have to help save the planet.'" No preliminary discussion occurred prior to the drawing session other than to introduce the activity as part of a project on children and the environmental crisis. All drawing sessions were conducted by the author or by classroom teachers following the research protocol. Drawing sessions were of approximately 20 to 30 minutes duration. At the conclusion of each session, children were given an opportunity to discuss their drawings (in a group setting) in response to the question, "Can you tell us what is going on in your picture?" These brief (approximately five minute) discussions were tape recorded or copied onto the back of each child's drawing and were later used for assistance in content analysis. Because some children drew more than one picture, a total of 354 drawings were collected. All were used in constructing thematic categories, but only a child's *first* drawing was tabulated for comparison across grade, gender, race, race/class, and geographical region.

Using a qualitative method of content analysis, I analyzed each picture so as to discover thematic categories of children's environmental concern. My method was exploratory, interpretive, and systematic (cf. Glaser and Strauss 1967). Drawings were initially sorted according to their manifest content, including (but not limited to): subject choice; inclusion or exclusion of human figures; inclusion or exclusion of signs of environmental degradation; the use of slogans; and/or positive or negative sanctions. Gradually piles of drawings began to take on distinctive characteristics—a particular emotional tenor, and/or ideational theme. These data then functioned in a dialectical fashion to inform the categorization of subsequent drawings. A pattern emerged in the content and classification of these childrens' drawings, leading to the construction of six thematic categories of children's environmental concern: (1) everything's okay; (2) taking personal action; (3) calling for action; (4) depicting the problem; (5) indicting the problem makers; and (6) recasting the problem.

RESULTS

An overwhelming majority of children in this study are aware of environmental crisis (87 percent). Nearly one-half of all the children (48 percent)—including 64 percent of the kindergarten and first graders, and almost one-half of all the girls (47 percent) and boys (47 percent)—depict themselves or others taking personal action for positive social or environmental change (see Tables 1 and 2). Descriptive data show that, although some children express (in their drawings and in subsequent interviews) a daunting awareness of the power and effort required to "save the planet," many children feel empowered, not unduly burdened, to heed the call for global stewardship. A detailed description of each thematic category is provided below, to illustrate different aspects of children's environmental awareness and concern and to raise issues and questions of potential theoretical significance about the environmentalization of children.

CATEGORIES OF CHILDREN'S ENVIRONMENTAL CONCERN

Everything's Okay (n = 33, 10% of total)

These drawings are imbued with an aura of deep tranquility. Each picture reveals an apparent absence of stress and evokes a quiet sense of repose. Reminiscent of the Garden of Eden, one young girl's picture is replete with butterflies, a deer, two smiling girls, a fancy bird. Even an intricately drawn green and red-eyed snake is shown amicably curled around a sturdy tree. Nature is presented to us as serene, home as secure. Flowers, rainbows, trees, even one child's dark cloud and rainy scene conjure up the pastoral image of nature at peace and in balance. People-populated landscapes are curiously absent here—comprising only 15 percent of the category—whereas animals, including among others a horse, dog, birds, turtles, snakes, and frogs, are more frequently represented (25 percent). Homes when they appear are happy-look-

Table 1   Themes in Children's Drawings by Grade (%)

	Grade			
	K-1 %	2-3 %	4-5 %	6-8 %
Everything's Okay	8.5%	21.8%	3.6%	0.0%
Personal Action	63.9%	37.3%	55.1%	28.1%
Call for Action	10.6%	18.2%	27.7%	46.9%
Depict Problem	2.1%	10.9%	8.0%	15.6%
Problem Makers	12.8%	7.3%	10.9%	9.4%
Re-cast Problem	2.1%	4.5%	0.7%	0.0%
	100.0%	100.0%	100.0%	100.0%
	(47)	(110)	(138)	(32)

Table 2   Themes in Children's Drawings by Gender

	Gender	
	Girls	Boys
Everything's Okay	9.6%	11.0%
Personal Action	47.1%	46.7%
Call for Action	25.7%	16.3%
Depict Problem	11.2%	6.0%
Problem Makers	4.8%	17.0%
Re-cast Problem	1.6%	3.0%
	100.0%	100.0%
	(187)	(135)

ing places, nestled in a landscape devoid of any indication of problems, pollution, damaged ozone layers, or recyclable trash.

Although we might assume that young children drawing such pictures are simply arrested at a pictographic stage of arcadian landscape production (i.e., little children *always* draw sunny scenes and pretty flowers)—and are thus quite likely unaware of "save the planet" messages—let us first look carefully at the data. Almost one-half of all the drawings in this category (45 percent) include some rendition of a healthy, happy planet earth. In one engaging variant, a 9-year-old Girl Scout draws the earth as a smiling global figure wearing top hat and flowers, a continent for a nose, and arms and legs that protrude from its benign rotundness. Some children portray the earth in space amidst other planets in the solar system, and others place it high or low in the

Figure 1. Everything's okay.

Drawn by a white girl going into second grade in upstate New York. Note the serpent curled around the tree.

sky of their cheerful landscapes, often right between simultaneous depictions of the sun and the moon. At the very least, these children can be seen to have recognized and acknowledged a significant element of the "save the planet" message.

Assuming that these children are unaware of environmental crisis, we might expect a correlation of chronological age/grade, with the youngest children representing the least environmentally aware. However, this is not borne out in the present study. In fact, 23 percent of the 2nd and 3rd graders drew unpolluted nature scenes as compared to 9 percent of the youngest participants in kindergarten and 1st grade (see Table 1).

Given the undeniable ubiquity of environmental crisis messages to children, it is significant that those in the (relatively) higher grades are overrepresented in a category that seems to imply total innocence or blissful obliviousness about "saving the planet." Perhaps the appellation, "Everything's Okay," is too simplistic, too unidirectional to adequately describe this kind of environmental concern. Pictures of planets and incongruities of age differences in this category seem to mitigate against sheer obliviousness as its defining factor. Could it be these children are *too* aware of environmental crisis, and are expressing psychological avoidance, fanciful escape from overwhelming, stressful "planetary" demands? Perhaps. But there are reasons to doubt such a premise. The content of these pictures evinces much pleasure in natural scenes. And there are virtually no indicators of the bizarre or the strange—content that might reasonably be expected in representations of children's repressed fear. Another reading—going beyond the apparent, yet consistent with the overt content of the drawings—suggests that these idyllic scenes might depict the world put right again, after the work of saving the planet has been done. Or perhaps these children are painting a portrait of a world worth saving, a motivational goal for would-be "planeteers." This is supported by the comments of one 3rd grade boy, describing his pastoral scene, "It's a forest with a waterfall and a river really clean, and it's nice and clean and there's no garbage on the ground." Another child, whose first drawing depicts smiling figures picking up garbage (and therefore is not included in this category), drew a second picture of a house, a bird, and a flower. She reports, "This is the earth, and this is Pluto. And here is me, I'm cleaning up all the garbage and putting it into the wastebasket. And there's one more piece [of garbage to pick up]." Referring to her second picture, she says, "This is it all cleaned up. And I'm inside, playing with my friends."

Although such examples suggest that some of these children *are* responding to environmental concern, if in a subtle mode, it remains possible that many are simply unaware of environmental crisis. For, when asked about their drawings, most failed to mention directly any specific environmental problem or issue. Thus, despite some ambiguity between the content and descriptions of their drawings, children in this category appear to be unaware of any crisis in "save the planet" messages.

Taking Personal Action (n = 152, 48% of total)

Almost one-half (48 percent) of all the children in this study drew pictures of themselves and/or others actively participating in some kind of environmental activity; if not, the artist provided clear, spontaneous verbal comments indicating such activity is implied in the picture. One child's picture of a landscape, with objects circled and slashed with a line, illustrates this latter type. The 8-year-old girl describes, "There's a whole bunch of junk on the ground, and I pick it up . . . I made a [no] sign." Several of the younger children express their personal action in this way, verbally but not figuratively locating themselves in their pictures.

Almost two-thirds (64 percent) of the K-1st grade youngsters drew and/or described themselves in environmental activity (see Table 1). Examples of such kiddie eco-actions include releasing dolphins from underwater cages, stopping people from capturing animals in the rainforest, "help[ing] elephants live forever so they don't do what the dinosaurs did (they all died)," and picking up garbage, including on the moon: "I went to the moon when I was 2 years old. They have garbage there too. I helped pick it up." These youngest children (5–6 years old) exhibit a remarkable, if idiosyncratic, awareness of environmental issues, along with a marked sense of personal agency in the face of global problems.

Teaching or enlisting others to help save the planet is a common theme throughout these drawings. Describing his picture—a bright and smiling figure bending cheerfully to pick up an object—one 5-year-old boy states, "I went outside and found some poison that bad boys left on the ground. It was sickness poison. I put it in the garbage. Kids should learn from their parents that poison is bad." This is a rare example of a child directly citing his parents as socializing agents about environmental issues. More typically these children depict themselves as socializers "environmentalizing" others, as, for example, in a fifth-grade South Carolina girl's drawing of two smiling girls and a scowling male figure, of whom she wrote, "The girls are showing the man to not pulite [sic]. Throw trash in the trashcan." Throwing away trash and picking up garbage are dominant themes, with 60 percent of all the drawings including some rendition of people personally "cleaning up" the environment.

All the children depict themselves and/or others performing some kind of constructive action to improve environmental conditions. There are, however, qualitative differences in the ways children render the degree of effort required to "save" a planet. Although an overwhelming majority draw smiling, cheerful figures busily picking up garbage or recycling trash, a few children (7 percent) add representational details or dialogue that underscore the hard work they perceive as necessary for getting the monumental job done. Preparing to clean up a messy park, one little girl in a drawing tells her friends, "We better put our shoes on." "Whew!," a girl in another drawing declares, "all of this work I did will pay off." "It means it's a difficult . . .," a boy writes at the top of his page. "Yuck," protests another child's figure, working at sorting and picking up trash. Several children draw figures wiping sweat from their brow, and one picture in particular seems to sum up the theme that saving the planet is hard work. Smiling bravely, a little girl holds the entire earth on her back. "The fate of the world is on our shoulders," the fifth-grader's heading declares.

A perfectly equal gender division occurs in this category, with almost half of all the girls (47 percent) and boys (47 percent) drawing someone taking personal action to help the environment. Some gender differences in theme preference can be detected, however, with more girls drawing "protecting, preventing and nurturing" themes—such as planting trees or saving animals— while a few boys depict "avenging" as taking personal action. Instances of avenging polluters include a figure with a gun "kill[ing] Captain Dirt Man," and a huge hand holding a pistol, shooting "the Litter Man."

Both boys and girls draw themselves using technology to repair environmental problems. Technical solutions range from the pleasantly mundane (vacuum-cleaners suctioning up garbage from the surface of the earth, children sweeping the planet with brooms), to the celestial. In one third-grader's drawing, two girls in spacesuits, attached by thick tubes to their rocketship, approach the planet crying, "I will save the Earth!" In another the power of the sun is used to propel a young boy's solar car. One child, a 6-year-old boy, uses a brightly striped hot air balloon to depict himself picking up beer bottles floating in the sky, against the backdrop of a multiringed planet.

Throughout every thematic variation, which includes one instance of a child (a black boy from South Carolina) drawing himself walking up

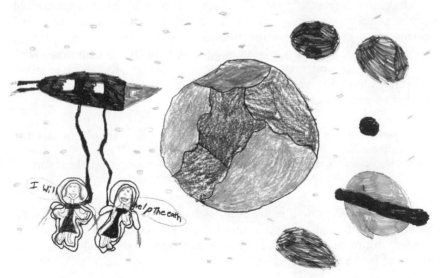

Figure 2. Taking personal action.

These girls in spacesuits helping to repair the earth were drawn by a third grade white girl in upstate New York.

the steps of the White House to inform the president about "bad polluters who should go to jail," the dominant response to environmental
concern is a sense of personal agency. These children unambiguously
convey, in visual and/or verbal terms, that they feel they *can* do something about the "problems with the planet." The meanings and implications of this kind of environmental empowerment for children will be
examined further in the discussion section.

Calling for Action (n = 71, 22% of total)

Looking at these drawings, one is immediately struck by the incessant
prevalence of the imperative, as over and over the viewer is exhorted to
"HELP SAVE THE PLANET!" and "MAKE OUR EARTH A HAPPIER
PLACE!" Words take on a special significance in this (second largest)
category of children's environmental concern (22 percent), where drawings are distinguished by an absence of human figures, a surfeit of positive sanctions, and a heavy reliance on slogans and signs demanding
environmental action. The dominant message is a rallying call to others
to eradicate environmental problems.

For some children the effort to persuade others to environmental
activism results in a pure symbolic gesture. Many children simply draw
recycling cans, or even more succinctly, the circular arrows of the
"reduce, reuse, recycle" symbol. Several incorporate the circular symbol
of the peace sign along with the recycle sign or with a picture of the
earth. Most children combine images of environmentalism—planets,
recycling cans, and natural landscapes are the most common—with
words, slogans, and text. In some pictures the text threatens to overwhelm, as in one 12-year-old girl's drawing, where almost half the page
is written commentary:

Q: What do you think of when someone says you have to help save the
   planet[?].
A. Recycle. pick up trash. Try to help people be aware of problems such as
   the holy [sic] ozone. If you see a piece of litter pick it up.

Other children quite literally plant signs in their pictures' front yards,
reminiscent of local election campaigns, with pointed messages about
the environment. The slogans below are from individual signs in a
drawing by an 8-year-old girl:

"Recicle! [sic]". "help save our earth!". "You can save our animal friends
by saving their homes." "don't ploute [sic]." "Save rainforests." "You can
help us save the earth." "Have composts!"

Drawing posters or signs, rather than human figures in action, can be interpreted as a kind of political activism:

> another aspect of children's art: the traditional function of poster art and the traditional prerogative of such serious and renowned and diverse artists as Goya, Kollwitz, Picasso, Hopper, Remington—[is] social comment, rhetorical assertion. (Coles 1992:49)

There are several ways children approach this aesthetic and political stance in their drawings about environmental crisis. Some try to educate their viewers, using their drawings as a way to show others proper environmental actions. One fourth-grade South Carolina boy demonstrates a remarkably informed knowledge of environmental issues in his drawing, including suggestions for positive actions such as using solar energy and joining Greenpeace.

Other children use "before and after" techniques, dividing the page into two frames, with the earth (or a landscape scene) depicted first as polluted or damaged, and then as repaired or cleaned up. "See what happens when you don't take care of the Earth," one fourth-grade girl writes. "See what you can do when you clean up." This can also work in reverse, as in another fourth grade girl's drawing, "Make your world a better place" (smiling, green and blue planet) . . . "not worse" (orange and brown plan-

Figure 3. Calling for action.

This fourth grader, a white boy from South Carolina, displays a wide range of calls for environmental action.

et "all steamed-up," emitting red rays and an angry grimace).

Many of these children demonstrate political commitment and concern in their pictures of "saving the planet." But another, more complex, quality emerges when the drawings are taken as a whole. Revealed in the repetitiveness of content and tone—the incessant imperative, the sameness of the slogans, the planets, the message, almost as by rote—a sense arises that, for some, politics is reduced to a treacly slogan on a Hallmark card: "Saving my planet means a lot to me. Tell me what saving your planet means to you _____ ." Perched atop a pretty rainbow and a shiny sun, this second-grader's sentiment can easily be described as "cute."

Similarly, the sheer redundancy of virtually interchangeable depictions of the earth with "Recycle," "Save the Earth," or "Save the Planet" at the head, suggest the possibility of some subtle contradictions here— commitment and trivialization, impassioned pleas and pat phrases, social comment and social reproduction—in the expression of some children's environmental concern. Paired and contrasted with "taking personal action," drawings they raise complex questions about issues of children's empowerment, political engagement, and the social uses of environmentalization.

Depicting the Problem (n = 29, 9% of total)

A distinct qualitative shift occurs in the content and mood of these children's drawings. Looking at them, one is left with a tangible sense of warning, anxiety, and foreboding. Here environmental problems are depicted without any sign of personal action, solutions, or perpetrators. "If we do nothing the planet could look like this!" one seventh-grade boy exclaims, beneath a ragged-edged, orange, black and purple earth. "No polluting or the animals will die," a nameless third grader warns. Pictures with planets with bites taken out or with garish colors are a recurrent theme, as are garbage-strewn rivers and fields. Several children, boys and girls alike, depict bombs exploding, some as pulsating abstract energy, others as mushroom clouds complete with BOOM! and BOSH! sound effects and children crying AH! or "SUE! SUE!" (The artist, an 8-year-old girl, explains "Sue" is a person not a legal action.) One kindergartner, a boy from Brooklyn, describes the bird in his drawing as wearing "one of those soda-rings around his neck." The happy-looking home from the "Everything's Okay" category is mutated here into an anthropomorphic figure wearing band-aids and a fiery roof crying "HELP!" - "SAVE OUR HOME," a frowny-face in the O of the "our," standing firmly printed by its side.

Figure 4. Depicting the problem.

A seventh grade white boy in a special education class in South Carolina draws the earth as ugly and eaten away by pollution.

Confronted with personal responsibility to save the planet, these children (9 percent) respond with graphic images of decay and destruction, things gone wrong, the ecosystem awry. Significantly, none locate any agent of decay, any specific causal factor in the problems they depict. Nor do they find refuge in arcadia, satisfaction in slogans, or power in personal action. Of course, it is important to remember that each descriptive category represents only one kind of response children may have to environmental crisis messages. Individual children may draw second or third pictures from completely different perspectives, reaffirming the commonplace that we all are capable of holding simultaneously contradictory notions. Still, the data here clearly reveal that at least some children, at some times, respond to messages about global environmental crisis with serious worry, without easy or immediate recourse or relief, and without any apparent awareness or understanding of the root causes of the problems with which they are being faced.

Given its somewhat "negative" cast (emphasizing problems without indicating solutions, or providing only negative sanctions), it is interesting to note grade, regional, race/class, and to a lesser extent, gender differences arising in this category of environmental concern. Drawings from the youngest children (K-1 grade) are virtually absent here (the kindergartner's drawing described above—of a bird with a soda ring around its neck—represents that child's second drawing), whereas there are twice as many 6th to 8th graders as might be expected by chance (see Table 1). Similarly regional differences arise, with fewer southern children (3 percent) and slightly more northern children (12 percent) drawing environmental problems. Race alone does not appear to be a significant factor in these children's depiction of environmental problems, but when race is combined with class, twice as many low-income black children (5 of 17—29 percent) draw more problem scenes than would be expected by chance. There also appears to be a trend in gender differences, with more girls and fewer boys emphasizing problems in their drawings of the environment (see Table 2). Generalizations from these data need to be carefully qualified, given the small numbers and the study's non-random sample. Even so, the data raise theoretical implications of an intersection of race, class, and gender issues in environmentalization that merits further consideration.

Indicting the Problem Makers (n = 32, 10% of total)

As in the previous category of concern "Depicting the problems," drawings here focus on environmental problems—not solutions, personal actions, or calls for change. However, these drawings are distinguished by pointing out the problem makers and indicting those considered responsible for creating environmental problems.

Are children who draw "eco villains" demonstrating a keen awareness of the institutional origins of environmental crisis? A close look at the data reveals who and what these children see as responsible for planetary problems. Air polluters rank as the most frequently mentioned environmental culprits (59 percent). Included are billowing smokestacks of nameless factories, car, truck, and jet plane exhaust, people burning garbage or trash; and even radioactive emissions from a nuclear power plant. Some children point to users of aerosol cans as direct destroyers of the earth's protective ozone layer. None drew the

Figure 5. Depicting the problem.

This kindergartner, a 6-year-old white boy from upstate New York, draws a logger, a frequently depicted "villian."

store where the aerosol cans are sold or the chemical plant where the offending ingredients are developed and produced. Other commonly cited problem makers include people who cut down, destroy, or otherwise damage trees (38 percent), water polluters (28 percent), and garbage dumpers and litters (22 percent). Thirty-one percent of the drawings include some other kind of environmental offender.

One picture features a frightened- (and frightening-) looking character at a computer terminal. The artist, a 14-year-old boy from a special ed class, explains: "It's a scientist working on a computer. We need to send messages to all the scientists in the world telling this, Don't mess up the environment or we won't have one. Scientists ought to think of more ways to save the planet than rockets and bombs." This child's drawing is an astute mixture of indictment and recruitment. Scientists are cited as creators of "rockets and bombs" and other (implied) technology that "mess[es] up the environment." At the same time, scientists are depicted as having an express responsibility to "think of ways to save the planet."

Few children so specifically cite personal representatives of big capital and/or nation states as responsible for environmental damage, although one girl draws the *Exxon Valdez* spilling oil into the sea, as others draw nameless oil tankers, and many children draw anonymous smoky factories emitting air pollution and dumping toxic waste. In yet another (dramatic) depiction a whaling ship is shown trying to capture and kill a great whale.

For many children individual responsibility for environmental crisis is the dominant focus in their drawings. "A lot of people think only about themselves. They need to think about the Earth," states one kindergarten boy, drawing two menacing figures carrying chainsaws toward a tall tree. "If you don't recycle water you will not have any. . . . Turn the water off," an 11-year-old Girl Scout admonishes, the girl in her picture brushing her teeth with the water running, oblivious to its rapid depletion.

These children, then, see artifacts of capital and technology—factories, vehicles, aerosol sprays—as primarily responsible for environmental pollution. Loggers or others who cut down trees are a frequently cited culprit, perhaps in response to messages about saving the rainforest and old-growth forests in the Northwest, and the much-publicized controversy over the endangered northern spotted owl. Few children directly name institutional polluters, although the Alaskan oil spill by the *Exxon Valdez* has left its trace in many of these children's drawings. It appears that contrary to the "Taking personal action" category where in general children view eco-problems as individually created and resolved by "you and me," in the "Problem maker" category children display a budding awareness of the institutional origins of environmental crisis but offer few, if any, structural solutions in their drawings.

Although grade levels seem to be significant in children's preference for depicting problems (older children are much more likely to emphasize environmental problems than are kindergarten and first graders), they do not appear to be a factor in children's depiction of problem makers (see Table 1). However, a developing pattern of race, class, and gender differences in children's reception of environmental crisis themes continues here, with almost three times as many boys as girls drawing pictures depicting environmental problem makers (17 percent and 5 percent, respectively; see Table 2) and no black children drawing problem makers. Keeping in mind that this category of concern represents a small percentage of drawings by children in the study (10 percent), it still appears that race, class, and gender play a role in children's reception of environmental crisis themes, particularly for those children who do not draw themselves or others taking some kind of personal action to "save the planet."

Recasting the Problem (n = 9, <3% of total)

These last drawings represent a very small percentage (less than 3 percent) that seem to have dramatically changed or recast the original "save the planet" message. Unlike the first category (Everything's Okay), where the planet itself is the element that seems to leave the clearest trace (and thus fuels speculation that the message has been understood on some level by children drawing those pictures), here it is the "saving" part, or the depiction of some other than environmental danger, that is most evident in the children's drawings.

Does recasting environmental messages constitute a category of environmental concern? These drawings are intriguing in the diverse ways they appropriate the notion of saving the earth. One unique, somewhat inscrutable, drawing, by an upper-middle class fifth-grade black girl from coastal South Carolina, fills a page with the gaping mouth of a huge Jawslike killer whale, brilliantly colored in green and blue, with an impressively rendered double-set of razor-sharp white teeth. Two other drawings, both by younger girls from different summer camps, depict a figure drowning. In one picture a child sits in a small wooden boat with a long ladder falling into the water. Another, smaller child, is apparently struggling in deep water nearby a black life ring floating on the surface of the lake. "Save the earth [sic]" the smiling girl in the boat cries out.

Aliens or creatures from outer space are a common theme, particularly among boys. One third grader, a 9-year-old black boy from South Carolina, draws a picture that features two ringed planets in the sky, with several alien creatures involved in a set piece. "I am diaing [sic]" calls a prostrate antennaed alien. "We need to help him," another alien impassively replies. A woman dressed in orange calls out, "We have to save our plantet [sic]." "Yes we do," the small extra-terrestrial next to her responds.

Several of the boys' drawings depict planetary dangers and rescues in overtly aggressive and militaristic terms. Two third-grade boys draw pictures of ships under attack by airborne enemies descending by parachute or supercape. In another the earth is shown under assault by extra-terrestrials who are fiercely resisted by flying creatures with blazing rockets, "Tring [sic] to save the earth." Unlike the drawings which show "Taking personal action," these pictures—albeit action-packed—lose track of the notion of environmental crisis.

These drawings could be completely missing the intended message environmentally minded adults are seeking to convey. On the other hand, they may be demonstrating an implicit continuum of cultural messages that children, and especially boys, are getting from commer-

This third grader from South Carolina, a middle-class black boy, draws a dying alien from outer space saying, "we have to save our planet"[sic].

cial cartoons and environmentalist rhetoric. Some children are primed to see saving the planet as not only the environment, but the entire universe at stake. As Engelhardt (1986) notes, cartoons such as *He-Man* and *Masters of the Universe* engage young children with the thrill (and chill) of Star Wars military technology, along with ads for innumerable action-figure toys that are even more blatant in their visual (and commercial) aggressiveness (pp. 89–94). The enviro-tainment cartoon *Captain Planet and the Planeteers* cleverly exploits this lucrative cultural phenomenon, blending "the Universe of the Action-Figure Superhero," and plots about preventing environmental destruction, with a vast merchandising and licensing enterprise (King 1994).

That so few children recast saving the planet messages suggests that the environmentalization of children is an extremely effective project. Even when the message is recast by children in a number of ways, their alternate themes seem linked to concerns for "saving the planet." For the most part, children are getting the message in much the way socializing agents are intending it to be conveyed. Implications of this pervasive and persuasive environmentalization of children remain to be critically explored.

DISCUSSION AND CONCLUSION

Children are not social incompetents when it comes to understanding and interpreting environmental messages. Even very young children are getting "save the planet" messages quite clearly and are responding to environmentalist socialization in often thoughtful and creative ways. Similarly, most children are not experiencing themselves as vulnerable victims, hopeless and helpless in the face of overwhelming global responsibility. They are neither cynical nor apathetic—although older children are more likely to draw environmental problems than are younger ones, supporting evidence that children's political attitudes become increasingly negative with age (Palonsky 1987). Contrary to popular myths portraying eco-activist children as environmentally correct bullies, children in this study do not terrorize others with stringent, self-righteous, or unreasonable demands, nor do they express themselves in rigid or tyrannical terms.

Most children respond to social messages about environmental crisis with a clear and confident sense that they can do something about the problem, either through some kind of personal ecological activity, or by urging others to do their share to save the planet. However, what is the meaning of this empowerment for children who experience it? What does it signify for the society that promotes it? And, should we adults rest assured knowing that children are feeling empowered in this way?

In the late 1960s similar questions were raised as to the effectiveness of political socialization in the schools. Hess (1968) maintains that children in the United States were being presented with a "picture of unity, equality, and freedom that ... is distorted, over-simplified, and, to a degree, false" (p. 529). Schools, he argues, created "an attitude of complacency" and a willingness in children to embrace "inaccurate representations" of the nation as "powerful, wise, and of good intent" (p. 531). He points out that the young child, socialized to believe, for example, in the effectiveness of the vote, learns nothing of the "realities of political influence ... [and, consequently] overestimates his [sic] own power until he attempts to have an effect upon politics or institutions in government" (p. 531). He also asserts that teaching democratic political values in the form of slogans, rather than as concepts to be applied to social issues, leads to superficial acceptance of egalitarian principles—principles that often disappear when lived social and political contexts require tolerance for the expression of opposing, controversial, or non-conforming views. Summing up his critique, Hess states: "In short, much of the political socialization that takes place at elementary and high-school levels is lacking in candor, is superficial with respect to basic issues, is cognitively fragmented, and produces little grasp of the implications of principles and their application to new situations" (p. 532).

More than a quarter of a century later, much the same issues arise in the environmental socialization of children. Children are cheerfully targeted for environmental concern. They are told to pick up the trash, recycle plastic, bottles, and cans, conserve trees and water, and buy "environmentally friendly" products. In this way, saving the planet is a comfortable arena for feeling socially and politically committed, even better suited to white middle-class concerns than, for example, "brotherhood," with its inevitable, uncomfortable, acknowledgment of long-standing racist oppression or "nuclear winter," with its attendant gloomy focus on the international proliferation of military weapons of mass destruction.

Saving the planet messages accommodate capitalist social relations in an effective, if paradoxical, fashion. Pictures of the earth are plastered on commodities as diverse as t-shirts and toilet paper. Children as young as 3 and 4 are being cultivated as a major consumer market (McNeal 1987, 1992), with environmentalism being sold to kids in any number of ways (King 1994).

The discourse of environmental disaster encompasses a broad range of social, political, economic, biological, and cultural concerns. But the rhetoric of liberal environmentalism, expressed in the pat phrases of many children's drawings, promotes the notion that global environmental degradation—the end result of multinational corporate, military/industrial, and nation state practices of consumption and production—is really "everybody's fault." The reduction of complex global problems to simplistic, individualist solutions serves corporate interests more effectively than it does children willingly accepting responsibility for stewardship of a planet that is, in most ways, not under their control. Borrowing from Bourdieu, one could argue that liberal environmentalism is a form of "symbolic violence," where the consent of children is sought to maintain the hegemony of global capitalism.

However, inextricably intertwined in the liberal environmental paradox is the message to little children that they *can* do something. Children are not cultural dopes (Hall 1981). They actively interpret, appropriate, and occasionally subvert or resist, messages aimed at them by society—whether they be from school, home, their friends, TV, or the mall. A sense of empowerment, that actions have effects, and words the power to persuade, is one many children in this study easily embrace.

Hess's caveat—that children supplied with a superficial sense of empowerment are being set up for a fall—needs to be heeded in the context of liberal environmentalism. Tentative findings in this study also suggest that race, class, and gender differences affect the quality of children's environmental concern, particularly when children *do not* directly express the sense that they personally can help "save the planet."

REFERENCES

Alanen, L. 1990. "Rethinking Socialization, the Family and Childhood." *Sociological Studies of Child Development* 3:13–28.

Ambert, A. 1986. "Sociology of Sociology: The Place of Children in North American Sociology." *Sociological Studies of Child Development* 1:11-31.

Ariès, P. 1962. *Centuries of Childhood*. New York: Random House.

Best, J. 1990. *Threatened Children*. Chicago: University of Chicago Press.

Bolotin, S. 1990. "Woodman, Spare That Tree!" Book Review Section, *New York Times* May 20:47.

Bookchin, M. 1990. *Remaking Society: Pathways to a Green Future*. Boston: South End Press.

Bourdieu, P., and J. Passeron. 1977. *Reproduction in Education, Society and Culture*. Beverly Hills, CA: Sage.

Cahill, S. 1990. "Childhood and Public Life: Reaffirming Biographical Divisions." *Social Problems* 37:390–402.

Coles, R. 1986. *The Moral Life of Children*. Boston: Atlantic Monthly Press.

_____. 1992. *Their Eyes Meeting the World: The Drawings and Paintings of Children*. Boston: Houghton Mifflin.

Coward, R. 1990. "Greening the Child." *New Statesman & Society* 3(102):40–41.

Dalla Costa, M. 1972. "Women and the Subversion of the Community." Pp. 19–54 in *The Power of Women and the Subversion of the Community*, edited by M. Dalla Costa. Bristol, UK: Falling Wall Press.

Dennis, W. 1966. *Group Values Through Children's Drawings*. New York: John Will & Sons.

Denzin, N. K. 1979. *Childhood Socialization*. San Francisco: Jossey-Bass.

Elkin, F., and G. Handel. 1989. *The Child and Society*. New York: Random House.

Engelhardt, T. 1986. "The Shortcake Strategy." Pp. 68–110 in *Watching Television*, edited by T. Gitlin. New York: Pantheon.

Fiske, J. 1989. *Reading the Popular*. Boston: Unwin Hyman.

Garelik, G. 1991. "The Enforcers: Teach Your Parents Well." Cover story, USA Weekend Magazine, *Daily News* August 9–11:4–5.

Glaser, B., and A. Strauss. 1967. *The Discovery of Grounded Theory*. Hawthorne, NY: Aldine de Gruyter.

Hall, S. 1981. "Notes on Deconstructing the Popular." Pp. 227–41 in *People's History and Socialist Theory*, edited by R. Samuel. London: Routledge & Kegan Paul.

Hebdige, D. 1988. *Hiding in the Light*. London: Routledge.

Hess, R. D. 1968. "Political Socialization in the Schools." *Harvard Educational Review* 38:528–36.

Katz, C. 1990. "A Cable to Cross a Curse: Everyday Cultural Practices of Resistance and Reproduction among Youth in New York City." Unpublished manuscript.

King, D. L. 1994. "Captain Planet and the Planeteers: Kids, Environmental Crisis, and Competing Narratives of the New World Order." *The Sociological Quarterly* 35:103–20.

_____. (In progress). "Using Children's Drawings in Sociological Research."

La Farge, P. 1987. *The Strangelove Legacy: The Impact of the Nuclear Threat on Children.* New York: Harper & Row.

Laslett, B., and J. Brenner. 1989. "Gender and Social Reproduction: Historical Perspectives." *Annual Review of Sociolgy* 15:381–404.

McNeal, J. U. 1987. *Children as Consumers.* Lexington, MA: Lexington Books.

_____. 1992. *Kids as Customers.* New York: Lexington Books.

McRobbie, A. 1988. *Zoot Suits and Second-Hand Dresses: An Anthology of Fashion and Music.* Wincester, MA: Unwin Hyman.

_____. 1991. *Feminism and Youth Culture.* Boston: Unwin Hyman.

Mesnikoff, W. S. 1989. *The Place of Nuclear Threat in Young People's Everyday Concerns and Expectations.* Unpublished doctoral dissertation, Graduate Center, City University of New York.

Palonsky, S. B. 1987. "Political Socialization in Elementary Schools." *The Elementary School Journal* 87:493–505.

Postman, N. 1982. *The Disappearance of Childhood.* New York: Delacorte Press.

Power, M. B. 1986. "Socializing of Emotionality in Early Childhood: The Influence of Emotional Associates." *Sociological Studies of Child Development* 1:259–82.

Quindlen, A. 1990. "Thou Shalt Nots." *New York Times* October 14:E19.

Reeves, J. B., and N. Boyette. 1983. "What Does Children's Art Work Tell Us about Gender?" *Qualitative Sociology* 6:322–333.

Rothman, B. K. 1989. *Recreating Motherhood: Ideology and Technology in a Patriarchal Society.* New York: Norton.

Slesin, S. 1991. "Newest Parental Nightmare: Eco-smart Child." *New York Times* July 11:C1.

Waksler, F. C. 1986. "Studying Children: Phenomenological Insights." *Human Studies* 9:71–82.

Warren, M. L. 1991. "Educating for Global Citizenship through Children's Art." *School Arts* 90(April):53–57.

Willis, P. 1977. *Learning to Labor.* New York: Columbia University Press.

_____. 1990. *Common Culture.* Boulder, CO: Westview Press.

Winn, M. 1983. *Children without Childhood.* New York: Random House.

WMHT. 1990. "Save It! Operation Earth, Public TV." Albany, New York.

Zelizer, V. 1985. *Pricing the Priceless Child: The Changing Social Value of Children.* New York: Basic Books.

Biographical Sketches of the Contributors

Joel Best is Professor and Chair of the Department of Sociology at Southern Illinois University at Carbondale. Specializing in social problems and deviance, his books include *Threatened Children* and *Organizing Deviance* (with David F. Luckenbill). He received his Ph.D. from the University of California, Berkeley.

York W. Bradshaw is Associate Professor of Sociology and African Studies at Indiana University, Bloomington. His research interests are in the area of Third World economic and social development, with a particular focus on Kenya. His forthcoming book (coauthored with Michael Wallace) is titled *Global Transitions: Emerging Patterns of International, Regional, and National Inequality.*

Claudia Buchmann is a Ph.D. candidate in Sociology at Indiana University, Bloomington. Her research interests are in the area of comparative education and women in the Third World. She recently conducted research in Kenya under the support of a Social Science Research Council (SSRC) 12-month predissertation training grant. Her most recent publication is "Borrowing Against the Future: Children and Third World Indebtedness," which appeared in *Social Forces* in 1993 (coauthored with Rita Noonan, Laura Gash, and York Bradshaw).

Spencer Cahill received his Ph.D. from the University of California, Santa Barbara. He is currently an Associate Professor of Sociology at Skidmore College.

Phillip W. Davis is Associate Professor of Sociology at Georgia State University. He received his Ph.D. from UCLA and has research interests in punishment as ritual drama, naturally occurring violence against children, and parents' folk techniques of child-rearing.

Carol Brooks Gardner is an Associate Professor of Sociology and Women's Studies at Indiana University, Indianapolis. She is interested in social problems and gender, and especially in those social problems said to affect women and children. By training, she is a social interactionist and was a student of Erving Goffman. Among her other interests are the structure of social interaction; behavior in public, especially public harassment; and gender in everyday interaction.

Donna Lee King earned her Ph.D. in Sociology at the Graduate School and University Center of the City University of New York, where she wrote her dissertation on children and the environmental crisis. Her most recent publication, "Captain Planet and the Planeteers: Kids, Environmental Crisis, and Competing Narratives of the New World Order" appears in *The Sociologycal Quarterly*. Currently she teaches sociology and psychology at Orange County Community College in Middletown, New York.

Marion Kloep works as senior lecturer at the Department of Human Resource Development at Mid-Sweden University, Ostersund. She received her doctorate in Educational Sciences at Rhenish-Westphalian Technical University in Aachen, Germany. Her main research interest is the impact of social and economic crises on the development of children and adolescents.

Joseph A. Kotarba is an Associate Professor of Sociology at the University of Houston. He received his Ph.D. from the University of California at San Diego. Dr. Kotarba teaches courses in social theory, ethnographic research methods, the sociology of health, and the sociology of popular music. He is currently writing on the relationship between various social institutions (e.g., the family, religion, medicine and sports) and rock music. Dr. Kotarba recently completed an ethnographic study of the effects of the fall of communism on rock music and youth culture in Poland.

Jacquelyn Litt is an Assistant Professor of Sociology and Chair of Women's Studies at Allegheny College in Meadville, Pennsylvania. She is currently writing a book on Jewish-American and African-American mothering practices before 1950, entitled *Science in the Kitchen: Motherhood and Medical Expertise in Historical Perspective.*

Donileen Loseke received her Ph.D. from the University of California, Santa Barbara. She is currently an Associate Professor of Sociology and a member of the Women's Studies teaching faculty at Skidmore College. Her book, *The Battered Woman and Shelters: The Social Construction of Wife Abuse*, is published by the State University of New York Press.

Paul Mbatia is a Ph.D. candidate in Sociology at Indiana University, Bloomington, and a Lecturer in Sociology at the University of Nairobi, Kenya. His research interests are in the areas of health-care delivery and development, with a particular focus on East Africa. He has completed numerous research projects and served as a consultant to organizations in Kenya. He is a MacArthur Scholar during the 1993-94 academic year.

Maureen McNeil is currently Nancy Rowell Jackman Chair of Women's Studies at Mount Saint Vincent University, Halifax, Nova Scotia, Canada. She is on leave from her permanent post as Senior Lecturer in the Cultural Studies Department at the University of Birmingham, England. Her publications include: *Under the Banner of Science: Erasmus Darwin and His Age* (University of Manchester Press, 1987); as editor, *Gender and Expertise* (1987) and as editor with I. Varcoe and S. Yearly, *The New Reproductive Technologies* (1990). In the midst of a number of research projects and teaching, she is writing a book about cultural studies of science and technology.

Shan Nelson-Rowe received his Ph.D. at State University of New York at Stony Brook and teaches sociology at the University of Wisconsin, Milwaukee. His interests include the social construction of education and childhood. He is currently researching the origins of educational toys.

Atsushi Yamazaki is a journalist for the Japanese newspaper *Kahoku Shimpo*. He received a Bachelor of Law degree from Meiji Gakuin University, and an M.A. in sociology from Southern Illinois University at Carbondale.

Index